Practical Standards

Microsoft® for

Visual Basic®

James D. Foxall

Practical Standards for Microsoft Visual Basic

Published by Microsoft Press
A Division of Microsoft Corporation
One Microsoft Way
Redmond, Washington 98052-6399

Library of Congress Cataloging-in-Publication Data
Foxall, James D.
    Practical Standards for Microsoft Visual Basic / James D. Foxall.
        p.   cm.
    Includes index.
    ISBN 0-7356-0733-8
    1. Microsoft Visual BASIC.   2. BASIC (Computer program language)   I. Title.

    QA76.73.B3 F695 2000
    005.26'8--dc21   99-056695

Printed and bound in the United States of America.

    2 3 4 5 6 7 8 9 QMQM 5 4 3 2 1 0

Distributed in Canada by Penguin Books Canada Limited.

A CIP catalogue record for this book is available from the British Library.

Microsoft Press books are available through booksellers and distributors worldwide. For further information about international editions, contact your local Microsoft Corporation office, or contact Microsoft Press International directly at fax (425) 936-7329. Visit our Web site at mspress.microsoft.com.

Acquisitions Editor: Ben Ryan
Project Editor: Devon Musgrave
Technical Editor: Steve Perry

This book is dedicated to Laura (my incredibly supportive and encouraging wife), Ethan (my son, who teaches me something new and makes me belly-laugh every day), and my yet-to-be-named daughter. (I promise we'll have a name for you before you get here.) You, my family, are everything to me.

Contents at a Glance

Table of Contents

Part 3   Coding Constructs

Acknowledgments

First and foremost I would like to thank Ben Ryan, Devon Musgrave, Steve Perry, and all the other wonderful people at Microsoft Press. This troupe of talented individuals is by far the most gifted and diligent group of people with which I've had the pleasure of working. You guys are great! Ben, thanks for listening to my ideas and being so receptive. Devon, I really appreciate how you kept me on track and contributed so many good ideas for the book. Steve—what can I say?—you are amazing. You should be writing books of your own. All of you worked *with* me and allowed me to contribute ideas, not just text. For that I will always be grateful.

Thanks also to Ed Spence, for his willingness to set everything aside to give my writing a once-over before I sent it to Press, and a special thanks to Matt Wagner at Waterside Productions for always believing in me and sticking with me through the not-so-fun times.

For all of you—including Mike Hartman, Jim White, Dave Foxall, Linda Foxall, Chris Wright, and Lisa Brink—who helped in ways you might not realize, thank you.

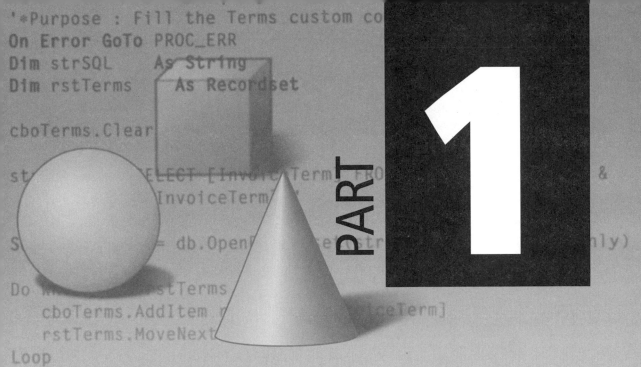

Design

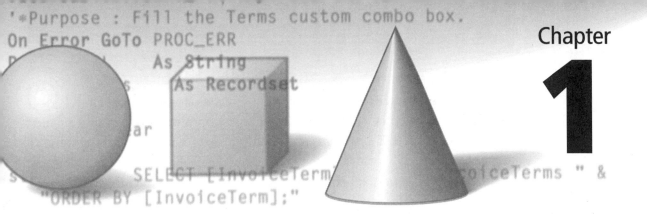

Introduction to Standards

As members of a functional society, we adhere to standards every day of our lives. Often we don't think about these standards; rather, we take them for granted and apply them naturally. For instance, when you pull up to an intersection that's a four-way stop, you stop your car and check for cross-traffic. Once any cars already crossing the intersection are through, you determine who has the right of way (the car first to arrive at a stop sign and then whichever car is on the right) and cross the intersection at the appropriate time. You might do this 50 times a day. You might do this while eating a donut, drinking coffee, or talking to a carful of passengers. When you were first learning to drive, it took a considerable amount of attention to figure out the procedure, but once you became comfortable with the situation the process became second nature. This is how programming standards should be.

One of the standards that affects our everyday lives is the electrical standard of 110 volts. When you plug a new appliance into a wall outlet, you don't have to check the appliance's documentation and use a voltmeter on the outlet to determine whether the appliance and the outlet will work together. You can rest assured that both devices adhere to strict standards. If a device doesn't need the full 110 volts, it uses a mechanism such as a transformer to step down the power so that it can function connected to a

110-volt system. When more power is required—for instance, clothes dryers require 220 volts—the device's plug is a completely different size and shape, which makes it incompatible with a 110-volt system. Obviously, if such standards weren't adhered to, injury or death could result. These standards are so critical that an organization certifies components and makes sure they meet the necessary standards and pass certain safety checks, which is why almost all electrical components carry the UL (Underwriters Laboratories) logo.

Employing interface and coding standards may not save someone from an electrical shock or prevent two cars from colliding in an intersection, but strict adherence to a published set of standards does offer benefits. Code written to a set of standards is easier to maintain and enhance, and often the correct utilization of accepted standards creates improved code—studies have shown that code written to standards usually contains fewer errors.

For a good example of the benefits of standardization when applied to a user interface, you need look no further than the Microsoft Office suite. Whether or not you like the interface, it's easy to understand and respect the benefits that the suite's set of visual standards gives the end user. I know that nothing is perfect, and I could come up with a list of changes I'd like to see made in the Office interface, but I really awoke to the interface's benefits—a direct result of applied standards—when I wrote my first Microsoft Office Compatible commercial program. It was a lot of work to get that certification, and it even required a waiver because of the inability of the tool I was using at the time to create certain required features—no, it wasn't Microsoft Visual Basic, but it was a Microsoft product. My fellow programmers and I found ourselves writing a good bit of code that we could have gotten by without had we not wanted the certification. We also spent an insane amount of time on toolbars, menus, and accelerator keys. However, when our customers started using the product, we received a large number of compliments and kudos.

What the customers told us was that the amount of internal training and support required for the implementation of our application was far lower than expected. Users were able to focus on the functions and features of our program rather than on the mechanics of the interface, such as navigation. For example, when a user wanted to print, he or she knew where to find the Print button. The button was located as it is in Office, and it displayed the printer icon that the user was already familiar with. Likewise, users familiar with Office's standard hot keys could simply press Ctrl+P to print. In the end, our initial investment in development paid major dividends for our customers. When it comes to an application's interface, the consistency that standards produce is key. Although it might be a little less apparent, consistency and standards are also key when it comes to writing code.

Why This Book Is Necessary

Visual Basic has the largest user base of any development language in the world, and the ranks are growing. Estimates put the number of users of Visual Basic at about 3 million. Once considered a hobbyist's language, it has quickly gained the respect of serious developers and is now widely used in corporate and other commercial environments. Visual Basic's generous flexibility combined with its focus on maintaining backward compatibility make it an extremely powerful language. Unfortunately, these attributes also seem to encourage sloppy programming.

For instance, Visual Basic will actually let you create what I call *voodoo variables*. A voodoo variable is a variable created on the fly simply by its name being referenced. If you haven't included the *Option Explicit* statement in a module, you can create a voodoo variable by referencing the name of a variable not already declared or in use. Voodoo variables are often created by mistake, and they can be very difficult to debug. Visual Basic *shouldn't even allow you to turn off* the requirement to explicitly declare variables. This feature is available for backward compatibility, but it has no place in modern programming, not in applications written for fun and certainly not in distributed applications. To make matters even more difficult, when you install Visual Basic the default settings do not require variable declaration. If you don't know to turn on this feature, you're creating potential land mines in your code.

Many developers have been getting by with sloppy code for years, either their own code or the code of someone on their team. The repercussions of poor programming techniques are numerous. For example, have you ever needed to make a small change to a procedure and ended up having to rewrite the entire procedure because the code wasn't easily modifiable (extendable)? When processes are cobbled together in a routine, they tend to make enhancements and modifications difficult, if not impossible. Correctly written code, on the other hand, is generally much easier to modify as the need arises.

Have you ever had to modify someone else's code and discovered that you needed hours, days, or even weeks just to understand how certain processes worked? Have you ever revisited your own code after some time has passed only to find that you weren't very generous with your comments and you can't remember exactly how you implemented the processes? When you're forced to deal with your own sins, the benefits of standards become much more obvious. Code written to strict standards contains sufficient comments to make it easy to understand what is occurring in a procedure as well as how the tasks are being accomplished. The visual presentation of the code, such as its indentation and use of white space, and the proper naming of variables can also make code dramatically easier to understand.

Many developers still don't give enough thought to the data types of their variables. This problem ranges from using variants where they aren't necessary to using the Single data type where Double is required. In these situations, it's possible for Visual Basic to perform type coercion or unanticipated rounding, giving you unexpected results. For example, if you put a number with a decimal value into an Integer variable, the value is rounded but no error occurs. If, however, you attempt to put a value into a variable larger than its data type allows, a run-time error occurs. At design time, it's almost impossible to test for some of these conditions without putting huge amounts of test data through the program. You need to define variables correctly from the beginning, or problems won't be known until they start manifesting themselves on your customer's computer.

Performance is always a top priority for developers. So, although comput-
ing horsepower is climbing at a phenomenal rate, you should remember
that not everyone is using equipment like the state-of-the-art development
machine you have on your desk. Code written to meet certain standards
often runs faster than code that doesn't meet those standards, such as
strict data typing and the use of the proper loop for a given task.

Another consequence of not adhering to proper coding standards affects
you, the developer, alone: you may not get and you may even lose a job
because of lax coding. As an employer of Visual Basic programmers, I've
found that most of the applicants I've chosen *not* to employ were dis-
qualified because of their code, not their resumes. I review code samples
of every developer that applies to work for our company. The most common problem—code that lacks liberal and accurate comments—is often
just the tip of the iceberg when it comes to bad code. What I've seen is
truly amazing and often pitiable. I've reviewed code in which not a single
variable was explicitly declared—there were voodoo variables every-
where! I've even reviewed code in which all the variables were declared
at the module level. Out of curiosity, I performed searches on some ran-
domly chosen variables. Most were used in only one procedure. Many
weren't used anywhere! When I queried the author of the code about this,
he informed me that he felt he might need those variables in the future, so
he was just planning ahead! If none of this sounds like weak programming practice, this book should prove valuable to you indeed.

If you think that I'm being picky, you might be right. However, I can tell
you that I'm not alone. Many people realize that someone who writes
good, sound code that adheres to solid programming standards can learn
to code just about any process. If you're looking for a job, take the principles in this book to heart and modify your code *before* sending it to a
potential employer for review.

As I've said, Visual Basic's power and flexibility, coupled with its built-in
allowance for backward compatibility, create numerous problems. These
problems multiply when you consider that a large number of Visual Basic
programmers are self-taught, lacking the formal development training that

would help them recognize the pitfalls of bad programming techniques. These facts make the need for published standards all the more necessary.

Although applications developed with standardization techniques have been shown to contain fewer errors, to be easier to maintain, and to be easier to enhance—this just can't be said enough—some programmers argue against standardization. Unfortunately, such arguments often originate in arrogance, a lack of understanding, resistance to change, or simple laziness. For example, claiming that it requires too much effort to add a three-character naming prefix to a variable to denote its data type is like claiming that it takes too much typing to call a variable *TotalStudents* rather than calling it *X*. Sure, typing *X* is easier than typing *TotalStudents*, but who can argue that the time savings is worth it when you consider the later confusion created?

The benefits of standards multiply as more developers are added to a project, and therefore it's often the corporate and commercial shops that make the first attempts to standardize. In development shops using some level of standardization, the standards employed usually come from a high-level manager, someone who has to review and maintain code written by others. However, the standards used are often a small subset of those that should be employed, and often they're standards created internally, comprising many unique characteristics rather than universally adopted techniques. When hired at such a place, a developer might be forced to learn development techniques that differ greatly from those already familiar to the developer. This, of course, adds unnecessary work and increases the possibility of error.

Every person who writes code should employ some common standardization techniques, even when writing only a few lines of code. The need for standardization increases exponentially as the number of developers who work on the code increases and the number of lines within a program increases. Whether you're a hobbyist or a corporate or commercial developer, standardization techniques should be part of your base set of skills.

At my company, we did an analysis a long time ago and discovered that we were using a hodgepodge of standards—each developer was doing essentially whatever he or she wanted to do. I *know* what a long road it is to universally adopt standards in development because I've traveled it. It's not easy, but it's worth it.

About This Book

If you've been looking for a set of Visual Basic–specific programming standards, you've probably been frustrated by the lack of available material. Steve McConnell's *Code Complete* (Microsoft Press, 1993) is a good book on programming standards, but it's directed primarily at C programmers and you'll rarely find a Visual Basic code example. A number of other languages, such as Pascal, are discussed, but Visual Basic comes across as a second-class citizen. Add the fact that much of *Code Complete* is higher-level theory supported by statistics, and you've got to *really* want to learn the material to make it through the book if you're a Visual Basic programmer.

In this book, I've tried to create a professional coding book for Visual Basic programmers, and *just* for Visual Basic programmers. If you're a C++ person, you might find the interface chapters worth a look, but overall you're not going to get your money's worth here. However, if you're a Visual Basic programmer, whether a student or a pro, the cost of this book will be paid back to you in spades if you learn about, and adhere to, even a few of the standards presented.

This book is not about application architecture, needs analysis, design specs, or testing; it *is* about development. Some of the topics, such as designing modules and procedures, certainly contain material you might find in a software design book, but it's presented here as practical guidance rather than as theory. You won't learn *how* to program here, but you will learn how to program *better*.

This book focuses on the practical aspects of standardization, with "practical" being the key word. Code samples are used liberally, showing both good and bad coding techniques. Where necessary, alternate methods are shown and discussed. I've also taken a lot of time to format the code in this book to look much like the code you work with in Visual Basic's code editor. I've used color and boldface accordingly, and I hope you find that it makes the code easier to read and adds a bit of character to what might otherwise be many dull code listings.

For clarity's sake, I've attempted to present the material in each chapter in a uniform way. The content of some chapters does not lend itself to fitting a strict mold, so, where necessary, some minor deviation occurs. Generally, however, each chapter begins with a general discussion of the ideas and topics covered in the chapter, including problems or issues that the standards address. The purpose of this beginning section is not necessarily to teach you the standards and methods to apply to overcome the problems, but to educate you concerning the issues themselves. I've tried to refrain from putting too much code in this section and instead reserved the detailed code examples for later in each chapter.

Following the general information is a bulleted list of goals related to the specific programming issues covered by the chapter. If you choose not to implement a standard discussed in a chapter, you should still make sure that you are meeting the goals listed in the chapter. The best approach to the particular programming issues is to follow the standards presented in the chapter, but, as I'm sure you're aware, many of these issues can quickly divide a team of developers into factions. If you feel strongly that a standard I'm arguing for is not appropriate, employ some other technique that meets the goals—just meet the goals.

In every chapter you'll find a number of *directives*—that is, specific standardization techniques intended to direct and guide you. Each directive is numbered with the chapter number and directive number (for example, 10.1). This numbering scheme serves two purposes: it makes it easy for you to cross-reference directives within the book, and it allows managers and teachers to compile a specific list of directives to use within their development projects or instruction. Each directive section includes text explaining how and why to implement a specific standard and usually code samples that apply and fail to apply the directive.

Sometimes within a directive section I will offer one or more *practical applications*—even more detailed directives related to the directive they follow and illustrating specific components of that directive. (An "application" in this context refers to the application of a technique, not to a program.) Almost every practical application includes a code example that doesn't adhere to the related standard, as well as the same code process written according to the standardization rules. At times, alternate examples are given when there is more than one acceptable solution. These examples go far beyond *Debug.Print "Hello World"*. Most, if not all, of the code examples come from real-world commercial projects, and many are full procedures. I hope this code will make the benefits of a given technique more readily apparent and make the technique easier to implement in your own projects.

Some directives and practical applications will be more relevant to your situation than others, and that's OK. In certain cases, I try to point out standards and techniques that are very important—that is, areas where deviation should not occur. Even in those cases, however, you might decide differently than I do. The key in the end is to accept a formal set of standards and to apply those standards consistently. The benefits of doing so are there for the taking. After reading this book, you will write better code.

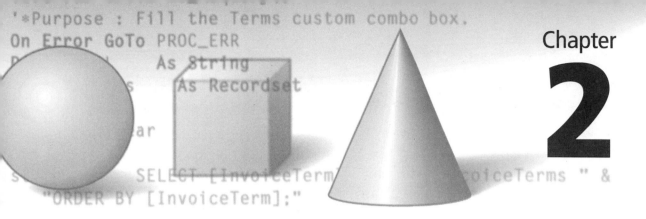

Creating Object and Project Templates

If you or your development team creates numerous projects, you can save considerable development time and promote application consistency by creating and using object and project templates. Consultants, for instance, often create many different applications for many different clients. When consultants reduce their work through code and object reuse, they enjoy higher profits and shorter development cycles.

If you develop numerous applications, chances are good that you create components that are often very similar, if not identical, from project to project. You might use a common splash screen or a common About box and copyright form. Or you might have a common switchboard form or a custom browse-for-file class. In these cases, you can make some small changes to the objects, add them to your integrated development environment (IDE) as templates, and use them to kick-start new development projects and ensure a more consistent look and feel across all of your applications.

Using Object Templates

When you choose to add a new object to a project, Microsoft Visual Basic displays a dialog box (for example, the Add Form dialog box) from which you can select an existing object or create a new object (either a generic object or an object based on a template). (See Figure 2-1.) Although Visual Basic ships with a number of predefined object templates (most notably a number of form templates), you aren't limited to just those that are provided. Any standard object (for example, a form or a module) you create and save in Visual Basic can be made into an object template.

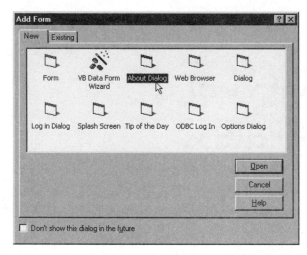

Figure 2-1.   *The Add Form dialog box displays the form templates contained in the Template\Forms folder.*

When Visual Basic displays an Add *<object>* dialog box with a number of object template icons, as shown in Figure 2-1, those object templates aren't displayed from a static list. Instead, Visual Basic looks at the Template folder located in the main Visual Basic folder. Within the Template folder are a number of subfolders, one for each type of object that can have templates. (See Figure 2-2.) Visual Basic looks within the appropriate subfolder and adds each of the objects within that subfolder to the Add *<object>* dialog box as a template icon. If a file placed within a subfolder isn't of the correct type, it's ignored.

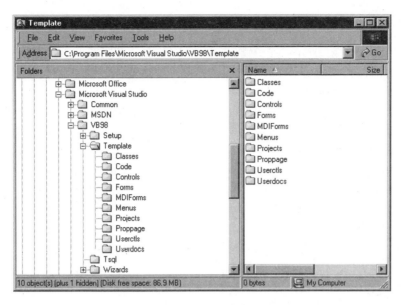

Figure 2-2. *The Template folder contains subfolders for the various objects that can have templates.*

Suppose for instance that you've created a form object, and you want it to appear in the Add Form dialog box each time you choose Add Form from the Project menu. Simply place a copy of your form file in the Forms subfolder of the Template folder. If the form has a binary file associated with it (that is, an .frx file), that file must also be placed in the subfolder. To prevent an object from appearing as a template, delete or move the object's files from the appropriate subfolder of the Template folder.

When a template object is added to a project, a new instance of that object is created; changes made to the object are not propagated to the template itself. When you save the project, Visual Basic prompts you for a filename and path for the object. The next time an object is created based on that template, the template will be the same as it was originally.

 OTE To make changes to an object template, add the object to a project by using the Existing tab of the Add *<object>* dialog box, make your changes, and save the object.

Using Project Templates

It seems as though software development these days is largely focused on reuse. Programming with objects is one of the hottest topics for programmers, and objects are really all about code reuse. It only makes sense that if you can take advantage of previous development by using some or all of an existing object, you can reduce development and testing time. Creating object templates as I discussed at the beginning of this chapter is a great way to make common objects easily accessible to new and existing projects. In addition to enabling you to make object templates, Visual Basic also gives you the ability to create complete project templates.

Exploring Visual Basic Project Templates

Project templates can be skeletal templates containing a few base objects, such as a form and a module, or they can be half-completed applications containing intricate code, such as a multiple-document interface (MDI) front end. To see examples of project templates, you need go no further than starting up Visual Basic itself. If you haven't disabled the New Project dialog box shown in Figure 2-3—see "Enabling and Disabling Templates" later in this chapter—it will be displayed each time you start Visual Basic. The default project templates displayed in this dialog box are installed with Visual Basic. These project templates are located in the Template\Projects folder in the main Visual Basic folder. (See Figure 2-4.)

When you double-click a project icon in the New Project dialog box, Visual Basic creates a temporary copy of the corresponding project file

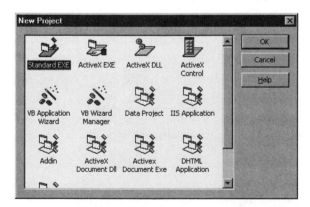

Figure 2-3.   *Visual Basic's available projects for new development are simply default templates.*

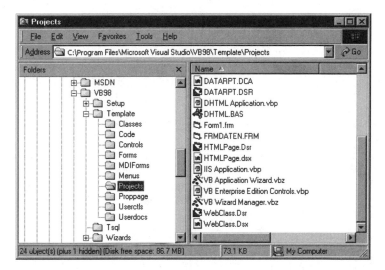

Figure 2-4. *Visual Basic project templates are located in the Template\Projects folder.*

from the Template\Projects folder. When you save the project, Visual Basic asks you to name all the objects within the project as well as the project itself. This behavior is much the same as when you are adding objects based on templates to a project—Visual Basic never overwrites the original template files.

You can make changes to Visual Basic's default templates, except to the basic projects: Standard EXE, ActiveX EXE, and ActiveX DLL. To modify any of the existing project templates, you must open the projects directly. When you open a project template directly, rather than create a new project based on the template, Visual Basic treats the template like any other project. When you save changes, the actual template files are overwritten with your modifications. This is a great way to tweak standard project templates so that they're more immediately usable in your environment.

Creating Custom Project Templates

Modifying the existing project templates is one way to promote consistency and jump-start your new projects, but it's not the only way. A much better approach is to create your own project templates. By creating custom project templates, you remove the risk of having your templates overwritten in the event that you need to reinstall Visual Basic. To create a new project template, simply create a new project of any type and set all of its properties to the appropriate values. Next create the objects (such as forms and modules) just as you want them to appear in projects based on the template. When you're finished, save the project file along with all of its object files in the Template\Projects folder.

 OTE Since every module (including form modules) should have full error trapping (as I'll discuss in Chapter 7, "Error Handling"), you should add the proper error handling to each object template. The idea is to make each object template as complete as possible. If objects based on a common template need to have the same work done to them each time they're added to a project, that work should be done in the template file itself.

Customizing Template Behavior

If you don't use object templates when developing, you can streamline the development process a bit by turning off specific object templates. Suppose, for example, that you want to add a form to a project. If form templates are enabled, Visual Basic displays an Add Form dialog box like the one shown in Figure 2-5, and you have to select a particular type of form, even if you just want to add a standard form. However, you can eliminate this step by disabling form templates. Similarly, you can eliminate the appearance of the Add *<object>* dialog box for other types of objects.

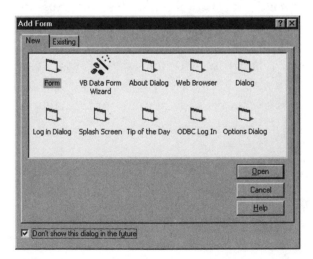

Figure 2-5. *If you don't use templates, the Add* <object> *dialog box can add an unnecessary step to your development process.*

Enabling and Disabling Templates

To disable templates for an object type, display Visual Basic's Options dialog box by choosing Options from the Tools menu and then click the Environment tab. (See Figure 2-6.) If you don't want to use templates of a certain type, clear the appropriate check box. When the templates are disabled for a type, adding an object of that type causes a new standard object of that type to be added to the project, without the intermediate step of the Add *<object>* dialog box appearing.

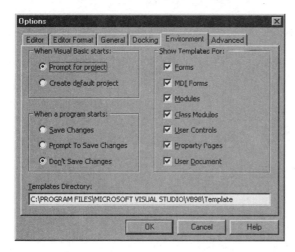

Figure 2-6. *You can pick and choose what types of templates to enable or disable.*

Setting the Templates Folder

You can add another level of consistency to your team development environment by specifying a custom template folder. The folder specified in the Templates Directory text box on the Environment tab of the Options dialog box—take a look at Figure 2-6 again—is the parent folder in which Visual Basic looks for object templates. For example, when you have enabled templates and you choose Add Form from the Project menu, Visual Basic looks in the specified folder for a subfolder named Forms and then adds all the form files it finds there to the dialog box.

To create your own custom template folder, you must create a root folder (that is, the folder you specify in the Templates Directory text box) as well as the proper subfolders. To simplify the process, just copy the Template folder in your Visual Basic folder to a shared drive, remove the templates you don't want to use, and set the path in the Templates Directory text box to the new folder you've created. Then place all your company's object templates in this custom template folder and have all the developers enter the path to the new folder in their Templates Directory text boxes. Whenever a developer adds a template object to a project, he or she will be using the same template as everyone else.

> ### Goals of Using Object and Project Templates
>
> The primary goals of using object and project templates include
>
> - Promoting and encouraging code reuse
> - Reducing development time of new and existing projects

Directives

2.1 Never hard-code application-specific or component-specific values in object templates.

Object templates should be made as generic as possible. Since you can rarely know in advance the project in which the objects might end up, you have to design your objects accordingly. There are essentially three mechanisms you can use to ensure that the data used and displayed by a template object is the proper data for the project in which the object resides. You can

- Reference the App object properties whenever possible.

- Provide functions and properties that the host project can call to set values within the object.

- Use a common set of global constants (and variables, if absolutely necessary).

Using parameters of public procedures is probably the best way to share data from a project with a template object. This mechanism allows you to create template objects as independent units. A developer only has to call the procedures in the object, passing the appropriate arguments, for the object to be integrated. This creates very modular and "black box"-like objects. You can design objects that rely on global variables or constants from the project to which they are added, but this reduces the modularity of the objects and generally means more work must be performed during the integration of the object.

 OTE It's important to use constants in place of hard-coded "magic" numbers within an object template so that developers can easily understand and replace the values.

Practical Applications

If any values within an object will be dependent on the project to which the object is added, do not hard-code those values. Make your object templates as "ready-to-go" as possible by minimizing the amount of code that needs to be added or modified within the object when the object is added to a project.

2.1.1   Never hard-code paths in an object template. Paths change from application to application and from installation to installation. Just as you should never hard-code a path in any object whatsoever, you should also never hard-code a path in an object template. The developer using the template might not realize that the hard-coded path exists, and this could cause the project to fail, crash, or, worse yet, modify inappropriate files.

Incorrect:
```
Me.Picture = LoadPicture("C:\Program Files\MyApp\Splash.bmp")
```

Correct:
```
Me.Picture = LoadPicture(App.Path & "\Splash.bmp")
```

Also correct (but using a global variable is not preferred):
```
Me.Picture = LoadPicture(g_strPath & "\Splash.bmp")
```

2.1.2   Never hard-code the application name in an object template. Because each application has its own name, never hard-code an application name in an object template.

Incorrect:

```
'* NOTE: Need to change application title when
'*       added to a project.
Me.Caption = "About Application"
```

Correct:

```
Me.Caption = "About " & App.Title
```

2.1.3 Never hard-code a version number in an object template.

A common form template is the About box, which often shows version information. If a template object displays data that can be retrieved from the App object, always pull that information from the App object.

Incorrect:

```
'* NOTE: You must replace X.X.X with the current version of the
'*       application when this object is added to a project.
lblVersion.Caption = "Version X.X.X"
```

Correct:

```
lblVersion.Caption = "Version " & App.Major & "." & _
                     App.Minor & "." & App.Revision
```

2.1.4 Expose properties for template objects to accept data from the host applications.

Rather than expose public variables or use global variables, use Property procedures. Property procedures allow you to perform data validation and execute code when the values change.

Incorrect:

```
Public m_strUserName As String
```

Correct:

```
Private m_strUserName As String

Public Property Get UserName() As String
   UserName = m_strUserName
End Property

Public Property Let UserName(strNewUserName As String)
   m_strUserName = strNewUserName
End Property
```

2.2 Provide extensive comments in object templates, particularly where modifications are required.

It's rare that you'll be able to add a template object to a project and not have to make *some* changes to it. You need to make it is as easy as possible for a developer (including you) who adds the template object to a project to know where and what changes are necessary to integrate the object with the project. One way to do this is to use a consistent mechanism for denoting comments that explain required changes and to document this notation in the Declarations section of the module. A developer can then easily search for the comments and make the changes as necessary.

For instance, you could denote comments that show where changes are necessary like this:

```
If txtPassword = "password" Then
    '* NOTE: Place code here to pass the
    '*       success to the calling procedure.
    LoginSucceeded = True
    Me.Hide
Else
    MsgBox "Invalid Password, try again!", , "Login"
    txtPassword.SetFocus
    SendKeys "{Home}+{End}"
End If
```

You could then document this in the Declarations section of the module as follows:

```
'* All areas of code where modifications are necessary
'* to integrate this object with a project are documented
'* with comments denoted by Note:.
'* To locate these comments, search for '* NOTE:.
```

Do this consistently in all your object templates, and you'll reduce the time and effort necessary for objects based on your templates to be integrated into projects. The more documenting (commenting) that you perform within the object template, the more efficiently the object can be used in other projects. Also, the work put into designing the template is paid back in multiples—the more the object is used in new projects, the higher the payback on the initial investment of development time. Finally, you'll also reduce the chance of something important being missed.

Incorrect:

```
'* Set tip file.
Const c_Tip_File = "TipOfDay.txt"
```

Correct:

```
'* NOTE: Change this constant to the name of the tip file.
'*       If you prefer, you can use a variable instead and
'*       set the value at run time.
Const c_Tip_File = "TipOfDay.txt"
```

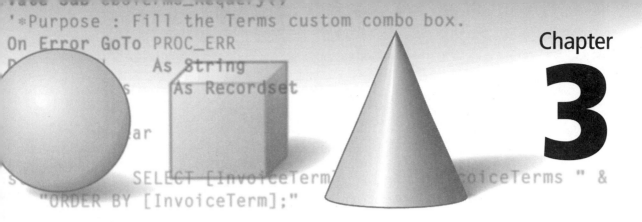

Designing Modules and Procedures

Since Microsoft Visual Basic is a visual language, much of your work involves designing user interfaces. However, you still have to write code to make your application do something. Modules and procedures are the framework for the code of your application, and building this framework requires careful consideration. There are proven techniques for creating better modules and procedures, and you should use these techniques when developing your project.

You'll often hear many different terms when modules and procedures are discussed. Take a look at the following table for descriptions of some of these terms.

Term	Description
Procedure	A named sequence of statements dedicated to a specific process. A procedure can have a set of parameters through which it can communicate with other portions of the program, and it can also return a value that can be used by other portions of the program. "Procedure" is a broad term covering Sub procedures, Function procedures, and Property procedures.

(continued)

continued

Term	Description
Sub procedure	A procedure declared with the keyword *Sub*. Sub procedures do not return values.
Function procedure	A procedure declared with the keyword *Function*. Function procedures return values.
Property procedure	A procedure declared with the keywords *Property Get*, *Property Let*, or *Property Set*. Property procedures are used to create object properties that can be read (*Property Get*) or set (*Property Let* or *Property Set*).
Routine	A generic term for a procedure.
Module	A named collection of (preferably related) procedures in a Visual Basic project.

Create Modules That Have Strong Cohesion

The importance of procedures is usually better understood than that of modules—a procedure is a section of code that performs a unified function. Unfortunately, for many developers the role of the module is a bit more confusing. A module is often wrongly thought of as a mere container used to store procedures. Some developers even take this idea to an extreme and put *all* their procedures into a single module—ugh!

One reason that modules don't always get the consideration they require is that the implementation of modules really doesn't affect the execution of a program. When a project is compiled, it doesn't matter if all the procedures are in a single module or in dozens of modules. But while the number of modules doesn't matter much to the actual execution of code, it matters a great deal when it comes to creating code that is easier both to debug and to maintain.

Modules should be used to organize sets of related procedures. In most applications, it's fairly easy to group procedures by some sort of commonality. For example, you might group all the routines in a contact management program that manipulate a contact record. You would put these related procedures in a single module with a name that describes the common purpose of the procedures, such as *mdlContact*. A procedure that opens a contact database, however, and that doesn't directly manipulate a contact record probably wouldn't belong in the contact module.

When a module contains a set of procedures that are tightly related, the module is said to have *strong cohesion.* When a module contains a number of more or less unrelated procedures, it's said to have *weak cohesion.* You should strive to create modules with strong cohesion.

Most projects contain a number of procedures that don't quite fit into a group with other procedures. In such cases, it's perfectly acceptable to create a catchall module for these loners, perhaps named *mdlGlobal, mdlUtilities,* or *mdlSupport.* As the project grows, however, keep an eye on these modules and watch for situations where groupings appear—then consider creating new modules for the groupings. By creating specialized modules, you'll promote stronger cohesion. The quantity of modules in a project is not nearly as important as the quality of the organization. A very large Visual Basic project might contain only a dozen or so modules, but they should be very well constructed modules.

A set of organized modules might look something like this:

Module	Procedure
mdlContact	*CreateContact*
	DisplayContact
	DeleteContact
mdlDatabase	*CloseDatabase*
	CreateDatabase
	OpenDatabase
mdlUtilities	*ShowOpenFileDialog*
	ShowSaveFileDialog

When building modules, think of what the term "modularization" means. The principal idea with modules is to create fairly self-contained units. The ultimate module is one that can be added to another project and used immediately by calling its public procedures. Such a universal module doesn't rely on global data or on procedures within other modules.

In reality, this second point is very hard to implement; it's difficult to create modules that don't contain at least a few calls to procedures in other modules, but it's a worthy goal.

If you're familiar with programming Visual Basic's class modules to create reusable objects, the general principles of modules should sound familiar to you. Creating an entity that contains all of its code (local procedures) as well as its own data (module-level variables) is known as *encapsulation,* and this is the principal idea behind object-oriented programming. If you're able to create perfectly encapsulated modules, you should seriously consider creating them as class modules (rather than standard modules) and manipulating them as objects.

Create Loosely Coupled, Highly Specialized Procedures

Visual Basic makes creating procedures easy, but this simplicity masks the art and science of building well-crafted procedures. Visual Basic places few rules on procedures—it doesn't limit the number of statements you can place within a procedure, nor does it limit how many tasks can be performed by a procedure. Although Visual Basic doesn't enforce such limitations, you should perform some self-governing in these areas to create better procedures. In the following sections, I'll describe how to do that.

Make All Procedures Perform Specialized Functions

The first thing to keep in mind is that every procedure should perform a specific function, and it should do it *very* well. You should avoid creating procedures that perform many different tasks. This frequently requires some forethought because it's not always obvious what constitutes a task. For instance, in an inventory management application you might need to create a posting routine to post receipts generated from a purchase order. The steps involved in posting might include

- Retrieving the ID and cost of a received item

- Confirming that the ID exists in the master table of inventory items

- Updating the quantity on hand in the inventory table

- Updating total, average, and latest costs for the item in the database

- If FIFO (first in, first out) or LIFO (last in, first out) accounting practices are being used, updating the FIFO or LIFO records

You can use a number of approaches to code this functionality. You could create a single posting procedure that performs all these actions, or you could create more specialized procedures such as those in the following list:

- *PostPurchaseOrderReceipt* (main entry procedure)

- *ValidateItemExistsInMasterInventoryTable*

- *UpdateQuantityOnHand*

- *UpdateItemCosts*

- *UpdateFIFOLIFO*

Creating specialized procedures has a number of advantages. First, debugging becomes easier. If you're getting incorrect latest costs on your inventory valuation reports, you'd know to begin your search for bugs in the *UpdateItemCosts* procedure. If you placed all this code in a single *PostPurchaseOrderReceipt* procedure, you'd have to wade through the other functionality to get to the cost-related code. When you create specialized procedures, you won't always locate errors in the first procedure in which you look, but you'll reduce the amount of time you spend hunting for them.

Perhaps an even more important advantage of creating specialized procedures is the ease with which you can make planned or unplanned modifications to the code. Continuing to use the example above, let's say that a change within your organization causes certain business rules to change or causes a change in the data storage tier. Consider that you are no longer going to keep inventory in a single location but rather are going to spread it across multiple warehouses. When an item is received in inventory, it must be received in your inventory management application in a specific location. If you've isolated the code that adds the item to inventory—the *UpdateQuantityOnHand* procedure here—you'll know exactly where to go to make the changes and you'll affect only a small and specialized area of the code. If instead you placed all the posting-related code in one procedure, adding features would cause the procedure to bloat, making it increasingly more difficult to manage.

There are no hard-and-fast rules as to how to split a process into specialized procedures. You want to create efficiently maintainable procedures, but you don't want to have to keep track of dozens of tiny procedures that would be better utilized as parts of a larger procedure. When in doubt, have someone review your code; it usually helps to get a different perspective. This is an area where experience really improves your skills. Over time, you'll start to get a feel for how parts of code are maintained and modified.

Make Procedures as Self-Contained as Possible

Besides making procedures as specialized as possible (within reason), you should also make procedures as self-contained as possible. When a procedure relies on calls to other procedures, it's said to be *tightly coupled* with those other procedures. Tightly coupled procedures make debugging and modifying more difficult because more factors are involved. When you create procedures that rely on few or no calls to other procedures, you create *loosely coupled* procedures. Loose coupling is superior to tight coupling, but of course it's impossible to make every procedure a self-contained entity. Nonetheless, strive to reduce the coupling of procedures as much as possible.

One way to make procedures more self-contained is to minimize global and module-level variables. Procedures that use global or module-level variables are not self-contained because they rely on data outside of their full control. For more information on controlling the scope of variables and on the evils of global variables, refer to Chapter 6, "Variables."

As you're developing your procedures, try to think of each one as a black box—other routines shouldn't require knowledge of the inner workings of the procedure, nor should the procedure require knowledge of items outside of it. This is why your procedures should rely on parameters rather than global data. When a procedure accepts parameters through the front door, the parameters become data local to the procedure. (Every procedure has a single entry point, known as the front door, and should contain only one exit point, the back door.) When a procedure uses global or module-level variables, it's accessing data outside of its own confines.

When creating specialized procedures, consider the following guidelines:

- Put complex processes in specialized procedures. If an application utilizes complex mathematical equations, consider putting each equation into its own procedure. That way other procedures that use the equations won't be burdened with the actual code for that equation. This also makes it easier to debug problems related to the equations.

- Hide data input/output (I/O) in specialized procedures. It might be necessary later to change the way data I/O is handled. For instance, you might modify an application that uses text files so that it uses a database engine such as Microsoft Jet. If the application's data I/O functionality is isolated in specialized procedures, it'll be much easier to make the necessary modifications.

- Isolate areas of code likely to change in specialized procedures. If you know that a certain process might change over time, place the volatile code into specialized procedures to make it easier to modify later and to lessen the likelihood that you'll inadvertently cause problems with other processes.

- Encapsulate business rules in specialized procedures. Often, business rules fall into the category of code likely to change and should be isolated from the rest of the application. Other procedures shouldn't know the business rules, only the procedures to call to apply the business rules.

Minimize Fan-In and Fan-Out

Fan-in and *fan-out,* illustrated in Figure 3-1, are technical terms used to describe, respectively, the number of procedures that call a single procedure and the number of procedures called from within a procedure. When a given procedure is called (and therefore relied on) by numerous other procedures, it's said to have a high degree of fan-in, which is good. A procedure with a high degree of fan-in is generally a well-encapsulated procedure, and it supports the concept of code reuse. A procedure that makes calls to numerous other procedures has a high degree of fan-out, which is not so good. A high degree of fan-out means that the procedure relies on many other procedures to get its job done—in other words, it's a tightly coupled procedure. This makes debugging more difficult because of the added complexity of following the execution path.

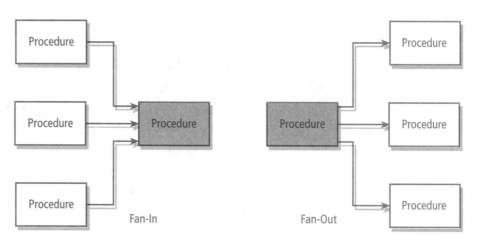

Figure 3-1.   *A procedure with fan-in and a procedure with fan-out.*

When maximizing fan-in and minimizing fan-out, you'll have to accept some give-and-take; there's no perfect solution in a given project. If you follow all the principles of creating specialized procedures, you're bound to encounter situations in which some procedures have a high degree of fan-out because they're delegating various tasks to other specialized procedures. Achieving a balance of specialized procedures with loose coupling, strong cohesion, higher fan-in, and lower fan-out is a continuing goal that's never fully met.

Attempt to Alphabetize Procedures Within a Module

If you don't work with Visual Basic's code window in multiple-procedure mode, you should. This mode allows you to scroll in the code window to view multiple procedures at one time, as shown in Figure 3-2. To put the code window in multiple-procedure mode, choose Options from the Tools menu, and select the Default To Full Module View check box. When you're working in this mode, it helps to have the procedures sorted alphabetically so that you can more easily find a particular procedure when scrolling—making the scroll bar much more useful.

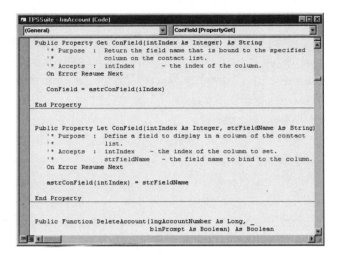

Figure 3-2. *Viewing multiple procedures in the code window helps increase productivity.*

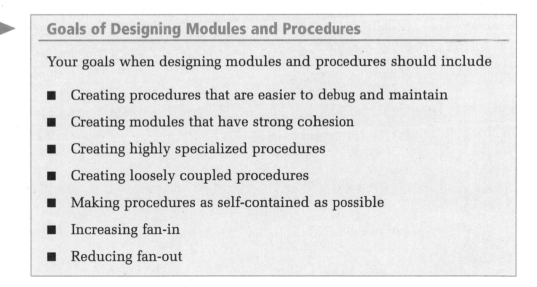

Goals of Designing Modules and Procedures

Your goals when designing modules and procedures should include

- Creating procedures that are easier to debug and maintain
- Creating modules that have strong cohesion
- Creating highly specialized procedures
- Creating loosely coupled procedures
- Making procedures as self-contained as possible
- Increasing fan-in
- Reducing fan-out

Directives

3.1 Give procedures and modules descriptive names.

One of the easiest ways to make your code more understandable is to give your procedures descriptive names. Function names such as *DoIt*, *GetIt*, and *PrintIt* aren't nearly as understandable as *CalculateSalesTax*, *RetrieveUserID*, and *PrintSpreadsheet*.

The first thing to remember when naming a procedure is that DOS is gone (not dead and gone, but for the most part gone). Many programmers from the DOS days are still trying to break old habits that hinder rather than benefit development. For instance, some languages commonly used in the past limited the number of characters you could use to define a procedure name. We still see programmers choosing procedure names such as *CALCTAX*, *GETIT*, *GETREC*, and *DELREC*. If you're doing this, it's time to make a change. Code consisting of abbreviated procedure names is difficult (at best) to understand and maintain, and there's simply no valid reason to do this anymore. Certainly, procedure names such as *Calculate-SalesTax*, *RetrieveEmployee*, and *DeleteEmployee* are much more self-explanatory than the older names.

Correctly naming procedures can make all the difference in the world when it comes to debugging and maintaining a project. Take naming procedures seriously; don't reduce understandability for the sake of reduced typing.

Incorrect:

```
Private Function InvoicePost() As Boolean
Private Function PrintIt() As Boolean
Public Sub SaveItem()
Public Sub DeleteRecord()
```

Correct:

```
Private Function PostInvoice() As Boolean
Private Function PrintSpreadsheet() As Boolean
Public Sub SavePicture()
Public Sub DeleteContact()
```

Practical Applications

3.1.1   Use mixed-case letters when defining procedure names. In the past, some languages limited you to uppercase procedure names. This limitation does not exist in Visual Basic, and you should define all procedure names in mixed-case letters. IT'S HARDER TO READ SENTENCES IN ALL UPPERCASE THAN IT IS TO READ THEM IN MIXED CASE, and the same holds true for procedure names. By the way, all-lowercase names are almost (but not quite) as difficult to read as all-uppercase names. For instance, compare *EmployeeAge* to *EMPLOYEEAGE* and *employeeage*. Also, it's OK to use an underscore in a variable name to simulate a space (for example, *Employee_Age*), but if you do use underscores, use them consistently. Note that you cannot use spaces in variable names.

Incorrect:
```
Private Function POSTINVOICE() As Boolean
Public Sub savepicture()
```

Correct:
```
Private Function PostInvoice() As Boolean
Public Sub SavePicture()
```

3.1.2 Don't abbreviate when defining procedure names. If you ask two people how to abbreviate a given word, you'll probably end up with two different answers. If you believe that specific items within your application should be abbreviated, document those situations and make sure everyone uses those abbreviations all the time. Definitely don't abbreviate certain words in some procedures but not in others.

Incorrect:
```
Private Function SaveEmp() As Boolean
Public Sub DelContact()
Public Sub CalcTax()
```

Correct:
```
Private Function SaveEmployee() As Boolean
Public Sub DeleteContact()
Public Sub CalculateSalesTax()
```

3.2 Give every procedure a single exit point.

Debugging code in an event-driven application can be quite challenging—procedures are called from within procedures (fan-out), and code execution often bounces around like a billiard ball on a bumper pool table. The simple statements *Exit Function* and *Exit Sub* can compound this complexity. Every procedure has a single entry point, and this makes sense. You wouldn't want different calling procedures to be able to enter a given procedure in different code locations—that would be a nightmare.

Although it's not as obvious, every procedure should also have a single exit point.

When you can be assured that control always exits a procedure in the same way, at the same line of code, debugging becomes considerably easier. If you allow a procedure to be exited from anywhere within the code, how can you be sure that cleanup code is always executed before the procedure is exited? Sure, you might be able to remember exactly what is occurring within a procedure, but what about when another developer edits the procedure to add just one more *Select Case* clause and uses an *Exit Sub* to exit the procedure? Any code that *should* be executed to clean up the procedure sits unused, and problems can easily result.

The solution is to create a label called *PROC_EXIT* in every procedure. Underneath this label, place all necessary cleanup code and an appropriate Exit statement (*Exit Sub*, *Exit Function*, or *Exit Property*). Whenever you need to exit the procedure, include a *GoTo PROC_EXIT* statement rather than directly invoking the Exit command.

Creating single exit points makes procedures more like black boxes. Execution comes in one door and leaves through another door, resulting in fewer errors and a less difficult debugging process. The act of creating single exit points is amazingly trivial, but the rewards are tremendous. It's not often that the rewards will be so much greater than the effort required, so make sure to take advantage of it!

Incorrect:

```
Public Function IsFormLoaded(strFormName As String) As Boolean
    '* Purpose  :  Determine whether a specified form is loaded.
    '* Accepts  :  strFormName - the name of a form.
    '* Returns  :  True if the form is loaded, False if not.
    On Error GoTo PROC_ERR
    Dim intCounter As Integer

    '* Since referring to a form loads the form, the proper
    '* way to determine whether the form is loaded is to loop
    '* through the Forms collection, which contains only
    '* loaded forms.
    For intCounter = 0 To Forms.Count - 1
        '* If the current form is the specified form,
        '* return True and get out.
```

```
        If Forms(intCounter).Name = strFormName Then
            IsFormLoaded = True
            Exit Function
        End If

    Next intCounter

    '* Form was not found; return False.
    IsFormLoaded = False

PROC_ERR:
    MsgBox "basMain | IsFormLoaded" & vbCrLf & "Error: " & _
            Err.Number & vbCrLf & Err.Description
    Resume Next
End Function
```

Correct:

```
Public Function IsFormLoaded(strFormName As String) As Boolean
    '* Purpose  :  Determine whether a specified form is loaded.
    '* Accepts  :  strFormName - the name of a form.
    '* Returns  :  True if the form is loaded, False if not.
    On Error GoTo PROC_ERR
    Dim intCounter As Integer

    '* Since referring to a form loads the form, the proper
    '* way to determine whether the form is loaded is to loop
    '* through the Forms collection, which contains only
    '* loaded forms.
    For intCounter = 0 To Forms.Count - 1

        '* If the current form is the specified form,
        '* return True and get out.
        If Forms(intCounter).Name = strFormName Then
            IsFormLoaded = True
            GoTo PROC_EXIT
        End If

    Next intCounter

    '* Form was not found; return False.
    IsFormLoaded = False

PROC_EXIT:
    Exit Function

PROC_ERR:
    MsgBox "basMain | IsFormLoaded" & vbCrLf & "Error: " & _
            Err.Number & vbCrLf & Err.Description
    Resume Next
End Function
```

Practical Application

3.2.1   Create robust exit code. Don't get complacent when adding cleanup code to a procedure. If the proper exit process depends on the states of certain variables, check the values of those variables and respond accordingly in your cleanup code.

Incorrect:

```
Private Sub cboTerms_Requery()
    '* Purpose  :  Fill the Terms custom combo box.
    On Error GoTo PROC_ERR
    Dim strSQL     As String
    Dim rstTerms   As Recordset

    cboTerms.Clear

    strSQL = "SELECT [InvoiceTerm] FROM tblInvoiceTerms " & _
             "ORDER BY [InvoiceTerm];"
    Set rstTerms = dbSales.OpenRecordset(strSQL, dbOpenForwardOnly)

    '* Add all of the invoice terms to the Terms combo box.
    Do While Not rstTerms.EOF
        cboTerms.AddItem rstTerms![InvoiceTerm]
        rstTerms.MoveNext
    Loop

PROC_EXIT:
    rstTerms.Close
    Set rstTerms = Nothing

    Exit Sub

PROC_ERR:
    Call ShowError(Me.Name, "cboTerms_Requery", Err.Number, _
                   Err.Description)
    GoTo PROC_EXIT

End Sub
```

Correct:

```
Private Sub cboTerms_Requery()
    '* Purpose  :  Fill the Terms custom combo box.
    On Error GoTo PROC_ERR
    Dim strSQL     As String
    Dim rstTerms   As Recordset
```

```
cboTerms.Clear

strSQL = "SELECT [InvoiceTerm] FROM tblInvoiceTerms " & _
         "ORDER BY [InvoiceTerm];"
Set rstTerms = dbSales.OpenRecordset(strSQL, dbOpenForwardOnly)

'* Add all of the invoice terms to the Terms combo box.
Do While Not rstTerms.EOF
   cboTerms.AddItem rstTerms![InvoiceTerm]
   rstTerms.MoveNext
Loop

PROC_EXIT:
   '* If a database error occurred, rstTerms won't be set to
   '* a valid recordset.
   If Not (rstTerms Is Nothing) Then
      rstTerms.Close
      Set rstTerms = Nothing
   End If

   Exit Sub

PROC_ERR:
   Call ShowError(Me.Name, "cboTerms_Requery", Err.Number, _
                  Err.Description)
   GoTo PROC_EXIT

End Sub
```

3.3   Give every procedure a clearly defined scope.

Scope refers to the visibility of a variable or procedure within a project. Procedures can be defined as having either module-level, global, or friend scope. When a procedure is declared with the *Private* keyword, it has module-level scope and can be called only from procedures within the same module. A procedure declared with the *Public* keyword has global scope and can be called from any module within the project. In addition, public procedures of public class modules are available to external programs. Declaring a procedure (in a public class module) with the *Friend* keyword makes the procedure public to all modules within the project, but it does not make the procedure public to external programs.

When creating a procedure, always explicitly define its scope. Although it's possible to define a procedure without using *Public*, *Private*, or

Friend, you should avoid doing this. Take a look at the following procedure definition in a standard module. Is this procedure private to the module, or is it public to all modules within the project?

```
Sub DisplayConfirmationMessage()
    ⋮
End Sub
```

The previous procedure is actually a public procedure because Visual Basic uses *Public* scope as the default. If your intent really is to create a public procedure, make that clear to the reader by explicitly declaring the procedure with the *Public* keyword like this:

```
Public Sub DisplayConfirmationMessage()
    ⋮
End Sub
```

Often, procedures declared without *Public*, *Private*, or *Friend* are really intended to be module-level (*Private*) procedures. However, without being specifically declared as *Private*, they are inadvertently created as *Public* procedures. Reduce the amount of effort required of the reader by giving each and every procedure a clearly defined scope. Also make sure that you're giving a procedure the scope that makes the most sense. If a procedure is called by only one other procedure within the same module, make it *Private*. If the procedure is called from procedures in multiple modules, explicitly declare the procedure as *Public*.

Practical Application

3.3.1 Every procedure definition should begin with *Public*, *Private*, or *Friend*. If you have existing procedures without one of these keywords, go through your project to determine the proper scope for each procedure and modify their declarations accordingly.

Incorrect:

```
Sub CalculatePOTotals()
    ⋮
End Sub
```

Correct:
```
Public Sub CalculatePOTotals()
    ⋮
End Sub
```

3.4 Use parameters to pass data between procedures.

Although they're not quite as problematic as global variables, module-level variables should be avoided as much as possible as well. In general, the smaller the scope of a variable the better. One way to reduce module-level and global variables is to pass data between procedures as parameters, rather than having the procedures share global or module-level variables.

Practical Applications

3.4.1   Specify a data type for each and every parameter. This can't be stressed enough. When creating procedures with parameters, always explicitly declare each parameter as a specific data type. For more information on data types, see Chapter 6, "Variables." When you omit the *As* <type> portion of a parameter declaration, the parameter is created as a Variant. I'll discuss the problems inherent with the Variant data type in Chapter 6. If you want to create a Variant parameter, do so explicitly using *As Variant.*

Incorrect:
```
Private Sub CreateStockRecord(ItemID, Repair, Quantity)
```

Correct:
```
Private Sub CreateStockRecord(strItemID As String, blnRepair _
    As Boolean, sngQuantity As Single)
```

3.4.2   Pass data *ByVal* or *ByRef*, as appropriate. Visual Basic passes data to procedure parameters *by reference* unless told to do otherwise. When a variable is passed by reference (*ByRef*) to a parameter of a procedure, the procedure receives a pointer to the original variable. Any subsequent changes made to the parameter are made to the original variable. On the other hand, when a variable is passed by value (*ByVal*) to a parameter, the procedure receives a copy of the variable. (String variables are an exception to this rule.) Any changes made to the parameter are made only to the copy, and the original variable remains unchanged. One possible standard would be to preface each parameter with *ByRef* or *ByVal*. That way you're explicitly declaring which process to use, and the code is more self-documenting. However, the discipline required to preface every parameter with *ByRef* or *ByVal* is great.

Another, and definitely easier, solution is to preface a parameter with *ByRef* only when that parameter will be used to change the value of the original variable (also called the argument). In that case, this practical application would read, "When a parameter is used to change the value of its argument, explicitly declare the parameter as *ByRef*." Then you can add a comment to the Accepts section of the procedure comment header stating that the parameter is being used as an output parameter—that is, to change the value of its argument. This approach gives you the best of both worlds.

Incorrect:

```
Public Sub ParseName(strFullName As String, strFirstName As String, _
    strMiddleInitial As String, strLastName As String)
```

Correct:

```
Public Sub ParseName(strFullName As String, _
                 ByRef strFirstName As String, _
                 ByRef strMiddleInitial As String, _
                 ByRef strLastName As String)
'* Purpose   :  Parse a full name such as "John Smith" or "John D.
'*                Smith" into the proper separate components.
'* Accepts   :  strFullName - the name to parse.
'*                strFirstName, strMiddleInitial, and strLastName are
'*                used as output parameters. This procedure populates
'*                the corresponding arguments with the proper values.
```

3.4.3   Always validate parameters—never assume that you have good data.   A common mistake among programmers is to write procedures that assume they have good data. This assumption isn't such a problem during initial development when you're writing the calling procedures. Chances are good then that you know what the allowable values for a parameter are and will provide them accordingly. However, the following situations can be troublesome if you don't validate parameter data:

- Someone else creates a calling procedure, and that person isn't aware of the allowable values.

- Bad data entered by a user or taken from a database is passed to the parameter. When you hard-code values, you have more control. When the data can come from "outside the box," you can't be sure what data is coming into a procedure.

- You add new calling procedures at a later time and mistakenly pass bad data.

- A procedure is made a public member of a public object. When that happens, you can't be sure of the data passed to the parameter from an external program.

Given these possibilities, and given the fact that it doesn't take much effort to validate incoming data, it's simply not worth the risks *not* to validate incoming data. Validating parameters is one of the first tasks you should perform in a procedure.

Incorrect:

```
Public Function DuplicateContact(lngContactNumber As Long) As Boolean
    '* Purpose  :  Create a new contact that is a duplicate of
    '*               the specified contact.
    '* Accepts  :  lngContactNumber - the unique ID of the contact to
    '*               duplicate.
    '* Returns  :  True if successful, False otherwise.
    On Error GoTo PROC_ERR
    :
End Function
```

Correct:

```
Public Function DuplicateContact(lngContactNumber As Long) As Boolean
    '* Purpose  :  Create a new contact that is a duplicate of
    '*               the specified contact.
    '* Accepts  :  lngContactNumber - the unique ID of the contact to
    '*               duplicate.
    '* Returns  :  True if successful, False otherwise.
    On Error GoTo PROC_ERR
```

```
'* Make sure a valid contact number has been specified.
If lngContactNumber <= 0 Then GoTo PROC_EXIT
    ⋮
PROC_EXIT:
    Exit Function

End Function
```

3.4.4 Use enumerations when a parameter accepts only a small set of values. Chapter 5, "Using Constants and Enumerations," describes enumerations in great detail, but they bear mentioning here also. If a parameter accepts only a small set of values, create an enumeration for the parameter. Using enumerations reduces the potential of data entry errors in coding. Remember, however, that declaring a parameter as an enumerated type does not ensure that a value passed to the parameter is a member of the enumeration; you must still validate the data. Enumerations are powerful and have many advantages—whenever possible, consider using an enumeration.

Incorrect:

```
Public Sub PrintReport(strRptFileName As String, _
    lngDestination As Long)

    If lngDestination < 0 Or lngDestination > 1 Then GoTo PROC_EXIT
    ⋮
PROC_EXIT:
    Exit Sub

End Sub
```

Correct:

```
Public Sub PrintReport(strRptFileName As String, _
    lngDestination As tpsPrintDestination)

    '* Make sure a valid destination has been specified.
    If lngDestination <> tpsScreen And _
        lngDestination <> tpsPrinter Then
        GoTo PROC_EXIT
    End If
    ⋮
PROC_EXIT:
    Exit Sub

End Sub
```

3.5   Call procedures in a consistent and self-documenting manner.

Visual Basic offers numerous shortcuts you can take when writing code. Generally, these shortcuts don't affect performance, but they often do sacrifice the readability of your code in favor of saving a few keystrokes at development time. You should attempt to make your code as self-documenting as possible. One area in which you can take shortcuts, but shouldn't, is when calling procedures.

You can call a procedure in a number of ways. When calling a Sub procedure, you can use the word *Call* or leave it out. For instance, the following statements will both call the same Sub procedure:

```
Call ShowError("clsApplication", "ShowRep", _
                Err.Number, Err.Description)

ShowError "clsApplication", "ShowRep", Err.Number, Err.Description
```

Although you can omit the word *Call* and save yourself having to type two parentheses to boot, you should avoid this technique. The *Call* keyword specifically indicates that the statement is calling a Sub procedure as opposed to a Function procedure, and it makes the code more easily readable.

Visual Basic lets you call a Sub procedure and a Function procedure in exactly the same way. Consider this function:

```
Public Function DisplayContact(lngContactNumber As Long) As Boolean
    ⋮
End Function
```

You can call this function by using any of these statements:

```
Call ShowRep(lngRepNumber)
ShowRep lngRepNumber
blnResult = ShowRep(lngRepNumber)
```

To make code as self-documenting as possible, differentiate between calling Sub procedures and calling Function procedures. Always use the *Call* keyword when calling Sub procedures, and always retrieve the value of a Function call—even if you aren't going to use the value. The first statement in the previous example is misleading; it looks like a Sub procedure call rather than a Function procedure call. Although the second statement is better than the first, it does not retrieve the result of the function. This is not nearly as legible as the third statement, which does retrieve the result. If you aren't going to use the result of a Function call, consider placing a comment in front of the Function call stating what is returned from the function and why you don't need it.

Practical Applications

3.5.1 **Always use the *Call* keyword when calling Sub procedures.** By using *Call* when calling Sub procedures, it's easier to distinguish the call from a Function call.

Incorrect:
```
PerformWordMerge8 strMergeFile, strTemplateName
```

Correct:
```
Call PerformWordMerge8(strMergeFile, strTemplateName)
```

3.5.2 **When setting a variable to the result of a function, include the parentheses in the Function call even if there are no arguments.** When calling a Function procedure, it isn't necessary to use the parentheses if the procedure doesn't accept any arguments. However, the code becomes a little more self-documenting when you include the parentheses anyway. The parentheses make it easy to tell that the symbol is a function name as opposed to a variable name.

Incorrect:
```
strDefaultWareHouse = GetDefaultWarehouse
```

Correct:
```
strDefaultWareHouse = GetDefaultWarehouse()
```

3.5.3 **Always retrieve the return value of a function, even if you aren't going to use it.** Although Visual Basic lets you call a Function procedure without retrieving the function's return value, you should always retrieve the return value even if you aren't going to use it. This improves readability and can greatly aid the debugging process. Many functions return a result code, indicating whether the function was successful. Although you might not need to use the result code right away, it might become important later.

Incorrect:

```
Public Sub OpenDocument(strFileName As String)
    '* Purpose  :  Launch the associated program of the specified
    '*               document.
    '* Accepts  :  A full path and file name of a document.
    On Error GoTo PROC_ERR

    ShellExecute frmMain.hwnd, "Open", strFileName, 0, 0, 1

PROC_EXIT:
    Exit Sub

PROC_ERR:
    MsgBox Me.Name & " | OpenDocument" & vbCrLf & "Error: " & _
           Err.Number & vbCrLf & Err.Description
    Resume Next

End Sub
```

Correct:

```
Public Sub OpenDocument(strFileName As String)
    '* Purpose  :  Launch the associated program of the specified
    '*               document.
    '* Accepts  :  A full path and file name of a document.
    On Error GoTo PROC_ERR
    Dim lngResult As Long

    '* The ShellExecute function returns a value indicating the result
    '* of trying to open the document. We might need this value later.
    lngResult = ShellExecute(frmMain.hwnd, "Open", _
                             strFileName, 0, 0, 1)

PROC_EXIT:
    Exit Sub

PROC_ERR:
    MsgBox Me.Name & " | OpenDocument" & vbCrLf & "Error: " & _
           Err.Number & vbCrLf & Err.Description
    Resume Next

End Sub
```

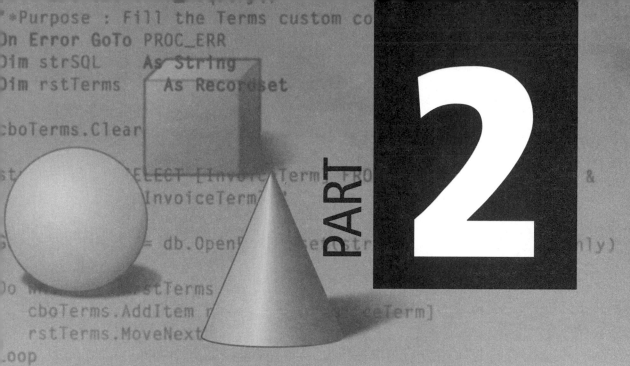

```
*Purpose : Fill the Terms custom co
On Error GoTo PROC_ERR
Dim strSQL      As String
Dim rstTerms    As Recordset

cboTerms.Clear

                ELECT [InvoiceTerm FRO                    &
        InvoiceTerm

        = db.Open                                    nly)

Do                rstTerms
    cboTerms.AddItem                       ceTerm]
    rstTerms.MoveNext
Loop

E_EXIT
stTerms.Close
et rstTerms = Nothing

xit
```

Conventions

PART **2**

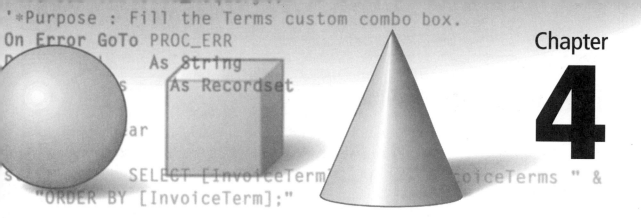

Naming Conventions

New objects and data types continue to emerge as Microsoft Visual Basic grows in complexity. Program code often references controls as well as variables, and in complex procedures it can be difficult to fully understand everything that is occurring in the code. How do you determine whether a particular statement references a variable or a control? Without some sort of convention to differentiate variables from controls, code is more difficult to read. For instance, can you tell exactly what is happening with this statement?

```
TotalDue = LineItemTotal - Discount + TotalTax
```

Without a way to distinguish variables of different data types from various objects, you can't tell what the statement is doing. Is *TotalDue* a variable or a text box? Or is it a label control? The same questions apply to the other items. If *LineItemTotal* is a variable, what type of variable is it? Currency? Single? Variant? To make code more self-documenting (always an important goal) and to reduce the chance of programming errors, you need an easy way to distinguish variables from controls and you need to make it easy to determine the exact data type of a variable or the exact type of a control.

Data Type Suffixes

One of the earliest methods of distinguishing data types was the use of Basic's *data type suffixes.* A data type suffix is a symbol representing a specific data type. You append these symbols to the ends of variable names. For instance, the type suffix for the String data type is the dollar sign ($). Using suffixes, you can create variable names such as *First-Name$* and *Address$*. Type suffixes have a number of drawbacks. The most apparent is that the suffixes aren't always intuitive. Do you know (or can you determine) the corresponding data types for these suffixes: %, &, !, and #? They are Integer, Long, Single, and Double, respectively. The difficulty of remembering type suffixes might not be enough reason to reject the convention. However, consider these variables:

■ *Send (Long)*—represents a count of the number of messages sent

■ *Send (Handle)*—a handle to the Comm (Communications) interface

Handles are actually Long integers. Reducing both of these variables to *Send&* doesn't help you to distinguish between the two.

Hungarian Notation

Developers moved away from data type suffixes toward the use of single-character prefixes (for example, *Dim lWidth As Long* and *Dim iHeight As Integer).* Prefixes make more sense because they are generally more intuitive than symbols and more of them are available. The single-digit prefix became popular but was doomed from the beginning. There are only 26 unique characters (a-z) available for single-character prefixes (still more than the number of available symbols), but there are many different types of variables and objects, and many of them share the same first letter.

A better naming convention eventually replaced the single-character prefix. This convention—using a three-character prefix to denote data types and control types—is known as Hungarian notation, partly because its creator, Charles Simonyi, was originally from Hungary, and partly because these prefixes tend to make variable names look like a foreign language. Prefixes can grow in length as additional information is denoted, such as scope or the fact that a variable is an array. Although the standard prefixes are usually three characters, with the possible addition of modifiers, conventions using larger prefixes are also referred to as Hungarian notation—Hungarian notation is a concept, not a specific implementation.

In Hungarian notation, a unique three-character prefix is assigned to each data type and to each type of control. The three characters allow for plenty of versatility and for prefixes that are logical and intuitive. Look at the following *Dim* statements and you'll see how the prefixes align fairly intuitively with the variables' assigned data types:

```
Dim strName      As String
Dim intAge       As Integer
Dim lngMiles     As Long
Dim curSalary    As Currency
```

Now consider once again the code statement shown earlier:

```
TotalDue = LineItemTotal - Discount + TotalTax
```

Each of the following statements is a possible equivalent of the previous statement. Three-character prefixes have been added. Also, for clarity, control references show their default properties.

```
txtTotalDue.Text = curLineItemTotal - txtDiscount.Text + curTotalTax
curTotalDue = curLineItemTotal - curDiscount + curTotalTax
txtTotalDue.Text = txtLineItemTotal.Text - txtDiscount.Text + _
                   txtTotalTax.Text
```

As you can see, prefixes make the statements much more understandable. Simply reading the statement tells you everything that is happening; you don't have to look at variable declarations to determine what's going on.

 NOTE There may well be no topic that causes more polarization among programmers than the use of Hungarian notation to denote type and scope. I firmly and unequivocally believe in the use of Hungarian notation and have personally enjoyed the benefits it provides.

Denoting a Variable's Data Type

The following table lists the prefixes you can use to denote a variable's data type.

Prefixes for Variable Data Types

Data Type	Prefix	Example
Boolean	*bln*	*blnLoggedIn*
Currency	*cur*	*curSalary*
Control	*ctl*	*ctlLastControl*
Double	*dbl*	*dblMiles*
ErrObject	*err*	*errLastError*
Single	*sng*	*sngYears*
Handle	*hwnd*	*hwndPicture*
Long	*lng*	*lngOnHand*
Object	*obj*	*objUserTable*
Integer	*int*	*intAge*
String	*str*	*strName*
User-defined type	*udt*	*udtEmployee*
Variant (including Dates)	*vnt*	*vntDateHired*
Array	*a*	*astrEmployees*

The *obj* prefix should be reserved for use when a specific prefix isn't suited. The most common use of this prefix is when referencing the Automation libraries of other applications. For instance, when automating Microsoft Word, you create an instance of Word's Application object. Since no prefix has been designated specifically for Word objects, *obj* works just fine, as shown in the following statement:

```
Dim objWord As Word.Application
```

User-defined data types (UDTs) are custom data structures. Your ability to create objects has rendered UDTs unnecessary in many cases, but you'll probably still have occasion to use a UDT. User-defined data types are composed of multiple variables, often of different types. When defined, the UDT should be prefixed with *type_*. However, each of the variables that make up the UDT should include the prefix of its type—or no prefix at all. Although it's generally a good idea to give the variables a prefix, some developers feel that doing so detracts from the object-oriented feel of using a UDT. If you use the Microsoft Windows API (application programming interface)—and you really should—you'll note that the

Windows API types don't use prefixes on the member variables. As with all aspects of applying standards, whichever method you choose, apply it consistently. The following code shows two possible ways to create a custom user-defined data type:

```
Private Type type_Printer
    DriverName  As String
    DeviceName  As String
    Port        As String
    Copies      As Integer
    Orientation As Long
End Type

Private Type type_Printer
    strDriverName  As String
    strDeviceName  As String
    strPort        As String
    intCopies      As Integer
    lngOrientation As Long
End Type
```

When creating a variable to hold a user-defined data type, use the *udt* prefix. Unfortunately, *udt* doesn't tell you anything about the specific UDT that it holds, but since the possibilities are endless and vary from program to program, it's impossible to assign them specific prefixes. The following statement is a sample declaration of the type created previously:

```
Dim udtPrinter As type_Printer
```

Prefixing a variable as an array is different from prefixing other types of variables. You use *a* to denote that the variable is an array, but you then follow *a* with the prefix for the array's data type—for example:

```
Dim asngGrades(9) As Single
```

Denoting a Variable's Scope

In addition to prefixing a variable to denote its data type, you can and should use a prefix to denote its scope. This scope designation character precedes the data type prefix and is separated from it by an underscore.

For example, to denote a module-level string variable, you can use a statement such as:

```
Dim m_strName As String
```

Prefixes for Variable Scope

Prefix	Description	Example
g	Global	*g_strSavePath*
m	Local to module or form	*m_blnDataChanged*
st	Static	*st_blnInHere*
(no prefix)	Nonstatic, local to procedure	*intIndex*

Other Prefixes

Prefixes aren't just for variables. All standard objects (including forms and controls) have a three-character prefix, as shown in the chapter's remaining tables. Learn and use these prefixes consistently—if you're not already. Correctly applying the standard three-character prefixes to all of your variables and objects makes your code more self-documenting and easier to maintain.

Prefixes for Standard Controls

Control	Prefix	Example
Check box	*chk*	*chkPrint*
Combo box	*cbo*	*cboTitle*
Command button	*cmd*	*cmdCancel*
Data	*dat*	*datBiblio*
Directory list box	*dir*	*dirSource*
Drive list box	*drv*	*drvTarget*
File list box	*fil*	*filSource*
Frame	*fra*	*fraLanguage*
Form	*frm*	*frmMain*
Group push button	*gpb*	*gpbChannel*
Horizontal scroll bar	*hsb*	*hsbVolume*

Control	Prefix	Example
Image	*img*	*imgIcon*
Label	*lbl*	*lblHelpMessage*
Line	*lin*	*linVertical*
List box	*lst*	*lstResultCodes*
MDI child form	*mdi*	*mdiContact*
Menu	*mnu*	*mnuFileOpen*
OLE container	*ole*	*olePhoto*
Option button	*opt*	*optSpanish*
Panel	*pnl*	*pnlSettings*
Picture box	*pic*	*picDiskSpace*
Picture clip	*clp*	*clpToolbar*
Shape	*shp*	*shpCircle*
Text box	*txt*	*txtAddress*
Timer	*tmr*	*tmrAlarm*
Vertical scroll bar	*vsb*	*vsbRate*

Prefixes for ActiveX Controls

Control	Prefix	Example
Common dialog	*dlg*	*dlgFileOpen*
Communications	*com*	*comFax*
Data-bound combo box	*dbc*	*dbcContacts*
Grid	*grd*	*grdInventory*
Data-bound grid	*dbg*	*dbgPrices*
Data-bound list box	*dbl*	*dblSalesCode*
List view	*lvw*	*lvwFiles*
MAPI message	*mpm*	*mpmSentMessage*
MAPI session	*mps*	*mpsSession*
MCI	*mci*	*mciVideo*
Outline	*out*	*outOrgChart*
Report	*rpt*	*rptQtr1Earnings*
Spin	*spn*	*spnPages*
Tree view	*tre*	*treFolders*

Prefixes for Database Objects

Object	Prefix	Example
Database	*db*	*dbCustomers*
Field (object or collection)	*fld*	*fldLastName*
Index (object or collection)	*idx*	*idxAge*
QueryDef	*qry*	*qrySalesByRegion*
Recordset	*rst*	*rstSalesByRegion*
Report	*rpt*	*rptAnnualSales*
TableDef	*tbl*	*tblCustomer*

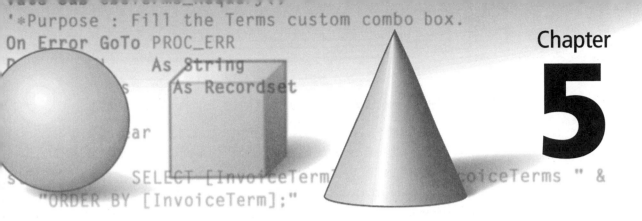

```
'*Purpose : Fill the Terms custom combo box.
On Error GoTo PROC_ERR
            As String
         As Recordset

           ar

         SELECT [InvoiceTerm                oiceTerms " &
"ORDER BY [InvoiceTerm];"

Set restTerms = db.OpenRecordset(strSQL, dbOpenForwardOnly)

Do WHile Not rstTerms.EOF
   cboTerms.AddItem rstTerms![InvoiceTerm]

Loop

OC_EXIT:
rstTerms.Close
Set rstTerms = Nothing

Exit Sub
```

Chapter

5

Using Constants and Enumerations

When you hard-code numbers in your procedures, a myriad of things can go wrong. Hard-coded numbers are generally referred to as "magic numbers" because they're often shrouded in mystery; the meaning of such a number is obscure because the digits themselves give no indication as to what the number represents. This chapter discusses the drawbacks of magic numbers and offers alternatives using constants and enumerations.

Using Constants

A constant is much like a variable; you create a name and assign it a value. However, unlike a variable, a constant is given its value at design time, and this value cannot be changed at run time. You should always use constants in place of magic numbers, for reasons I'll discuss in this section.

 NOTE   When you hard-code a string in a procedure, the effect is similar to that of using magic numbers. All the reasons for eliminating magic numbers also apply to eliminating hard-coded strings; if you know the value at design time, use a constant rather than hard-coding the text or the number.

59

Magic Numbers Are Prone to Data Entry Problems

One of the critical problems with magic numbers is that you can easily mistype a number, transposing its digits. When you type the number 10876, for instance, it's not at all difficult to mistakenly type 10867 or 18076. In contrast to the way it handles variables and reserved words, Microsoft Visual Basic's compiler takes no issue with transposed or incorrect numbers—it's happy to use whatever magic number you supply it. Sometimes the problems caused by a simple mistake don't surface immediately, and when they do they can appear as random miscalculations that are difficult to pinpoint. When you use a constant in place of a magic number, Visual Basic checks the validity of the constant at compile time. If the constant does not exist, Visual Basic tells you so and refuses to compile. This eliminates the problem of inaccurately typed numbers; as long as the single constant has the correct value, all the code that uses that constant will use the correct value as well.

 OTE If you don't include the *Option Explicit* statement within the Declarations section of a module and you mistype a constant name, Visual Basic implicitly declares a variable with the incorrect name of the constant, causing inaccurate results. This is just one more reason to explicitly declare your variables. See Chapter 6, "Variables," for more information on explicit vs. implicit variable declaration.

Magic Numbers Are Difficult to Update

Another serious drawback to magic numbers is that they're difficult to keep updated. Say you're developing a financial application and the current mortgage interest rate is 7.25 percent. Also assume that this value is hard-coded in a number of procedures that perform calculations based on the interest rate. What do you do when the rates change (which they do regularly)? You could perform a global search and replace, but that exposes your code to errors. Another loan rate used within the application might also have the value 7.25. If you perform a global search and replace on 7.25 percent, you'll change that loan rate as well. If you manually change each value in the code, you risk transposing or otherwise mistyping the new values. A selective search and replace with a confirmation on each change would be time-consuming. If you use a constant instead, you simply change the value once (in the constant's declaration), and every line of code that uses the mortgage interest rate instantly uses the new, updated rate.

Constants Make Code Easier to Read

A by-product of using constants to create more error-free code is code that is much more readable. Generally, magic numbers are anything but intuitive. They might be obvious to you, but they can be difficult for others to decipher. By intelligently naming your constants, the code that uses those constants becomes a bit more self-documenting and a lot easier to read. Consider the following two code statements. Which makes the most sense to you?

Magic numbers:
```
curInterestAmount = (curLoanAmount * .06) / 12
```

Named constants:
```
curInterestAmount = _
       (curLoanAmount * c_sngInterestRate) / c_intMonthsInTerm
```

One last note on constants: it's quite acceptable to give constants higher scope, unlike when you use variables, a situation in which it's highly advisable to reduce scope. As a matter of fact, you should never create the same constant twice within an application. If you find that you're duplicating a constant, move the original declaration to a higher scope until the constant becomes available to all procedures that reference it.

Using Enumerations

Enumerations are similar to constants in that they are named entities that are assigned values. However, enumerations behave like groups of public constants in a module. They're treated as data types, and you use them to create constants of suitable values for variables and properties. You might already be using enumerations in Visual Basic. For instance, when you use the *MsgBox* statement, Visual Basic's Auto List Members feature displays a drop-down list (commonly referred to as the "code helper drop-down list") for the *Buttons* parameter. (See Figure 5-1.)

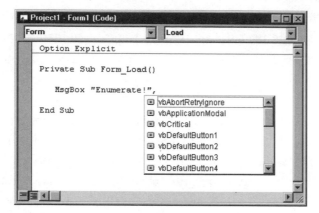

Figure 5-1.   *Enumerations eliminate the need to memorize many different parameter values.*

The time that the developers of the *MsgBox* statement invested to provide the *Buttons* parameter's values in an enumeration pays you dividends as a programmer. You never have to remember the numeric values of the parameter, and the chance of incorrectly specifying a value is greatly diminished. Although you can still specify a numeric value for a parameter rather than the name of an enumeration member, *you should never do so.* To actually use a magic number when an associated member name is available is just south of insane.

Creating Custom Enumerations

You create enumerations much like you do user-defined data types. In the Declarations section of a module, you type the word *Public* or *Private*, type *Enum*, and then type the name of your custom enumeration. The following is a sample enumeration:

```
Public Enum otBorderStyle
    otNone = 0
    otRaised_Light = 1
    otRaised_Heavy = 2
    otSunken_Light = 3
    otSunken_Heavy = 4
End Enum
```

This enumeration creates an enumerated type with five values. Although you always refer to the name of an enumeration member when you write code, the name simply represents its numeric value, much like a constant. All members of enumerations are long integers; you can't use other data types.

Using a Custom Enumeration

Once you've created an enumeration, you can use it as the data type for any variable, Function procedure, or Property procedure within the scope of the enumeration. For instance, to create a *BorderStyle* property that uses the enumerated type shown previously, you can declare a procedure like this:

```
Public Property Let BorderStyle(lngNew_BorderStyle _
    As otBorderStyle)
    ⋮
End Property
```

This property procedure accepts a value into the parameter *lngNew_BorderStyle. lngNew_BorderStyle* is a long integer because it is declared as an enumerated type and all members of enumerations are long integers. When you reference this property in code, Visual Basic displays the code helper drop-down list with all the enumeration members, as shown in Figure 5-2.

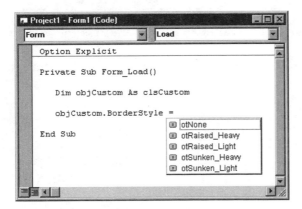

Figure 5-2.   *Custom enumerations offer the same advantages and behavior as system enumerations.*

You can also use an enumerated type as the data type returned by a function or a Property procedure. For instance, to create the Property Get procedure that corresponds to the previous Property Let procedure, you can use code like this:

```
Public Property Get BorderStyle() As otBorderStyle
    ⋮
End Property
```

Note that simply declaring a parameter as an enumerated type does not guarantee that the value passed to the parameter will be one of the defined enumeration members. As a matter of fact, this is one of the most common misconceptions about enumerated types. When you define an enumeration, you define a list of named values, but these are not the only values that a parameter of that enumerated type will accept. As mentioned previously, parameters that are defined as enumerated types are actually long integers. As such, they accept any value that fits into a long integer; Visual Basic does not confirm that the number passed into a parameter corresponds to a member of the enumeration. For this reason, you should always validate the data passed to a parameter declared as an enumerated type, as I'll discuss in Directive 5.8 on page 76.

> **Goals of Using Constants and Enumerations**
>
> The goals of using constants and enumerations include
>
> - Reducing errors caused by transposing or mistyping numbers
> - Making it easy to change values in the future
> - Making code easier to read
> - Ensuring forward compatibility

Directives

5.1 Prefix all constants with *c_* and a scope designator.

In the past, one convention for denoting a constant was to use all uppercase letters for the constant's name. For instance, when you created a constant to store a column index in a grid, you would use a statement like this:

```
Const COLUMN_INDEX = 7
```

Typing anything in code in all uppercase letters is now considered antiquated and undesirable. Mixed-case text is much easier to read. However, since variable and procedure names are also entered in mixed case, it's important to denote when an item is a constant. A better convention is to prefix the constant name with *c_*. For example, the constant shown above would be declared like this:

```
Const c_Column_Index = 7
```

This constant name is a bit easier to read, and you can still immediately tell that you're looking at a constant as opposed to a variable. The second underscore is optional. Some developers (including me) prefer not to use an underscore in this way. This is fine, as long as your approach is consistent. The same constant declaration without the second underscore would look like the following line of code. (Remember that you'll always have an underscore in the constant prefix.)

```
Const c_ColumnIndex = 7
```

 NOTE Labels for use with *GoTo* are one of the few exceptions to using mixed-case letters. Such labels, which should be used sparingly, appear in all uppercase letters. Refer to Chapter 11, "Controlling Code Flow," for more information on using these labels.

Another identifying characteristic of a constant as opposed to a variable is the lack of a data type prefix. For instance, if you were storing the column indicator in a variable, you would probably declare the variable by using a statement like this:

```
Dim intColumnIndex As Integer
```

 NOTE Some external libraries still use uppercase constants. For instance, if you use the API viewer to locate and copy API-related constants, you'll often see these constants in uppercase letters. In such cases, leave the constants as they are to promote cross-application consistency.

Many developers don't realize that you can actually create a constant of a specific data type. For instance, the following statement is completely legal:

```
Const c_InterestRate As Single = 7.5
```

You can specify a data type for a constant, but it adds complexity, and I don't know of a good reason to do so. If you decide to do it anyway, you should use the variable-naming prefixes discussed in Chapter 4, "Naming Conventions." The previous declaration, for instance, is not correct—according to the directives presented in this book—because the data type prefix is omitted. The proper declaration would be as follows:

```
Const c_sngInterestRate As Single = 7.5
```

Although the prefix for constants is different from the prefixes for variables, you should still use the same prefix scheme for indicating the scope of constants that you use for variables. For constants declared locally (within a procedure), no scope indicator is necessary. For constants declared as *Private* in the Declarations section of a module, you should use the prefix *m*. For global constants (constants declared as *Public* within a standard module), you should use the prefix *g*. The following are declarations of the same constant at different levels of scope:

Procedure:
```
Const c_InterestRate = 7.5
```
Module (private):
```
Private Const mc_InterestRate = 7.5
```
Global:
```
Public Const gc_InterestRate = 7.5
```

 OTE Constants are declared *Private* by default if you don't explicitly declare them with the *Public* keyword. As with procedures and variables, constants should always have a clearly defined scope. If you want to create a private constant, explicitly declare the constant using the *Private* keyword.

By consistently specifying the scope of a constant in addition to denoting the constant with *c_*, you'll make your code easier to read and to debug. If you're ever unsure where a constant is declared, simply place the cursor anywhere within the name of the constant and press Shift+F2. Visual Basic will take you directly to the constant's declaration.

Practical Applications

When you uniquely identify constants and denote their scope, you create more readable code.

5.1.1 Declare constants using mixed-case characters, prefixing each constant with *c_*. Remember that identifying constants by using all upper-case letters is out.

Incorrect:
```
Const USDATE = "mm/dd/yyyy"
Const KEYCONTROL = 17
```

Correct:
```
Const c_USDate = "mm/dd/yyyy"
Const c_KeyControl = 17
```

Also correct:
```
Const c_US_Date = "mm/dd/yyyy"
Const c_Key_Control = 17
```

5.1.2 Denote a constant's scope using a scope designator prefix. Knowing a constant's scope is extremely important for debugging. All constants declared in the Declarations section of any type of module need a *g* or an *m* designator.

Incorrect (module level or global level):
```
Private Const c_US_DATE = "mm/dd/yyyy"
Public Const c_KeyControl = 17
```

Correct:
```
Private Const mc_US_Date = "mm/dd/yyyy"
Public Const gc_KeyControl = 17
```

5.2 Use constants in place of magic numbers, regardless of scope.

I hope that the first part of this chapter has convinced you of the importance of replacing hard-coded numbers (magic numbers) with constants, regardless of scope. It might be tempting to use a hard-coded number within a procedure because it seems silly to create a constant for a single use in a single place. Certainly, maintaining the value is easy enough; you don't need to perform a search and replace when the number exists only once. However, readability is still a problem. Magic numbers are called "magic" for a reason. When someone else looks at the code, how can you be sure that the number will make complete sense to him or her? Regardless of scope, you should always replace magic numbers with constants. All together now: "Use constants in place of magic numbers, regardless of scope."

Incorrect:

```
'* Fill a most recently used list.
For intCount = 1 To 4
    strFileName = RetrieveRecentFileName(intCount)

'* If an entry was found, add it to the list.
    If strFileName <> "" Then
        Set objItem = lvwRecent.ListItems.Add()
        objItem.Text = strFileName
        objItem.SmallIcon = "Database"
    End If

Next intCount
```

Correct:

```
'* Fill a most recently used list.
Const c_Max_Recently_Used = 4

For intCount = 1 To c_Max_Recently_Used
    strFileName = RetrieveRecentFileName(intCount)

'* If an entry was found, add it to the list.
    If strFileName <> "" Then
        Set objItem = lvwRecent.ListItems.Add()
        objItem.Text = strFileName
        objItem.SmallIcon = "Database"
    End If

Next intCount
```

5.3 Use enumerations whenever they are available.

When a procedure or a parameter is declared as an enumerated type, it's common courtesy—nay, it's your duty—to reference the enumeration member names rather than their values. When you use an enumeration, your code is much easier to read and less likely to contain errors. Your code is also less likely to fail if someone later breaks backward compatibility by changing the values that correspond to the member names. For instance, say you're using an ActiveX component and one of its properties is *BorderStyle*. The developer has designated 0 - Flat and 1 - 3D as the possible values and has exposed them as members of an enumeration, as shown here:

```
Public Enum BorderStyle
    psFlat = 0
    ps3D = 1
End Enum
```

Say that you use the literal values rather than the enumeration's member names and you're updating to a new component. The developer has added a new *BorderStyle* value called *Chiseled* to the component. However, he wasn't really thinking of backward compatibility, and he changed the enumeration structure to the following:

```
Public Enum BorderStyle
    psFlat = 0
    psChiseled = 1
    ps3D = 2
End Enum
```

You can see that if you hard-code 1 to designate a 3-D border, you'll get unexpected results after you upgrade. Obviously, component developers should not break backward compatibility in this way, but it does happen. If you use the member's name rather than its value, your code will not be affected by such an oversight. Whether to use enumerations shouldn't even be a question. If a function supports them, use them. In new versions of software components, enumerations are often provided where there were none before. As enumerations and constants become available, make sure to change your code appropriately to use them.

Incorrect:

```
MsgBox "Print all documents?", 36
```

Correct:

```
MsgBox "Print all documents?", vbYesNo Or vbQuestion
```

5.4   Use constants when you refer to elements of a control array.

One area in which constants really shine but are often underused is as references to indexes of control arrays. When you create a control array, you end up with a number of controls all with the same name. To reference a particular control, you use its shared name and its unique index. When you hard-code an index, you create a magic number—complete with all the drawbacks discussed earlier. The problem with hard-coding index references is that your code can be difficult to debug if you've referenced the wrong index. Since controls within a control array are always of the same type, you can switch indexes all day long with little chance of generating an error message because all the actions you might perform on one member can be performed on another member.

To diminish the possibility of errors when you use control arrays, you should create constants that relate to each index. For example, say you have three text boxes that store a home phone number, work phone number, and mobile phone number, respectively. You use a control array because you have some standard code that runs on the *Validate* event to verify that each number is indeed a valid phone number. If you hard-code indexes, you have to remember which index references which type of phone number. If you're in a hurry or you haven't had your morning Mountain Dew, you can easily confuse the numbers. However, if you assign a constant to each index and always reference a control by its constant, never by its index directly, it's easier to ensure accuracy. Control arrays can make certain development situations much easier, and they can make an application less resource-intensive. However, the more elements you create for a control array, the more likely it is that an incorrect element will be referenced in code. Constants can help reduce the chances of this happening. In general, module-level scope is best for constants that reference elements of a control array, although local scope might be appropriate in some cases. The following constants have been given the prefix *txt* to denote that they reference the indexes of a text box control array.

Incorrect:

```
txtPhone(0).Text
txtPhone(1).Text
txtPhone(2).Text
```

Correct:

```
Const c_txtHomePhone = 0
Const c_txtWorkPhone = 1
Const c_txtFax = 2

txtPhone(c_txtHomePhone).Text
txtPhone(c_txtWorkPhone).Text
txtPhone(c_txtFax).Text
```

5.5 Use an application or company prefix for enumeration members.

Just as it's important to use a naming convention for variables, it's important to use a naming convention for enumeration members. You don't have to use a prefix to denote the type of an enumeration member because all members are always long integers. However, you should use a unique prefix that indicates that the values are from your application or component.

You should prefix your enumeration members with an identifier because when Visual Basic encounters an enumeration member name, it might get confused if other referenced type libraries contain the same name. For example, all of Visual Basic's system constants have the prefix *vb*. When you encounter a constant such as *vbFixedSingle*, you immediately know that the constant belongs to Visual Basic's type library. Although Visual Basic uses two-character prefixes, you should use three or four, but no more than that. If you were to use two characters, you would find it difficult to come up with an identifier that isn't used by another application or vendor. For instance, my company is called Tigerpaw Software. When we declare enumeration members, we use the prefix *tps*, as shown in the enumeration declaration on the following page.

```
Public Enum tpsPrintDestination
    tpsScreen = 0
    tpsPrinter = 1
End Enum
```

 NOTE   It's also acceptable to prefix the name of an enumeration (as well as the names of its members), as I have done in the previous example.

No application is an island. Even the simplest program uses many external libraries. To confirm this, just create a new Standard EXE and then choose References from the Project menu to see all the ActiveX components being referenced. With the increasing complexity of integrated components comes the need to be more aware of the potential for collisions between components. For this reason, give your enumeration members names that make such collisions unlikely.

Incorrect:

```
Public Enum BackTrackItem
    Account = 0
    ServiceOrder = 1
    Quote = 2
    Contact = 3
    PriceBookItem = 4
    PurchaseOrder = 5
    Task = 6
End Enum
```

Correct:

```
Public Enum BackTrackItem
    tpsAccount = 0
    tpsServiceOrder = 1
    tpsQuote = 2
    tpsContact = 3
    tpsPriceBookItem = 4
    tpsPurchaseOrder = 5
    tpsTask = 6
End Enum
```

Also correct:

```
Public Enum tpsBackTrackItem
    tpsAccount = 0
    tpsServiceOrder = 1
```

```
        tpsQuote = 2
        tpsContact = 3
        tpsPriceBookItem = 4
        tpsPurchaseOrder = 5
        tpsTask = 6
End Enum
```

5.6 Use system constants when enumerations aren't available.

Creating custom enumerations for your modules is highly encouraged, but Visual Basic has been slow to adopt them for all of its own objects. For instance, when you set the *WindowState* property of a form, there are only three possible values: 0 - Normal, 1 - Minimized, and 2 - Maximized. Looking in the Properties window shows you this. Each value (0, 1, and 2) has a name associated with it. These names look very much like members of an enumeration—well, in the Properties window, at least.

Although Visual Basic should use true enumerations for these properties, more often than not it doesn't. Figure 5-3 shows what the code window looks like when you attempt to change the *WindowState* property of a form. Notice that there is no code helper drop-down list in which you can select from a set of values.

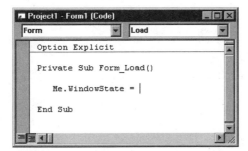

Figure 5-3. *When a parameter or property doesn't support an enumeration, you must remember the possible values; you don't get any help from Visual Basic.*

Visual Basic doesn't have defined enumerations for most of its objects, but it does often support *system constants* for the values. System constants are global constants that are part of the Visual Basic type library.

You don't have to define them or reference a library to use them because they're always available. However, since system constants don't appear in the code helper drop-down list, as enumerations do, many developers are unaware that these constants exist. Whenever you must type a numeric value as a parameter of a Visual Basic function or as the value of a standard Visual Basic object property, chances are good there's an associated system constant.

To determine whether a system constant exists for a property, type the property name (such as *WindowState*), place the cursor anywhere within the property text, and press F1. The help displayed for the property will usually include a list of any constants that are available, as shown in Figure 5-4.

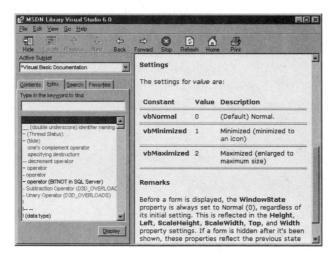

Figure 5-4.   *When you have to hard-code a value for a parameter, check online Help to see whether a system constant is available.*

 OTE   Many parameters, such as the *Buttons* parameter of the *MsgBox* statement, have associated system constants.

To use a system constant, you simply enter it as if you were referencing a constant that you've defined. For instance, to change a form to maximized, you can use a statement such as this:

```
Me.WindowState = vbMaximized
```

One way to know whether you've typed a system constant correctly is to type it in all lowercase letters. If the constant is valid, Visual Basic converts it to its proper case. If the constant remains in all lowercase letters, you've typed the name wrong and you have to correct it. Unlike enumerations, system constants can be used anywhere in code, not just with variables defined as an enumerated type. Therefore, you must be careful not to use the wrong constant because Visual Basic can't detect this type of error. Anything you can do to eliminate magic numbers is a good thing. If an enumeration is available for a procedure, use it. If not, check to see whether a system constant is defined. If that fails, consider creating your own constant to replace the magic number.

Incorrect:

```
With Me
    .BorderStyle = 1
    .WindowState = 0
    .ScaleMode = 3
    .DrawMode = 13
End With
```

Correct:

```
With Me
    .BorderStyle = vbFixedSingle
    .WindowState = vbNormal
    .ScaleMode = vbPixels
    .DrawMode = vbCopyPen
End With
```

5.7 Use an enumeration whenever a parameter accepts a limited number of values.

Even developers who truly believe in enumerations sometimes miss the opportunity to use them. As you develop code, you might not always think about creating an enumeration because an enumeration might seem like overkill in certain situations. In general, whenever a procedure accepts a limited set of values, use an enumeration. For instance, if you have a procedure in which a parameter can use one of two values only, that parameter is a prime candidate for an enumeration.

Creating an enumeration for two values might seem excessive, but it's not. You still get the benefits of avoiding magic numbers, including reduced data entry and greater legibility. Also, if you decide to add members in the future, an enumeration will make it easier to do so. Whether the values are strings or numbers is irrelevant; you can benefit from using an enumeration in both situations.

Incorrect:

```
Public Sub ShowAVIFile(lngType As Long)
```

Correct:

```
Public Enum tpsAVIFile
    tpsFileCopy = 0
    tpsFileDelete = 1
    tpsFileDeleteToRecycle = 2
    tpsFileNuke = 3
    tpsFindComputer = 4
    tpsFindFile = 5
    tpsFileMove = 6
    tpsSearch = 7
End Enum

Public Sub ShowAVIFile(lngType As tpsAVIFile)
```

5.8 Validate values that are passed as enumerated types.

You must validate any value passed to a parameter declared as an enumerated type to ensure that it is acceptable. When a parameter is declared as an enumerated type, it's really a long integer with a fancy code helper drop-down list. While other developers *should* use the named enumeration members, they are free to pass the parameter any valid long integer. Unfortunately, Visual Basic does not have the capability to automatically require that parameters be valid members of the enumeration. I hope this is added someday; it would greatly reduce the amount of code you have to write when you use many different enumerations.

There are essentially two methods you can use to validate the data:

■ If the values fall within a range (such as 1 to 10), use an *If...End If* construct to validate the data.

■ If the values form a discrete set that doesn't fit nicely in a range, use a *Select Case* construct.

In general, unless you are validating that the value falls within an acceptable range, use the *Select Case* construct rather than *If...End If*. The *Select Case* construct gives you more flexibility if you need to add more values to the enumeration later.

 NOTE When you use *Select Case*, always include an *Else* clause to deal with an invalid value passed into the procedure.

Practical Applications

Making assumptions is one of the leading causes of errors in code. Visual Basic won't ensure that values passed to an enumerated type actually correspond to named members within the enumeration. *Never assume you have good data.*

5.8.1 Always validate data by using comparisons to the named members, not to magic numbers. Refrain from using magic numbers for data validation, just as you refrain from using magic numbers elsewhere in your code.

Incorrect:

```
Public Enum tpsPrintDestination
    tpsScreen = 0
    tpsPrinter = 1
End Enum

Public Sub PrintReport(ByVal strFileName As String, _
        ByVal lngDestination As tpsPrintDestination)

    '* Verify that a valid location has been specified.
    If lngDestination < 0 Or lngDestination > 1 Then
        GoTo PROC_EXIT
    End If

    '* Print the specified report.
    ⋮

End Sub
```

Correct:

```
Public Enum tpsPrintDestination
    tpsScreen = 0
    tpsPrinter = 1
End Enum

Public Sub PrintReport(ByVal strFileName As String, _
      ByVal lngDestination As tpsPrintDestination)

    '* Verify that a valid location has been specified.
    If (lngDestination <> tpsScreen) And _
        (lngDestination <> tpsPrinter) Then
      GoTo PROC_EXIT
    End If

    '* Print the specified report.
    ⋮

End Sub
```

5.8.2   Use *Select Case* to validate that a value is a valid member of a discrete set of values. Don't forget to include the Case Else clause to handle invalid data.

Correct:

```
Public Sub PrintDocument(lngCallingForm As tpsCallingForm)

    '* Perform necessary actions based on the calling form.
    Select Case lngCallingForm
      Case Is = tpsContactView
          ⋮
      Case Is = tpsServiceOrderView
          ⋮
      Case Is = tpsCustomerInventoryView
          ⋮
      Case Else
          '* The value passed as the calling form parameter
          '* is invalid!
          MsgBox "An incorrect calling form " & _
                "has been specified!", vbInformation
          GoTo PROC_EXIT
    End Select

End Sub
```

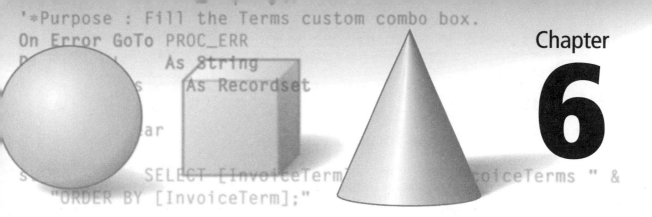
```
'*Purpose : Fill the Terms custom combo box.
On Error GoTo PROC_ERR
            As String
         As Recordset

        ar

      SELECT [InvoiceTerm]              oiceTerms " &
  "ORDER BY [InvoiceTerm];"

Set restTerms = db.OpenRecordset(strSQL, dbOpenForwardOnly)

Do WHile Not rstTerms.EOF
    cboTerms.AddItem rstTerms![InvoiceTerm]
          eNext
Loop
```

Variables

```
ROC_EXIT:
  rstTerms.Close
Set rstTe
  Exit Sub
```

Programming often involves manipulating variables. Most procedures contain at least one variable, and some have dozens. Because variables are so common, they're often taken for granted. In Chapter 4, "Naming Conventions," I discussed using Hungarian prefixes to denote the data types of variables. Although using these prefixes should be mandatory, it's only the beginning of properly handling variables. A well-defined variable has a clearly defined data type and scope. In addition, to correctly use variables you must explicitly declare them using intelligent variable names and you must give them focus.

Goals of Using Variables Appropriately

The goals of explicitly declaring variables and using a consistent variable-naming scheme are

- Making the purpose of each variable clear

- Making the data type and scope of each variable clear

- Making the processes in your code easier to understand

- Making debugging easier

- Making the storing and processing of variables more efficient

Directives

6.1 Define focused variables.

When you create and use variables, you should strive to make each variable serve a clearly defined purpose. It can be tempting to make variables serve double duty, but the small savings in memory is often negated by the resulting complexity of the code. A variable used for multiple purposes is said to be unfocused. If you need to perform unrelated actions or calculations on a variable, you'd be better served by having two focused variables rather than one unfocused variable. It's unnecessarily difficult to read and debug code that contains unfocused variables, and the code itself is more likely to contain errors.

Incorrect:

```
Public Sub AssignGroup(strGroup As String)
    '* Purpose  :  Add a group to the current account.
    '* Accepts  :  strGroup - Group to assign to account.
    On Error GoTo PROC_ERR
    Dim strTemp As String

    Const c_DuplicateRecord = 3022

    strTemp = "INSERT INTO tblAssignedAccGroups (AccountNumber, " & _
              "[Group]) VALUES (" & Me.AccountNumber & _
              ", """ & strGroup & """);"

    '* Capture any errors - specifically duplicate record errors.
    On Error Resume Next
    Err.Clear
    dbGroups.Execute strTemp, dbFailOnError

    '* Check to see whether there was a duplicate record error.
    If Err.Number = c_DuplicateRecord Then
        '* This is a duplicate entry; ignore and get out.
        strTemp = "The group you have specified (" & strGroup & _
                  ") already exists in the database."
        MsgBox strTemp, vbInformation
    End If

    On Error GoTo PROC_ERR

PROC_EXIT:
    Exit Sub
```

```
PROC_ERR:
   Call ShowError(Me.Name, "AssignGroup", Err.Number, Err.Description)
   GoTo PROC_EXIT

End Sub
```

Correct:

```
Public Sub AssignGroup(strGroup As String)
   '* Purpose  :  Add a group to the current account.
   '* Accepts  :  strGroup - Group to assign to account.
   On Error GoTo PROC_ERR
   Dim strSQL      As String
   Dim strMessage  As String

   Const c_DuplicateRecord - 3022

   strSQL = "INSERT INTO tblAssignedAccGroups (AccountNumber, " & _
            "[Group]) VALUES (" & Me.AccountNumber & _
            ", """ & strGroup & """);"

   '* Capture any errors - specifically duplicate record errors.
   On Error Resume Next
   Err.Clear
   dbGroups.Execute strSQL, dbFailOnError

   '* Check to see whether there was a duplicate record error.
   If Err.Number = c_DuplicateRecord Then
      '* This is a duplicate entry; ignore and get out.
      strMessage = "The group you have specified (" & strGroup & _
                   ") already exists in the database."
      MsgBox strMessage, vbInformation
   End If

   On Error GoTo PROC_ERR

PROC_EXIT:
   Exit Sub

PROC_ERR:
   Call ShowError(Me.Name, "AssignGroup", Err.Number, Err.Description)
   GoTo PROC_EXIT

End Sub
```

6.2   Give variables descriptive names.

The names you choose for variables are very important. Even if your code will never be seen by another person, you should write it as if it will be reviewed by dozens of other developers. Don't use the names of friends or pets, and don't use offensive words. When you're coming down from a caffeine high at three o'clock in the morning, you might be tempted to use all sorts of strange variable names. Using a bizarre reference to the Vincent Price movie you've been watching might help you release tension, but it will make your code considerably less readable.

 OTE   It's easier to name a variable that has been created for a well-defined purpose.

Giving your variables logical names is one of the easiest things you can do to make your code more understandable. Variables such as x, y, and i have almost no place in modern software development. They might be fine for loop counters (although better names are almost always available), but they should never hold important data. Not convinced? Have you ever seen code like this?

```
Dim rstCustomers  As Recordset
Dim i             As Integer

'* Print a list of the fields in the Recordset.
For i = 0 To rstCustomers.Fields.Count - 1

    Debug.Print rstCustomers.Fields(i).Name

Next i
```

Sure, i works in this example. However, what does i represent? In this instance, it represents an index of a field. With that in mind, consider how much more readable this code is:

```
Dim rstCustomers  As Recordset
Dim intIndex      As Integer
```

```
'* Print a list of the fields in the Recordset.
For intIndex = 0 To rstCustomers.Fields.Count - 1

    Debug.Print rstCustomers.Fields(intIndex).Name

Next intIndex
```

 N OTE   You should reserve *x*, *y*, and *z* for variables that hold coordinates. For instance, it's perfectly valid to have variables named *x* and *y* in a charting program.

For a more dramatic example, look at the next code snippet, which was taken directly from a well-known Visual Basic publication. I've left out the declarations of the variables on purpose.

```
av = Split(sCmdLine, " .," & sCRLF & sTab)
For Each v In av
    s = s & v
Next
```

Can you tell exactly what this code does? I can't. It's pretty obvious that this code would be much more understandable if the variables had descriptive names. Also, note the use of *sCRLF* and *sTab* (constants defined by the author). Using constants in place of magic numbers is good practice, but Microsoft Visual Basic includes built-in constants for these values (*vbCrLf* and *vbTab*, respectively). You should always use a system constant if one is available (as discussed in Chapter 5, "Using Constants and Enumerations").

An important thing to remember when you name variables is that the limitations that existed in older languages are gone. For instance, some languages limited the number of characters you could use to define a variable, so some developers still use variable names such as *EMPADD1*, *EMPADD2*, and *STXTOTAL*. Code consisting of deliberately shortened variable names is difficult to understand and maintain. There is no longer a valid reason for this practice. This is not to say that all variables should have long names; you should choose names that make the most sense—

whether they're short or long. The advantage of naming variables *EmployeeAddress1*, *EmployeeAddress2*, and *SalesTaxTotal* is clear: these names are more self-explanatory than their shorter counterparts.

Practical Application

6.2.1   Avoid naming variables *Temp*. One variable name you should avoid is *Temp*. It's easy to create variables such as *rstTemp*, *intTemp*, and *strTemp*, but all local variables are temporary by nature, so naming a local variable *Temp* is redundant. Generally, developers mean "scratch variable" when they say "temp variable," and you can almost always find an alternative for *Temp*. For instance, when you use the *InStr()* function to determine the location of a string within a string, it might be tempting to use a statement such as this:

```
intTemp = InStr(strBeginTime, "A")
```

A much better alternative is to give the variable a descriptive name like this one:

```
intCharacterLocation = InStr(strBeginTime, "A")
```

Or you can simply use this:

```
intLocation = InStr(strBeginTime, "A")
```

Incorrect:
```
Public Function StripDoubleQuotes(ByVal strString As String) As String
    '* Purpose  :  Double quotes cause errors in SQL statements.
    '*               This procedure strips them from the entered text
    '*               and replaces them with pairs of single quotes.
    '* Accepts  :  strString by value so that changes made to it aren't
    '*               also made directly to the variable being passed in.
    '* Returns  :  The original string, with all double quotes replaced
    '*               by pairs of single quotes.
    On Error GoTo PROC_ERR
    Dim intTemp        As Integer
    Dim blnQuotesFound  As Boolean

    Const c_DoubleQuote = """"
    blnQuotesFound = False
```

```
    '* Repeat as long as double quotes are found.
    Do
        '* Look for a double quote.
        intTemp = InStr(1, strString, c_DoubleQuote)

        '* If a double quote is found, replace it with a pair
        '* of single quotes.
        If intTemp > 0 Then
            strString = Left$(strString, intTemp - 1) & "'" & _
                        Mid$(strString, intTemp + 1)
            blnQuotesFound = True
        Else
            blnQuotesFound = False
        End If

    Loop While blnQuotesFound

    StripDoubleQuotes = strString

PROC_EXIT:
    Exit Function

PROC_ERR:
    Call ShowError(Me.Name, "StripDoubleQuotes", Err.Number, _
                   Err.Description)
    Resume Next

End Function
```

Correct:
```
Public Function StripDoubleQuotes(ByVal strString As String) As String
    '* Purpose  :  Double quotes cause errors in SQL statements.
    '*               This procedure strips them from the entered text
    '*               and replaces them with pairs of single quotes.
    '* Accepts  :  strString by value so that changes made to it aren't
    '*               also made directly to the variable being passed in.
    '* Returns  :  The original string, with all double quotes replaced
    '*               by pairs of single quotes.
    On Error GoTo PROC_ERR
    Dim intLocation     As Integer
    Dim blnQuotesFound  As Boolean

    Const c_DoubleQuote = """"

    blnQuotesFound = False

    '* Repeat as long as double quotes are found.
```

(continued)

```
    Do
        '* Look for double quotes.
        intLocation = InStr(1, strString, c_DoubleQuote)

        '* If a double quote is found, replace it with a pair
        '* of single quotes.
        If intLocation > 0 Then
            strString = Left$(strString, intLocation - 1) & "'" & _
                        Mid$(strString, intLocation + 1)
            blnQuotesFound = True
        Else
            blnQuotesFound = False
        End If

    Loop While blnQuotesFound

    StripDoubleQuotes = strString

PROC_EXIT:
    Exit Function

PROC_ERR:
    Call ShowError(Me.Name, "StripDoubleQuotes", Err.Number, _
                   Err.Description)
    Resume Next

End Function
```

6.3   Use mixed case in variable names.

IT'S HARDER TO READ SENTENCES IN ALL UPPERCASE THAN SEN-
TENCES IN MIXED CASE. In the past, some languages required all uppercase letters for variable names. This limitation does not exist in Visual
Basic, so use mixed case for all variable names. All lowercase is almost
as bad as all uppercase. For instance, *EmployeeAge* is far better than
EMPLOYEEAGE or *employeeage*. If you prefer, you can use underscore
characters to simulate spaces (for example, *Employee_Age*). However, if
you do this, do it consistently.

Incorrect:
```
Dim strFIRSTNAME    As String
Dim strlastname     As String
```

Correct:
```
Dim strFirstName    As String
Dim strLastName     As String
```

Also correct:
```
Dim strFirst_Name   As String
Dim strLast_Name    As String
```

6.4 Abbreviate only frequently used or long terms.

Although you should generally avoid abbreviating variable names, sometimes it makes sense to shorten a word or a term used for a variable name. Thirty-two characters is about the longest variable name you should create. Longer names can be difficult to read on some displays.

When you need to abbreviate, be consistent throughout your project. For instance, if you use *Cnt* in some areas of your project and *Count* in other areas, you add unnecessary complexity to the code.

One situation in which you might want to abbreviate variable names is when you're working with a set of related variables, such as these employee-related variables:

```
Dim strEmployeeName     As String
Dim strEmployeeAddress1 As String
Dim strEmployeeAddress2 As String
Dim strEmployeeCity     As String
Dim strEmployeeState    As String
Dim strEmployeeZipcode  As String
```

Here, abbreviation becomes more attractive. If you abbreviate, be consistent. For instance, don't use variations such as *EmpAddress1*, *Empl-Address1*, and *EmpAdd1*. Pick the abbreviation that makes sense and stick to it. Also, try to abbreviate only the part of the variable name that is the common component, not the part that is the unique specifier. In this case, abbreviating *Employee* is acceptable, but abbreviating *Address* is probably not a good idea.

Incorrect:
```
Dim strEmployeeName As String
Dim strEmplAdd      As String
Dim strEmployeeCity As String
```

Correct:
```
Dim strEmpName     As String
Dim strEmpAddress  As String
Dim strEmpCity     As String
```

6.5   Use qualifiers consistently.

Most projects contain variables that are related to one another. For in-stance, when you work with device contexts to perform drawing func-tions, you often have a source context and a destination context. You might also have variables that keep track of the first and last items in a set. In such situations, you should use a standard qualifier at the end of the variable name. By placing the qualifier at the end, you create more uniform variables that are easier to understand and easier to search for. For example, use *strCustomerFirst* and *strCustomerLast* instead of *strFirstCustomer* and *strLastCustomer*.

Common Variable Qualifiers

Qualifier	Description
First	First element in a set.
Last	Last element in a set.
Next	Next element in a set.
Prev	Previous element in a set.
Cur	Current element in a set.
Min	Minimum value in a set.
Max	Maximum value in a set.
Save	Preserves another variable that must be reset later.
Tmp	A "scratch" variable whose scope is highly localized within the code. The value of a *Tmp* variable is usually valid only across a set of contiguous statements within a single procedure.
Src	Source. Frequently used in comparison and transfer routines.
Dst	Destination. Often used in conjunction with *Src*.

Incorrect:

```
Dim strFirstCustomer      As String
Dim strLastCustomer       As String
Dim strPreviousCustomer   As String
```

Correct:

```
Dim strCustomerFirst      As String
Dim strCustomerLast       As String
Dim strCustomerPrevious   As String
```

6.6   Use the positive form in Boolean variables.

Boolean variable names deserve special mention. These variables have the value *True* or *False*—nothing else. When you name Boolean variables, always use the positive form—for instance, *blnFound*, *blnLoaded*, and *blnDone* rather than *blnNotFound*, *blnNotLoaded*, and *blnNotDone*. Using the negative form increases the chances that the variable will be handled incorrectly, particularly in complex expressions, where programming errors are more likely to occur. Positive names make Boolean variables more understandable and reduce the risk of programming errors. Notice in the incorrect example below that the negative nature of the *blnNotInHere* variable (used to keep track of whether or not the procedure is currently executing) means that the procedure never fully executes because a Boolean variable is initialized to False.

Incorrect:

```
Private Sub cmdPrint_Click(Index As Integer)
   '* Purpose  :  Print or cancel, depending on the button clicked.
   On Error GoTo PROC_ERR
   Static blnNotInHere  As Boolean

   Const c_Print = 0
   Const c_Cancel = 1

   '* Prevent this event from executing twice because of a user
   '* double-clicking the button.
   If Not(blnNotInHere) Then GoTo PROC_EXIT

   blnNotInHere = False

   '* Determine which button was clicked.
   Select Case Index
      Case Is = c_Print
```

(continued)

```
            '* Print the quote.
         Call PrintQuote

      Case Is = c_Cancel
         '* Unload the form.
         Unload Me

      Case Else
         '* No other index is expected.
   End Select

   '* Reset the variable that keeps track of whether we're in here.
   blnNotInHere = True

PROC_EXIT:
   Exit Sub

PROC_ERR:
   Call ShowError(Me.Name, "cmdPrint_Click", Err.Number, _
                  Err.Description)
   Resume Next

End Sub
```

Correct:

```
Private Sub cmdPrint_Click(Index As Integer)
   '* Purpose :  Print or cancel, depending on the button clicked.
   On Error GoTo PROC_ERR
   Static blnInHere  As Boolean

   Const c_Print = 0
   Const c_Cancel = 1

   '* Prevent this event from executing twice because of a user
   '* double-clicking the button.
   If blnInHere Then GoTo PROC_EXIT

   blnInHere = True

   '* Determine which button was clicked.
   Select Case Index
      Case Is = c_Print
         '* Print the quote.
         Call PrintQuote

      Case Is = c_Cancel
         '* Unload the form.
         Unload Me

      Case Else
         '* No other index is expected.
   End Select
```

```
'* Reset the variable that keeps track of whether we're in here.
blnInHere = False

PROC_EXIT:
   Exit Sub

PROC_ERR:
   Call ShowError(Me.Name, "cmdPrint_Click", Err.Number, _
                  Err.Description)
   Resume Next

End Sub
```

6.7 Explicitly declare variables.

When a variable is declared with *Dim*, *Private*, *Public*, or *Static*, it's explicitly declared. Visual Basic does not require that you explicitly declare your variables, but it should. Code that includes variables that aren't explicitly declared is far more prone to errors than code with explicitly declared variables and has no place in modern software development. This is one reason why explicit declaration of variables is one of the first things a code reviewer looks for. When code simply references variables as needed (implicit declaration), it can seem as though the developer didn't give much thought to the logic of the code or the data used. Variables are important, and they deserve a formal declaration. A formal declaration at least shows that the developer gave due consideration to the use of the variable and didn't just throw it in at the last minute.

Here is a simple illustration of the problems of not explicitly declaring variables:

```
Private Sub cmdTest_Click()

   strMessage = "This is a test."
   Debug.Print strMesage

End Sub
```

If you weren't paying close attention, you might have expected Visual Basic to print "This is a test." when the procedure was executed. However, Visual Basic prints an empty string. Here's what happens.

The first statement is fine. It implicitly creates a new variable called *strMessage* and places the string "This is a test." into the new variable.

Line 1:   `strMessage = "This is a test."`

But here's the problem. Notice the misspelling of the variable name:

Line 2:   **`Debug.Print`** `strMesage`

Since *strMesage* has not been declared as a variable and it's not a reserved word, Visual Basic automatically creates and initializes the variable "on the fly," just as it did for the variable *strMessage*. When variables are not explicitly declared as a specific data type, they are created as variants (which is a problem unto itself, as noted in Directive 6.9). A variant is initially empty, and therefore nothing prints. (Actually, an empty string is printed.) Note that all of this occurs without any compile-time or run-time errors.

You can easily prevent Visual Basic from allowing you to reference variables that aren't explicitly declared by adding *Option Explicit* to the Declarations section of a module. If Visual Basic encounters a variable that hasn't been explicitly declared in a module that contains *Option Explicit* in its Declarations section, an error is generated at compile time. Since you can't compile code with compile errors, you physically can't distribute these types of errors in compiled programs. Note, however, that *Option Explicit* applies only to the module in which it appears. Therefore, you must place it in the Declarations section of every module in your project (including Form and Class modules) for it to be fully effective.

Visual Basic can automatically add the *Option Explicit* statement to new modules. To enable this feature, choose Options from the Tools menu and then select Require Variable Declaration, as shown in Figure 6-1.

Note that when you enable this feature, Visual Basic does not place *Option Explicit* into any existing modules; you must manually add it to existing modules. The good news is that Require Variable Declaration is a systemwide setting, so all new modules created in any projects will have *Option Explicit* placed in their Declarations sections.

It's hard to fathom why, after all this time, *Option Explicit* is still an option. What's worse, it's not even the default option—when Visual Basic is

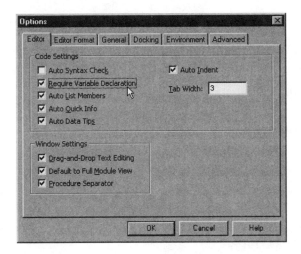

Figure 6-1.   *Select the Require Variable Declaration check box on the Editor tab of the Options dialog box to enforce explicit variable declaration.*

first installed, it does not enforce variable declaration; you have to turn on this feature. One of the first things you should do after installing Visual Basic is enable this feature. If you have a large project developed without *Option Explicit* in the Declarations sections of your modules, add *Option Explicit* to the modules and attempt to compile your code. You might be surprised at the results. If you find references to variables that haven't been declared, you'll probably want to put the code through some rigorous examination and testing.

Incorrect:
```
Private Sub cmdTest_Click()

    intValue = 6
    Debug.Print intValue / 2

End Sub
```

Correct:
```
Private Sub cmdTest_Click()
    Dim intValue As Integer

    intValue = 6
    Debug.Print intValue / 2

End Sub
```

6.8 Declare variables with carefully chosen data types.

Visual Basic provides many different data types for variables, and often, more than one data type will work in a given situation. Choosing the best data type for each variable can reduce memory requirements, speed up execution, and reduce the chance of errors. Also, different data types have different resource requirements, and the data type you use for a variable can affect the results of computations based on that variable. For instance, consider the following code:

```
Private Sub cmdCalculate_Click()
    Dim sngFirst    As Single
    Dim sngSecond   As Single
    Dim intResult   As Integer

    sngFirst = 3
    sngSecond = 0.5

    intResult = sngFirst + sngSecond

    Debug.Print intResult

End Sub
```

When this code is executed, the number *4* is printed in the Immediate window. The correct result should, of course, be *3.5*. However, Visual Basic does its best to follow your instructions and rounds the result of the calculation to fit in the Integer variable. Visual Basic doesn't raise a run-time error in situations like this—it simply forces the value to fit the data type. Such problems can be extremely tricky to debug. In this example, simply changing the type of the *intResult* variable to Single solves the problem.

Coercing (rounding) is not the only problem created by incorrect numeric data types. When you perform numeric calculations, you must be mindful of possible overflow errors. If you attempt to put a value into a variable and the value is greater than the maximum value for the data type, the run-time error "6 – Overflow" occurs. (See Figure 6-2.)

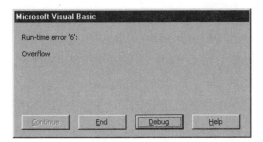

Figure 6-2. *When you attempt to put too large a value in a variable, this overflow error occurs.*

This type of error is easy to demonstrate. Consider the following code:

```
Private Sub cmdCalculate_Click()
    Dim intFirst   As Integer
    Dim intSecond  As Integer
    Dim intResult  As Integer

    intFirst = 32000
    intSecond = 32000

    intResult = intFirst + intSecond

    Debug.Print intResult

End Sub
```

The maximum value that can be stored in an Integer variable is 32,767. Since *intFirst* and *intSecond* are both assigned the value 32,000, no error is generated. However, when you attempt to place the result of adding these two numbers (64,000) in *intResult* (another Integer variable), an overflow error occurs. In this case, changing *intResult* to a Long solves the problem. Fortunately, overflow errors are easier to debug than rounding problems, but they often aren't apparent until the application is used live.

When you create a variable, consider whether the variable will hold the results of calculations based on other variables. In some cases, going to the next larger data type (Double from Single, Long from Integer) is the safest bet. In others, you might find that there is an even more specific data type available, such as the Currency data type for holding monetary values.

Incorrect:

```
Private Sub PrintTax(sngTaxableAmount As Single, lngTaxRate As Long)
    '* Purpose  :   Print the total tax (taxable amount * tax rate).
    '* Accepts  :   sngTaxableAmount - the dollar value to which tax
    '*              applies.
    '*              lngTaxRate - the local tax rate.

    On Error GoTo PROC_ERR
    Dim sngTax  As Single

    sngTax = sngTaxableAmount * lngTaxRate

    Debug.Print sngTax

PROC_EXIT:
    Exit Sub

PROC_ERR:
    Call ShowError(Me.Name, "PrintTax", Err.Number, Err.Description)
    GoTo Proc_Exit

End Sub
```

Correct:

```
Private Sub PrintTax(curTaxableAmount As Currency, _
                     sngTaxRate As Single)
    '* Purpose  :   Print the total tax (taxable amount * tax rate).
    '* Accepts  :   curTaxableAmount - the dollar value to which tax
    '*              applies.
    '*              sngTaxRate - the local tax rate.
    On Error GoTo Proc_Err
    Dim curTax  As Currency

    curTax = curTaxableAmount * sngTaxRate

    Debug.Print curTax

PROC_EXIT:
    Exit Sub
```

```
PROC_ERR:
    Call ShowError(Me.Name, "PrintTax", Err.Number, Err.Description)
    GoTo Proc_Exit

End Sub
```

The following table lists the Visual Basic data types.

Visual Basic Data Types

Data Type	Value Range
Byte	0 to 255
Boolean	True or False
Integer	−32,768 to 32,767
Long	−2,147,483,648 to 2,147,483,647
Single	−3.402823E38 to −1.401298E-45 for negative values 1.401298E-45 to 3.402823E38 for positive values
Double	−1.79769313486232E308 to −4.94065645841247E-324 for negative values 4.94065645841247E-324 to 1.79769313486232E308 for positive values
Currency	−922,337,203,685,477.5808 to 922,337,203,685,477.5807
Date	January 1, 100 to December 31, 9999
Object	Any object reference
Variable-length String	0 to approximately 2 billion characters
Variant	Numbers: any numeric value up to the range of a Double String: same range as for variable-length String

Here are some helpful guidelines for using data types:

- To store any type of text, use the String data type. This data type can contain any valid keyboard character, including numbers and nonalphabetic characters.

- To store only the values True and False, use the Boolean data type.

- To store a number that contains no decimal places, is greater than or equal to −32,768, and is less than or equal to 32,767, use the Integer data type.

- To store numbers with no decimal places but with values greater than or less than those that an Integer will allow, use the Long data type. Longs are often referred to as Long Integers, but they're defined using the keyword Long.

- To store numbers that contain decimal places, use the Single data type. Unless you're writing incredibly complex mathematical applications that require extremely large numbers or numbers very close to 0, this data type should work for almost all your values containing decimals. If you need to store larger numbers than the Single data type can hold, use the Double data type.

- To store dollar amounts, use the Currency data type. This data type uses a fixed decimal point of four places. However, unless you specify a value with four decimal places, only two are shown when you display the value.

- To store a date or a time value, use the Date data type. When you use this data type, Visual Basic recognizes common date and time formats. For example, if you store the value *7/22/1997,* Visual Basic does not treat it as a simple text string; it knows that it represents July 22, 1997.

6.9 Use the Variant data type only when absolutely necessary.

Visual Basic is extremely lenient on the typing of variables. It's quite content to "protect" you by coercing data when it feels it's appropriate. Nowhere is this more evident than in the use of the Variant data type. This data type is often abused, and there is almost always a better alternative to the Variant data type. When used correctly, a Variant is a great tool for certain tasks. You can create Variant variables that can hold any type of data, including objects. Visual Basic is even fairly smart at determining the type of data a Variant holds and applying the appropriate behavior to the determined type. For instance, take a look at the following code:

```
Dim vntA As Variant
Dim vntB As Variant

vntA = "1"
vntB = 2

Debug.Print vntA + vntB
```

When executed, the code prints *3*, even though the variable *vntA* contains a string. When Visual Basic encounters the + operator, it determines that, if at all possible, it must perform arithmetic using numbers. Visual Basic evaluates the two Variant variables in the preceding code and determines that they do indeed each contain a number. It then adds the two numbers and gets a result of 3. However, by changing a single character in the procedure, as shown below, the outcome is completely different:

```
Dim vntA As Variant
Dim vntB As Variant

vntA = "1"
vntB = 2

Debug.Print vntA & vntB
```

When this code is executed, *12* is printed. The ampersand (&) character is used for string concatenation; when Visual Basic encounters the ampersand, it evaluates the two variables to determine whether their values can be interpreted as Strings. Although only one of the variables (*vntA*) contains a String, Visual Basic decides that it can still represent the other variable's value as a String. This is called *coercion* or (somewhat less affectionately) *evil type coercion* (ETC). The result of such coercion is often unpredictable. Visual Basic can sometimes coerce strictly typed variables (variables declared as specific data types), but it is more likely to do this with Variants. The previous two code samples produce the same results even if the variables are declared as specific types such as String and Long. However, compare the following two code examples:

```
Dim strA As String
Dim strB As String
```

(continued)

```
strA = 1
strB = 2

Debug.Print strA + strB
```

and

```
Dim vntA As Variant
Dim vntB As Variant

vntA = 1
vntB = 2

Debug.Print vntA + vntB
```

The first code example prints *12*. When Visual Basic works with String variables, it treats the + symbol as a concatenation operator. However, recall that the default behavior of the + symbol is for arithmetic. In the second example, Visual Basic looks at the Variant variables to see if their values can be treated as numbers, which in this case they can. Therefore, it adds them and prints *3*. Other than the data types (and the names of the variables to enforce the naming prefixes), these two procedures are identical—but they produce different values.

 OTE Never use the + symbol for string concatenation—use an ampersand.

The simple fact that Visual Basic treats data in a Variant variable differently at different times should be enough to dissuade you from using Variants when they aren't necessary. Variants have other pitfalls as well. For instance, they consume more memory than any other Visual Basic data type—16 bytes for any numeric value up to the range of a Double and a whopping 22 bytes plus the string length when they hold string data! Arrays of any data type require 20 bytes of memory plus 4 bytes for each dimension—for example, *Dim MyArray(9, 5)* declares an array with 2 dimensions—plus the bytes for each data element itself. Consequently, if you create an array of Variants, you should have a darned good reason for doing so. Not only do Variants consume more memory than other data types, but manipulating the data within them is almost always slower than performing the same manipulation with strict data types.

Declaring a variable with *As Variant* isn't the only way to create a Variant variable. If you neglect to include an *As* <type> clause in a variable declaration, the variable is created as a Variant. For instance, the following two declarations yield the same result:

```
Dim MyVariable
```

```
Dim MyVariable As Variant
```

The same holds true for Function procedures. If you neglect to include an *As* <type> clause when you define a function, the return value of the function is always a Variant. The following definitions yield the same result:

```
Private Function MyFunction()
```

```
Private Function MyFunction() As Variant
```

For the reasons stated above, you should always declare variables and Function procedures as specific types. If you want to declare either one as type Variant, explicitly declare the variable or Function procedure by using *As Variant*.

In addition to omitting an *As* <type> clause when declaring a variable or Function procedure, there's another all-too-common way to inadvertently create Variant variables. Consider this line of code:

```
Dim VariableA, VariableB, VariableC As String
```

What are the data types of these three variables? If you said that they're all Strings, you're probably not alone, but you're definitely not correct. Visual Basic allows you to declare multiple variables on a single line to save space—not to make it easy to declare multiple variables of the same data type (which would be the obvious reason). When you declare multiple variables on the same line with a single *As* <type> clause, only the last variable in the *Dim* statement is given the specified type. All the other variables are allocated as Variants. For this reason, you should always declare each individual variable on a separate line. If you must declare multiple variables on a single line—and you should avoid this—declare each variable with an *As* <type> clause, like this:

```
Dim VariableA As String, VariableB As String
```

By paying close attention to your declaration of variables, you can keep the number of Variant variables to a minimum, resulting in leaner, quicker, and often more dependable code.

Incorrect:

```
Dim vntControl    As Variant

'* Loop through all controls on the form and print their heights.
For Each vntControl In Me.Controls
    Debug.Print vntControl.Height
Next vntControl
```

Correct:

```
Dim cntControl    As Control

'* Loop through all controls on the form and print their heights.
For Each cntControl In Me.Controls
    Debug.Print cntControl.Height
Next cntControl
```

· Practical Application

6.9.1 Declare only one variable per line if possible. To reduce the possibility of inadvertently creating Variant variables and to create more readable code, refrain from declaring multiple variables on the same line.

Incorrect:

```
Dim strName, strAddress As String
```

Also incorrect:

```
Dim intAge As Integer, strName As String, strAddress As String
```

Correct:

```
Dim intAge As Integer
Dim strName As String
Dim strAddress As String
```

6.10   Minimize variable scope.

The *scope* of a variable is its visibility to other procedures and modules. Visual Basic essentially offers three levels of scope: procedural, module, and global. These levels are explained in the following table.

Levels of Scope in Visual Basic

Scope	Description
Procedural	The variable is declared within the procedure and therefore can be seen and used only within the procedure. Variables with procedural scope are often called local variables.
Module	The variable is declared (with *Dim* or *Private*) in the Declarations section of a module and is visible to all procedures within the module.
Global	The variable is declared as *Public* within a standard module. The variable is visible to all procedures within all modules of the project.

You should try to minimize scope as much as possible. The smaller the scope of a variable, the lower the odds of errors related to the variable. Also, when variables go out of scope, their resources are reclaimed by the operating system. If the scope of a variable is wider than it needs to be, the variable might remain in existence and consume resources long after it's no longer needed. If data needs to be shared between procedures, pass the data as parameters between the procedures if at all possible.

Not all global variables are evil, but if you think of them as being generally demonic, you'll write better code. Unfortunately, some programmers treat the global variable as a panacea; they declare it once and use it for ever. Some even (gasp!) use a single global variable for multiple purposes!

The problems inherent with global variables are numerous. Their major problem is that they can be changed by any procedure within any module, and it's difficult to track where these changes take place. For instance, suppose that Procedure A makes use of a global variable. Procedure A reads the value of the variable and then calls Procedure B. Procedure B in turn calls Procedure C, which changes the value of the global variable. Procedure C ends and returns execution to Procedure B, which then ends and returns execution to Procedure A. Procedure A, meanwhile, is totally unaware of the change made to the global variable by Procedure C and proceeds to perform actions based on the original value of the global variable. Debugging in such scenarios is a nightmare.

As I mentioned earlier, consumption of resources is an important aspect of scope. With a single, ordinary variable, resource consumption is minimal. Imagine, however, the problems associated with creating global-level Recordset variables! Record locking and resource concerns are just a few of the issues associated with global-level Recordsets. Consider a procedure operating on the assumption that the Recordset is pointing to one record when it's actually pointing to another. With Recordset variables, minimizing scope can have a huge impact on the reliability of the application.

When you find yourself declaring a global variable, stop and look for a way to obtain the same functionality without using a global variable. You can usually find a better option, but it's not always obvious. For instance, if a module-level variable is used in only one procedure, you should make it a static variable local to that procedure. By doing so, you eliminate the possibility of another procedure inadvertently modifying the contents of the variable.

An excellent example of the use of a static variable can be found in the prevention of reentrancy. When we released our first Microsoft Windows program to our users, they experienced all sorts of errors. As developers, we took for granted that people knew to click buttons and toolbars only once. We came to find out that many users believed that double-clicking was the proper way to trigger all actions. Consequently, the Click event of a given button would execute on the second click of a double-click, but the event would still be in the process of executing from the first click. This is known as reentrancy, and it causes very strange and undesirable behavior. Users were also causing reentrancy when they double-clicked an item in a list or grid to perform an action. If the computer took slightly longer to perform the function than the user expected, they'd double-click the item again, causing the double-click to fire a second time while still executing code from the first time. Using a static variable, as shown in the following procedure, you can prevent reentrancy from causing problems in a procedure. Note, if you use a global variable instead of a static one, you run the risk of inadvertently changing the variable's value in another procedure that's performing the same technique.

```
Private Sub grdListFind_DblClick()
    '* Purpose  :  Display the selected record when the user
    '*               double-clicks a row on the grid.
    On Error GoTo PROC_ERR
    Static blnInHere As Boolean

    '* Protect this event from reentrancy caused by an overzealous user.
    If blnInHere Then GoTo PROC_EXIT

    '* Flag that we're in here.
    blnInHere = True

    Call ShowSelectedRecord

    blnInHere = False

PROC_EXIT:
    Exit Sub

PROC_ERR:
    Call ShowError(Me.Name, "grdListFind_dblClick", Err.Number, _
                Err.Description)
    Resume Next

End Sub
```

When you define variables, remember to use a scope prefix to clearly indicate the scope of the variable. The table on the following page lists the possible prefixes. (For more information on naming conventions and Hungarian prefixes, see Chapter 4.)

Scope Prefixes for Variables

Prefix	Description	Example
g	Global	g_strSavePath
m	Local to module or form	m_blnDataChanged
st	Static	st_blnInHere
(no prefix)	Nonstatic variable; variable is local to the procedure	

6.11 Concatenate strings by using an ampersand.

A common mistake that new Visual Basic programmers make is to use the plus sign (+) to concatenate Strings. The plus sign is used in arithmetic to add two numbers, so to many people it feels natural to use the plus sign to concatenate two Strings. Visual Basic even lets you use the plus sign for concatenation, but you should never do this; the ampersand is the official symbol for concatenating Strings. The main problem with using the plus sign arises when one of the variables that you're concatenating is not a String variable. If a variable has a numeric data type, Visual Basic performs arithmetic rather than concatenation. Consider the following code:

```
Dim strFirst   As String
Dim strSecond  As String

strFirst = "1"
strSecond = "2"

Debug.Print strFirst + strSecond
```

When this code is executed, *12* is printed in the Immediate window. Compare the previous code to the following:

```
Dim strFirst   As String
Dim sngSecond  As Single

strFirst = "1"
sngSecond = "2"

Debug.Print strFirst + sngSecond
```

The only difference is that the data type of *sngSecond* is now a Single. When this code is executed, the number *3* is printed. Because of this possible coercion, the only acceptable method of concatenation is to use the ampersand. The ampersand clearly conveys the intent of the function, removing any doubt a reader might have, and eliminates the possibility of incorrect results because of type coercion.

Incorrect:

```
Dim strFirstName    As String
Dim strLastName     As String
Dim strFullName     As String

strFirstName = "Ethan"
strLastName = "Foxall"

'* Concatenate the first and last names into a complete name.
strFullName = strFirstName + strLastName
```

Correct:

```
Dim strFirstName    As String
Dim strLastName     As String
Dim strFullName     As String

strFirstName = "Ethan"
strLastName = "Foxall"

'* Concatenate the first and last names into a complete name.
strFullName = strFirstName & strLastName
```

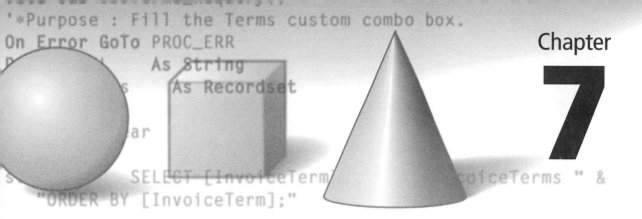

```
'*Purpose : Fill the Terms custom combo box.
On Error GoTo PROC_ERR
                As String
                As Recordset

                ar

         SELECT [InvoiceTerm                  oiceTerms " &
"ORDER BY [InvoiceTerm];"

Set restTerms = db.OpenRecordset(strSQL, dbOpenForwardOnly)

Do WHile Not rstTerms.EOF
   cboTerms.AddItem rstTerms![InvoiceTerm]

Loop

C_EXIT:
rstTerms.Close
Set rstTerms = Nothing

Exit Sub
```

Error Handling

The grandest of intentions and the most thorough planning can't eliminate errors in code. Errors can be programmer errors (usually caused by bad assumptions, such as that a denominator will never be 0), environmental errors (such as an attempt to save a file that is too large for the amount of free space on a disk), or timing errors (such as trying to set the focus to a form that isn't fully loaded). You should strive for error-free code, but you should also create every procedure with the assumption that an error might occur. This means that every procedure must contain an error handler.

There are practically an infinite number of possible program errors, but they basically fall into two types: compile errors and run-time errors. A compile error is an error that prevents Microsoft Visual Basic's compiler from compiling the code; Visual Basic won't execute a procedure that has a compile error in it, and you cannot distribute a run-time version of an application that has a compile error. Most compile errors are a result of erroneous syntax.

For example, if you attempt to call a procedure defined as

```
Public Sub MyProcedure(intMyVariable As Integer)
```

by using the statement below, a compile error occurs because of the added argument in the *Call* statement.

```
Call MyProcedure(intVariable1, intVariable2)
```

Run-time errors occur while the program is running and are usually the result of trying to perform an invalid operation on a variable. For instance, the following code doesn't generate a compile error. (It's syntactically correct if *intMyVariable* is a declared variable.)

```
Print 10 / intMyVariable
```

Under most circumstances, this code won't even generate a run-time error. However, if the value of *intMyVariable* is 0, Visual Basic halts with a run-time error because 10 can't be divided by 0. If a run-time error occurs when you run a project in the IDE, code execution stops at the offending line and an error message appears. In a compiled program, an unhandled error is fatal, causing the entire application to crash. You can prevent execution from stopping when run-time errors occur by creating error handlers.

Visual Basic's Compilation Options

Two Visual Basic settings greatly affect your ability to create consistently solid code: Compile On Demand and Background Compile. You set these on the General tab of the Options dialog box, shown in Figure 7-1.

When Compile On Demand is selected, Visual Basic doesn't fully compile your project when you click the Run button on the toolbar or press F5. Instead, procedures are compiled only as they're referenced. Compile On Demand often results in faster start times for larger projects or projects on slower computers, but it also causes some compile errors to go unnoticed.

 OTE   Pressing Ctrl+F5 or choosing Start With Full Compile from the Run menu causes the project to fully compile, regardless of the Compile On Demand setting.

Figure 7-1.   *The Compile On Demand and Background Compile options affect your ability to catch compile errors while developing.*

You cannot compile a project into a distributable file such as an .exe file or a .dll file until all compile errors are found and corrected, so selecting Compile On Demand won't allow you to distribute code with compile errors. However, selecting Compile On Demand might allow compile errors to build up over time and force you to make many corrections to your code when you finally attempt a full compile. If you're debugging your project in the IDE, you might become frustrated because Visual Basic often has to completely stop (not just halt) execution to allow you to correct the problem. This makes correcting numerous compile errors while debugging a running project a tedious process. If your computer can fully compile the project in a reasonable amount of time, you might consider turning off Compile On Demand. Or you can leave Compile On Demand selected but periodically run your project by pressing Ctrl+F5. This allows you to regularly correct compile errors as you develop rather than having to correct numerous errors all at once.

When you select Compile On Demand, you can choose whether to select the Background Compile option as well. Selecting Background Compile causes procedures and modules to be compiled as they're referenced, but

Visual Basic also uses idle time to compile modules that haven't yet been referenced. Over time, a project fully compiles. Using Background Compile allows you to enjoy the faster load times of running a project without full compilation while keeping compile errors to a minimum because you're alerted to errors in modules that are not being referenced. Once again, be aware that correcting compile errors often forces your project out of run mode, which can be a distraction during intense debugging sessions.

The *Err* Object

Before you can write effective error-handling code, you must understand Visual Basic's *Err* object, a run-time object that contains information about the most recent error. The properties of the *Err* object are populated when an error is encountered at run time or when you deliberately raise an error using the *Raise* method of the *Err* object.

The property values of the *Err* object are cleared when an *On Error* statement (such as *On Error Resume Next*) is encountered and after a procedure is exited via an *Exit Sub*, *Exit Function*, or *Exit Property* statement. To explicitly clear the *Err* object, you invoke its *Clear* method. The table below lists the properties of the *Err* object.

Property	Description
Number	The unique number that identifies the error.
Source	Name of the current Visual Basic project.
Description	A descriptive error message. If no such string exists for an error, the description says "Application-defined or object-defined error."
HelpFile	The drive, path, and filename of the Visual Basic Help file related to the error.
HelpContext	The Visual Basic Help file context ID for the error.
LastDLLError	On 32-bit Microsoft Windows operating systems, the system error code for the last call to a dynamic-link library (DLL). The *LastDLLError* property is read-only.

OTE When an error is raised, the *Err* object's properties are set to the appropriate values for the error. If you need to use any of these values, you should act on them immediately or store them in a variable before taking any other action because the *Err* object's property values might be reset. Also, the property values in the *Err* object reflect only the most recent error; the *Err* object does not maintain an error history list.

Types of Error Handlers

When you run a project as a compiled program, untrapped errors are fatal—they cause the program to terminate. You must make every effort to prevent this from happening. To prevent errors from stopping code execution (and terminating compiled programs), you create error handlers to trap the errors. When an error is trapped, Visual Basic doesn't display an error message or terminate the application. Instead, code that you've written to specifically handle the error is executed.

Every procedure should have an error handler, regardless of the amount of code it contains. It's best to place an *On Error* statement as the first line of code, immediately after the procedure header and just before the variable declarations. Be aware that errors can "bubble up" the call stack to error handlers in procedures higher in the stack (as I'll discuss later in this chapter). If a procedure's errors are allowed to bubble up in this manner, you should clearly explain this behavior in a prominent comment at the top of the procedure.

There are essentially two ways to trap errors:

- Divert code execution when an error occurs by using *On Error GoTo.*

- Ignore the error without interrupting or diverting code execution by using *On Error Resume Next.*

You can create multiple error handlers in a procedure, but no more than one error handler can be enabled at a time. Visual Basic treats the handler identified in the most recent *On Error* statement (discussed in the next section) as the enabled error handler. It's often advantageous to switch error handlers at different points within a procedure; understanding how the various error handlers work is crucial to taking advantage of this capability.

Ignoring Errors by Using *On Error Resume Next*

The simplest (and most dangerous) method of handling errors uses the *On Error Resume Next* statement. *On Error Resume Next* specifies that errors are completely ignored; the offending line of code is simply skipped and execution continues with the next statement.

For example, the following procedure has a run-time error—in this case, a divide-by-zero error—that is handled by the *On Error Resume Next* error handler:

```
Private Sub cmdGenerateError_Click()
    '* Purpose  :  Test On Error Resume Next
    On Error Resume Next

    Debug.Print 10 / 0

End Sub
```

The *Debug.Print* statement causes a divide-by-zero error. However, because there is an enabled error handler (specified by *On Error Resume Next*), the error is ignored and execution resumes at the next statement (that is, the *End Sub* statement).

Just because an error is ignored doesn't mean you'll be unable to know that an error has occurred. After a statement causes an error, the *Err* object contains information about the error even though an error message isn't displayed. The following procedure illustrates how you can test the *Err* object at any time to determine whether an error has occurred. When this procedure is called, a message box is displayed with the text *11: Division by zero*.

```
Private Sub cmdGenerateError_Click()
    '* Purpose  :  Detect an error using the Err object.
    On Error Resume Next

    Debug.Print 10 / 0

    '* If an error occurred, display its number and description.
    If Err.Number > 0 Then
        MsgBox Err.Number & ": " & Err.Description, vbCritical
    End If

End Sub
```

This technique has many uses. For instance, say that you want to create a new record in a database using data entered in a text box and that the table in which you're creating the record does not allow duplicate values. You can try to locate a record matching the entry in the text box before saving it as a new record, or you can simply try to create the new record and test for Error 3022 (duplicate record), as shown in the following procedure:

```
Private Sub CreateRecord()
    '* Purpose  :  Create a record in a database
    '*               from the data on the form.
    On Error Resume Next
    Dim rstMyTable As Recordset

    Const c_DuplicateRecordError = 3022

    '* Create a Recordset from the module-level Database variable.
    Set rstMyTable = m_dbMyDatabase.OpenRecordset( _
                    "MyTable", dbOpenDynaset)

    '* Attempt to add a new record to the database.
    rstMyTable.AddNew
        rstMyTable![Name] = txtName.Text
    rstMyTable.Update

    '* Test for duplicate value error.
    If Err.Number = c_DuplicateRecordError Then
        MsgBox "This name exists in the database, and duplicates " & _
                "are not allowed.", vbOKOnly
    End If

End Sub
```

OTE *On Error Resume Next* is often useful when you work with objects. Checking the *Err* object after each interaction with an object allows you to know with certainty which object caused the error—the object specified in *Err.Source*. This technique can require a considerable amount of code, however.

Diverting the Flow of Execution by Using *On Error GoTo*

Ignoring errors is very risky and is an inferior approach unless you're trapping an expected error, such as in the previous example. When an unexpected error occurs within a procedure, the procedure has problems. If you ignore the error, there might be serious repercussions for the user—such as data not saving or saving incorrectly. More often than not, you'll need to take some course of action when an error occurs by redirecting code execution to an error handler specified in an *On Error GoTo* statement. This statement has the following syntax:

```
On Error GoTo line
```

Note that *line* must refer to a statement in the same procedure as the *On Error GoTo* statement.

In this syntax, *line* has two possible meanings. The first is a literal line number to branch to when the error occurs. But the line number doesn't mean the physical position of the line in the procedure. Consider this next code example:

```
Private Sub TestErrorHandler()
    '* Purpose  :  Test the On Error GoTo statement by deliberately
    '*               generating a run-time error.
    On Error GoTo 4

    Debug.Print "Line 2"
    Debug.Print 10 / 0
    Debug.Print "Line 4"
    Debug.Print "Line 5"

End Sub
```

You might think that the division-by-zero error would cause code execution to continue at the statement that prints the text *Line 4* because this is the fourth statement of code (not counting comments). Not only does this not happen, but this code actually causes a compile error and won't execute at all. When you designate a line number, you must label a specific statement with that line number, as shown here:

```
Private Sub TestErrorHandler()
    '* Purpose  :  Test the On Error GoTo statement by deliberately
    '*               generating a run-time error.
    On Error GoTo 4

    Debug.Print "Line 2"
    Debug.Print 10 / 0
    Debug.Print "Line 4"
4   Debug.Print "Line 5"

End Sub
```

Even though the line beginning with *4* is not actually the fourth line of code, it's the statement that executes immediately after the division-by-zero occurs. The actual numbers you use are inconsequential—they need not correspond to physical line numbers or be in any sequential order.

 OTE You cannot use line number 0. This has a special use, which I'll discuss later in this chapter.

The second and more common use of *line* is to supply a line label. A line label is a string of text that identifies a single line of code. Line labels can be any combination of characters that starts with a letter and ends with a colon (:). Labels are not case sensitive and must always appear at the start of the line. For example, the procedure below contains a label. The *On Error GoTo* statement diverts execution to the line labeled *PROC_ERR* when the division-by-zero error occurs.

```
Private Sub TestAnErrorLabel()
    '* Purpose  :  Use a line label to divert code execution.
    On Error GoTo PROC_ERR

    Debug.Print "Line 2"
    Debug.Print 10 / 0
    Debug.Print "Line 4"

PROC_ERR:
    Debug.Print "Line 6"

End Sub
```

NOTE Labels should appear in all-uppercase letters for visual emphasis, as I'll discuss in Chapter 11, "Controlling Code Flow." Also, you should never put more than one statement of code on a single line—see Chapter 8, "Formatting Code." This rule applies to labels as well, since they are considered code statements. When control jumps to a label, execution will simply continue with the line following the label.

The *On Error GoTo* statement is used primarily to divert code execution to an error handler. To ensure that an error handler doesn't execute unless an error occurs, you should precede it with an *Exit Sub*, *Exit Function*, or *Exit Property* statement. (If you follow Directive 3.2 in Chapter 3, "Designing Modules and Procedures," the *Exit* statement will immediately follow the *PROC_EXIT* label and will be the procedure's single exit point.) The following is a skeleton procedure with a blank error handler and a labeled exit point:

```
Private Sub MyProcedure()
    '* Purpose  :
    On Error GoTo PROC_ERR
    ⋮
PROC_EXIT:
    Exit Sub

PROC_ERR:
    ⋮
End Sub
```

In this example, an error causes execution to jump to the *PROC_ERR* label, where it proceeds until it reaches the *End Sub* statement. You don't have to let the code run through the remainder of a procedure until it reaches an *End Sub*, *End Function*, or *End Property* statement. You can also do the following:

- Use an *Exit Sub*, *Exit Function*, or *Exit Property* statement to force code execution to leave the procedure. (Note that you should always use a single exit point rather than exiting the code directly from the error handler.)

- Use a *GoTo PROC_EXIT* statement to force execution to the procedure's single exit point.

- Use a *Resume Next* statement to force execution to continue with the line immediately following the statement that generated the error.

- Use a *Resume* statement to force execution to return to and continue executing the line that generated the error.

- Use a *Resume* <line> statement to redirect execution to a specific statement.

Using *GoTo PROC_EXIT* in combination with an *Exit Sub*, *Exit Function*, or *Exit Property* statement to force code execution to leave the procedure is straightforward:

```
Private Sub MyProcedure()
    '* Purpose :  Test the behavior of GoTo in an error handler.
    On Error GoTo PROC_ERR

    Debug.Print 10 / 0

PROC_EXIT:
    Exit Sub

PROC_ERR:
    MsgBox Me.Name & " | MyProcedure" & vbCrLf & Err.Number & vbCrLf & _
           Err.Description
    GoTo PROC_EXIT

End Sub
```

The following example shows how you can use the *ResumeNext* statement to force execution to continue with the line immediately following the statement that caused an error:

```
Private Sub MyProcedure()
    '* Purpose :  Test the behavior of Resume Next in an
    '*            error handler.
    On Error GoTo PROC_ERR

    '* Error is generated on the next line.
    Debug.Print 10 / 0
    Debug.Print "Code Returns Here"

PROC_EXIT:
    Exit Sub
```

(continued)

```
PROC_ERR:
    MsgBox Me.Name & " | MyProcedure" & vbCrLf & Err.Number & vbCrLf & _
           Err.Description
    Resume Next

End Sub
```

The error in this procedure causes execution to jump to the code within the *PROC_ERR* block. When *Resume Next* is encountered, execution continues with the statement immediately following the statement that caused the error.

You can branch to a specific code statement within the procedure in which the error occurs by using *Resume <line>*, as shown below. The *line* parameter works just like it does in the *On Error Resume <line>* statement.

```
Private Sub MyProcedure()
    '* Purpose  :  Demonstrate Resume <line> in an error handler.
    On Error GoTo PROC_ERR

    Debug.Print "Line 1"
    Debug.Print 10 / 0
    Debug.Print "Line 3"

ERR_CONTINUE:
    Debug.Print "Line 5"

PROC_EXIT:
    Exit Sub

PROC_ERR:
    Resume ERR_CONTINUE

End Sub
```

Perhaps the best thing an error handler can do is fix the error. If it can fix the error and return control to the offending statement, it's almost as if the error never occurred. Although the method used to remedy an error depends on the situation, returning to the offending line is simple and consistent. To force execution to return to the statement that caused the error, use the *Resume* statement, as shown here:

```
Private Sub cmdTestErrorHandler_Click()
    '* Purpose  :  Demonstrate the Resume statement in an
    '*               error handler.
    On Error GoTo PROC_ERR
    Dim intFileNumber As Integer
    Dim intRetries    As Integer

    Const c_MaxRetries = 10
    Const c_LockedFileError = 70

    intFileNumber = 1

    Open "C:\Test.txt" For Output As #intFileNumber

PROC_EXIT:
    Exit Sub

PROC_ERR:
    '* If the error indicates that the file is locked, attempt to open
    '* the file again until c_MaxRetries attempts have been made.
    If Err.Number = c_LockedFileError Then

        '* If the maximum number of attempts has been made, tell the
        '* user that the file is locked and get out.
        If intRetries > c_MaxRetries Then
            MsgBox "File is locked!", vbExclamation
            GoTo PROC_EXIT
        End If

        '* Call a custom Pause procedure that pauses a specified
        '* number of milliseconds.
        Call Pause(100)
        intRetries = intRetries + 1
        Resume
    End If

End Sub
```

This example attempts to open a file called C:\Test.txt. If the file is
locked by another application, an error occurs and execution is sent to
the error handler. The error handler then does the following:

- Checks to see whether the error is a locking error.

- If the error is a locking error, it checks *intRetries* to determine how
  many attempts have been made to open the file.

121

- If the error handler has been invoked fewer than the maximum times as specified by *c_MaxRetries*, it calls a custom Pause routine. Then *intRetries* is incremented and execution returns to the *Open* statement.

- If the error handler has been invoked more than the allowable number of times, a message is displayed to the user and the procedure is exited.

Error Handlers and the Call Stack

It's extremely important to understand how errors are passed up the call stack. A couple of terms are critical to such an understanding. The *enabled error handler* is the error handler most recently specified in an *On Error* statement. An *active error handler* is an error handler that is in the process of handling an error. Note that it is possible for a handler to be enabled but not active. Once an error handler is enabled, it remains enabled until another error handler is enabled or the procedure containing the error handler goes out of scope. When a procedure containing an enabled error handler goes out of scope, execution returns to the calling procedure and the last enabled error handler becomes enabled again.

Consider the following two procedures:

```
Private Sub cmdCreateErrorHandler_Click()
    '* Purpose  :  Enable an error handler and call another procedure.
    On Error Resume Next

    Call TestSub

End Sub


Private Sub TestSub()
    '* Purpose  :  Demonstrate error handlers and the call stack.
    On Error GoTo PROC_ERR

    Debug.Print 10 / 0

PROC_EXIT:
    Exit Sub

PROC_ERR:
    GoTo PROC_EXIT

End Sub
```

When the cmdCreateErrorHandler button is clicked, the *On Error Resume Next* statement enables an error handler. When the *TestSub* procedure is invoked, its error handler becomes enabled; any errors encountered within the *TestSub* procedure (such as the divide-by-zero error) are handled by the *PROC_ERR* error handler. When the *TestSub* procedure completes and code execution returns to the *Click* event of the command button, the *Click* event's error handler becomes enabled once more.

Next consider these two procedures:

```
Private Sub cmdCreateErrorHandler_Click()
    '* Purpose  :  Enable an error handler and call another procedure.
    On Error Resume Next

    Call TestSub

End Sub


Private Sub TestSub()
    ⋮
End Sub
```

When the command button is clicked, the *On Error Resume Next* statement within the *Click* event enables an error handler. When the *TestSub* procedure is invoked, error handlers in that procedure have the opportunity to become enabled. Since the *TestSub* procedure contains no error handler, the most recently enabled error handler (from the *Click* event) remains enabled throughout execution of the *TestSub* procedure.

What happens when an error is encountered within the *TestSub* procedure? The following two procedures illustrate this situation:

```
Private Sub cmdCreateErrorHandler_Click()
    '* Purpose  :  Demonstrate error handlers and the call stack.
    On Error Resume Next

    Call TestSub

    MsgBox "Statement in first procedure", vbInformation

End Sub
```

(continued)

```
Private Sub TestSub()

    '* Generate a run-time error.
    Debug.Print 10 / 0

    MsgBox "Statement after error", vbInformation

End Sub
```

When the *Click* event is fired, an error handler is enabled using *On Error Resume Next*. When execution transfers to the *TestSub* procedure, the error handler remains enabled because no error handler is enabled within the *TestSub* procedure. When the division-by-zero error occurs, what's printed? Since there is no error handler in the *TestSub* procedure, execution returns immediately to the calling procedure (the *cmdCreateError-Handler_Click* procedure) to be handled by its enabled error handler. Since the error handler is a *Resume Next* error handler, you might think that the statement immediately following the error (in the *TestSub* procedure) would be the next to be executed. It isn't. Instead, the statement immediately following the call to *TestSub* becomes the next statement, and the text "Statement in first procedure" is printed. An *On Error* statement cannot direct code execution outside of the procedure in which it exists.

This concept is true for multiple nested procedures as well. If an error occurs within a procedure that doesn't have an enabled error handler, the procedure that called the procedure with the error is checked for an enabled, but not active, error handler. This continues up the call stack until an enabled, but not active, error handler is found or the top of the call stack is reached. If the top of the call stack is reached, the error is treated as an untrapped error (and rightly so). If an enabled, but not active, error handler is encountered, it is executed, and then execution continues in the procedure that contains that handler.

Disabling Error Handlers at Run Time by Using *On Error GoTo 0*

Sometimes you might need to disable an enabled error handler at run time. Earlier in this chapter you learned that you can't use line number 0 when using *On Error GoTo*. This is because using line number 0 disables the currently enabled error handler.

Consider this procedure:

```
Private Sub cmdDisableErrorHandler_Click()
    '* Purpose  :  Demonstrate disabling an error handler
    '*                at run time.
    On Error GoTo PROC_ERR
    On Error GoTo 0

    Debug.Print 10 / 0

PROC_EXIT:
    Exit Sub

PROC_ERR:
    Call ShowError(Me.Name, "cmdDisableErrorHandler", Err.Number, _
                Err.Description)
    GoTo PROC_EXIT

End Sub
```

The first statement in this procedure enables an error handler. However, the *On Error GoTo 0* statement disables the error handler. Consequently, the division-by-zero error is not trapped and Visual Basic displays an error message.

 NOTE *On Error GoTo 0* disables the enabled error handler only in the current procedure. If an error is encountered after an *On Error GoTo 0* statement, the error is passed up the call stack as if there were no error handler in the procedure at all. If an enabled, but not active, error handler is found higher in the call stack, that error handler handles the error.

Enabling and Disabling Error Handlers in Debug Mode

Although you don't want errors to go untrapped in a compiled program, it's often advantageous when running a program in the IDE to let Visual Basic halt code execution if an error occurs. When execution halts, you receive a relevant error message and are shown the offending line of code; this greatly aids the debugging process. The approach Visual Basic takes to handling errors encountered at design time is determined by the *Error Trapping* property of the Visual Basic IDE. You set this property in the Options dialog box, shown in Figure 7-2.

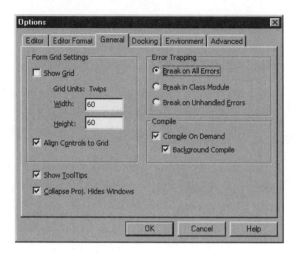

Figure 7-2. *You can change the way Visual Basic treats errors trapped at design time by selecting an option on the General tab of the Options dialog box.*

The *Error Trapping* property is a property of the Visual Basic environment, not of a specific project. Each project you work with—even after you shut down and restart Visual Basic—uses this setting. To set the error trapping option for the current session of Visual Basic only without changing the default for future sessions, use the Toggle command on the code window's shortcut menu. (See Figure 7-3.)

You can set the *Error Trapping* property to one of the following values:

- Break On All Errors

- Break In Class Module

- Break On Unhandled Errors

Break On All Errors essentially disables all of your error handlers. When an error occurs, regardless of whether an error handler is enabled, the code enters break mode at the offending statement and Visual Basic shows an error message. This allows you to deal with unexpected errors while testing within the IDE.

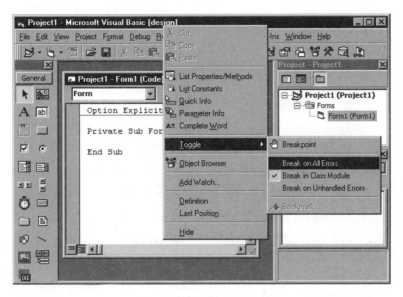

Figure 7-3. *You change the error-handling behavior of the IDE for the current session by choosing the Toggle command from the shortcut menu in any code window.*

The Break In Class Module setting is most useful when you debug ActiveX components. Ordinarily, the enabled error handler within a procedure that calls a method of an ActiveX component handles any errors that are not handled within the ActiveX component's procedure. The Break In Class Module setting specifies that errors not handled within the ActiveX component will cause the ActiveX project to enter break mode at the statement that caused the error. This prevents errors not handled within the ActiveX component from being passed up the call stack to the procedure in the client program, thus making it considerably easier to debug the ActiveX component.

The Break On Unhandled Errors setting closely models how errors are treated in compiled programs. Errors trapped by enabled error handlers are dealt with by those error handlers, and only unhandled errors cause the program to enter break mode.

Central Error Handlers

It's tedious to add error handling to all procedures in a project, but it's a necessity. Every unexpected error must be displayed to the user in the same format, and this can take a considerable amount of code. Adding a central error handler can help.

A central error handler is a procedure that you call when an error occurs. At a minimum, a central error handler displays a consistent error message to the user. However, you can add capabilities to the central error handler as you see fit. For instance, you can have your error handler send an e-mail to a support specialist whenever an unexpected error occurs, or you can actually include code to take a snapshot of the state of the machine and log the loaded applications and loaded DLLs, along with their versions.

The following is a typical central error handler:

```
Friend Sub ShowError(strModule As String, strProcedure As String, _
    lngErrorNumber As Long, strErrorDescription As String)
    '* Purpose  :   Provide a central error-handling mechanism.
    '* Accepts  :   strModule - the module in which the error was
    '*                  encountered (form, class, standard, and so on.)
    '*              strProcedure - the name of the procedure in which
    '*                  the error was encountered.
    '*              lngErrorNumber - the numeric identifier of the
    '*                  error.
    '*              strErrorDescription - the text description of
    '*                  the error.
    On Error GoTo PROC_ERR
    Dim strMessage As String
    Dim strCaption As String

    '* Build the error message.
    strMessage = "Error: " & strErrorDescription & vbCrLf & vbCrLf & _
                 "Module: " & strModule & vbCrLf & _
                 "Procedure: " & strProcedure & vbCrLf & vbCrLf & _
                 "Please notify My Software's tech support " & _
                 "at 555-1213 about this issue." & vbCrLf & _
                 "Please provide the support technician with " & _
                 "information shown in " & vbCrLf & "this dialog " & _
                 "box as well as an explanation of what you " & _
                 "were" & vbCrLf & "doing when this " & _
                 "error occurred."

    '* Build the caption for the message box. The caption shows
    '* the version number of the program.
    strCaption = "Unexpected Error! Version: " & _
                 Str$(App.major) & "." & Str$(App.minor) & "." & _
                 Format(App.Revision, "0000")

    MsgBox strMessage, vbCritical, strCaption
```

```
PROC_EXIT:
    Exit Sub

PROC_ERR:
    Resume Next

End Sub
```

To use this central error handler, you simply call the procedure in an error handler like this:

```
Private Sub frmMain_Click()
    '* Purpose  :  Generate an error by setting the focus to
    '*               an invisible control.
    On Error GoTo PROC_ERR

    '* Set the focus to an invisible control.
    txtCity.Visible = False
    txtCity.SetFocus

PROC_EXIT:
    Exit Sub

PROC_ERR:
    Call ShowError(Me.Name, "frmMain_Click", Err.Number, Err.Description)
    Resume Next

End Sub
```

When the error illustrated in the previous example occurs, the central error handler is called and it displays the dialog box shown in Figure 7-4. Imagine trying to display such a comprehensive error message from every error handler in every procedure in every module without using a central error handler!

Notice the use of *Me.Name* in the *ShowError* function call, which makes the line of code a bit more portable. You can copy this statement to the Clipboard and paste it into other procedures. In form procedures, all you change is the procedure name. This enables you to write the error handlers in your various procedures more quickly and allows you to change the way errors are handled or displayed by changing code in one location rather than hundreds or thousands of locations.

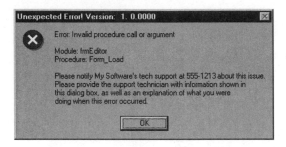

Figure 7-4.   *A central error handler makes it easy to display comprehensive error messages.*

For class modules, *Me.Name* doesn't work, so you have to use the literal class name. However, in this situation it's best to create a module-level constant and use the constant so that you can easily modify the error handlers in a class module when the module's name is changed. If you use a generic constant name, you can copy the *Call* statements from one module and paste them into another module without having to make major modifications.

Although the central error handler shown earlier displays the error message to the user in a consistent fashion, you must determine the code that each error handler will have in addition to calling the *Show-Error* procedure. For instance, does the error handler require a *Resume* or a *Resume Next* statement? Perhaps it requires a *GoTo PROC_EXIT* statement instead. You should make your error handlers as generic as possible but make sure that each one is appropriate for the procedure in which it resides.

Logging Errors to a Text File

It's often useful to have a log of any errors that occur. For instance, during the testing phase of your project, you need to know as much as you can about any errors that happen. Often, you can't rely on reports from users. When it's critical that you know about every error in your program, you should use a central error handler to create an error log.

Creating an error log is simple. First create a central error handler as discussed earlier. Then, within the central error handler, devise a mechanism to log the errors to a text file. The following code illustrates one way to log errors to a text file. This code is shown as it would appear as part of the central error handler shown previously. It assumes that the local variables in that procedure are present and that there is a global variable in the project called *g_strErrorLogFileName* that contains the path and name of the error log file.

```
Dim intLogFile    As Integer

'* Obtain a free file handle.
intLogFile = FreeFile

'* Open the error log text file in Append mode.
'* If the file doesn't exist, the Open statement
'* creates it.
Open g_strErrorLogFileName For Append As #intLogFile

'* Write the header.
Print #intLogFile, "*** Error Encountered " & VBA.Now & " ***"

'* Write the pertinent error information to the log file.
Print #intLogFile, "Error: " & lngErrorNumber
Print #intLogFile, "Description: " & strErrorDescription
Print #intLogFile, "Procedure: " & strProcedure
Print #intLogFile, "Module: " & strModule

'* Write a blank line to the log file.
Print #intLogFile, ""

'* Close the log file.
Close #intLogFile
```

This code attempts to open the text file specified in the global variable *g_strErrorLogFileName* in Append mode. If the file doesn't exist, it's created automatically and then opened. Once the file is opened, a log entry is written. In this example, five lines of text are written for each log entry, with each entry separated from the others by a blank line. Here is a sample of a text file created using the previous code:

```
*** Error Encountered 8/29/99 4:19:18 PM ***
Error: 5
Description: Invalid procedure call or argument
Procedure: ShowCustomer
Module: clsCustomer
```

(continued)

```
*** Error Encountered 8/29/99 4:20:08 PM ***
Error: 11
Description: Division by zero
Procedure: CalculateCoefficient
Module: mdlScience

*** Error Encountered 8/29/99 4:22:05 PM ***
Error: 6
Description: Overflow
Procedure: CalculateDrag
Module: mdlScience

*** Error Encountered 8/29/99 4:22:34 PM ***
Error: 11
Description: Division by zero
Procedure: CalculateCoefficient
Module: mdlScience
```

You can start to see a trend in this error log. Whoever wrote the *mdlScience* module needs to spend a little more time with the code. The information shown here is the minimum amount you'd want to include in a text file; you might want to include much more. For instance, you might want to include the user name of the person running the program when the error occurs, or you might want to include the machine name in the log entry. The possibilities are endless. Whatever you choose to put into the text file, make sure it's pertinent information that will help you find and correct the problem.

For clarity, the following is the complete error handler shown previously, with the inclusion of the error log code:

```
Friend Sub ShowError(strModule As String, strProcedure As String, _
    lngErrorNumber As Long, strErrorDescription As String)
    '* Purpose  :   Provide a central error-handling mechanism.
    '* Accepts  :   strModule - the module in which the error was
    '*                  encountered (form, class, standard, and so on.)
    '*              strProcedure - the name of the procedure in which
    '*                  the error was encountered.
    '*              lngErrorNumber - the numeric identifier of the
    '*                  error.
    '*              strErrorDescription - the text description of
    '*                  the error.
    On Error GoTo PROC_ERR
    Dim strMessage As String
```

```vba
Dim strCaption As String
Dim intLogFile As Integer

'* Obtain a free file handle.
intLogFile = FreeFile

'* Open the error log text file in Append mode.
'* If the file doesn't exist, the Open statement
'* creates it.
Open g_strErrorLogFileName For Append As #intLogFile

'* Write the header.
Print #intLogFile, "*** Error Encountered " & VBA.Now & " ***"

'* Write the pertinent error information to the log file.
Print #intLogFile, "Error: " & lngErrorNumber
Print #intLogFile, "Description: " & strErrorDescription
Print #intLogFile, "Procedure: " & strProcedure
Print #intLogFile, "Module: " & strModule

'* Write a blank line to the log file.
Print #intLogFile, ""

'* Close the error log text file.
Close #intLogFile

'* Build the error message for display to the user.
strMessage = "Error: " & strErrorDescription & vbCrLf & vbCrLf & _
             "Module: " & strModule & vbCrLf & _
             "Procedure: " & strProcedure & vbCrLf & vbCrLf & _
             "Please notify My Software's tech support " & _
             "at 555-1213 about this issue." & vbCrLf & _
             "Please provide the support technician with " & _
             "information shown in " & vbCrLf & "this dialog " & _
             "box as well as an explanation of what you " & _
             "were" & vbCrLf & "doing when this " & _
             "error occurred."

'* Build the caption for the message box. The caption shows
'* the version number of the program.
strCaption = "Unexpected Error! Version: " & _
             Str$(App.major) & "." & Str$(App.minor) & "." & _
             Format(App.Revision, "0000")

MsgBox strMessage, vbCritical, strCaption
```

(continued)

```
PROC_EXIT:
    Exit Sub

PROC_ERR:
    Resume Next

End Sub
```

Once your application is logging error messages, you must decide what you want to do with those logs. If you're on-site with the program, you can manually retrieve copies of the error logs. Or you can have users e-mail you their logs if they encounter problems. You might even write a program that automatically e-mails the logs to you on a preset schedule. Log files can be very useful for locating specific bugs as well as general program errors, and they are easy to create. You should seriously consider adding this feature to your programs. You might even elect to include the code but turn off the feature by default. Then you can enable or disable log file generation via your program's interface or a registry setting.

> **Goals of Error Handling**
>
> The goals of utilizing error handling are
>
> - Preventing your program from crashing
> - Gracefully correcting mistakes whenever possible
> - Notifying the user when errors occur so that the problems can be addressed

Directives

7.1   Use *On Error GoTo* to trap unexpected errors.

Most error handlers are designed to trap errors that aren't anticipated at design time. The *On Error GoTo* statement is the most common way of designating an error handler. You should use this as the default in all of your procedures unless you have a specific reason to use a different scheme.

Incorrect:

```
Private Sub imgEditor_MouseUp(Button As Integer, Shift As Integer, _
    X As Single, Y As Single)
'* Purpose  :  If the editor is in select (marquee) mode, display
'*               the Edit shortcut menu when the user right-clicks
'*               the Canvas.
On Error Resume Next

'* Display the shortcut menu only if the user clicked with
'* the right mouse button.
If Button = vbRightButton Then

    '* See if the active tool of the Canvas object is the
    '* marquee tool.
    If g_objCanvas.ToolIndex = bdMarquee Then
        '* Display the Edit shortcut menu using the active
        '* bar control.
        Me.ActiveBar.Bands("puEdit").TrackPopup -1, -1
    End If

End If

'* Tell the Canvas object to stop its current action.
g_objCanvas.ActionEnd Button, Shift, X, Y

PROC_EXIT:
    Exit Sub

End Sub
```

Correct:

```
Private Sub imgEditor_MouseUp(Button As Integer, Shift As Integer, _
    X As Single, Y As Single)
'* Purpose  :  If the editor is in select (marquee) mode, display
'*               the Edit shortcut menu when the user right-clicks
'*               the Canvas.
On Error GoTo PROC_ERR

'* Display the shortcut menu only if the user clicked with
'* the right mouse button.
If Button = vbRightButton Then

    '* See if the active tool of the Canvas object is the
    '* marquee tool.
    If g_objCanvas.ToolIndex = bdMarquee Then
        '* Display the Edit shortcut menu using the active
        '* bar control.
```

(continued)

135

```
            Me.ActiveBar.Bands("puEdit").TrackPopup -1, -1
        End If

    End If

    '* Tell the Canvas object to stop its current action.
    g_objCanvas.ActionEnd Button, Shift, X, Y

PROC_EXIT:
    Exit Sub

PROC_ERR:
    Call ShowError(Me.Name, "imgEditor_MouseUp", Err.Number, _
                    Err.Description)
    Resume Next

End Sub
```

7.2   Use *On Error Resume Next* to trap expected errors.

When you expect an error, such as Error 5 when you use *SetFocus* to move the cursor to a control on a form that is not fully loaded, or an error from a database action, use *On Error Resume Next.* But be careful—using *On Error Resume Next* can be dangerous because it can cause run-time errors to go unnoticed. Do not use it as a panacea; if you do not expect an error, don't use it. Also, just because you expect an error within a procedure doesn't mean that you should use *On Error Resume Next* for the entire procedure. Use *On Error GoTo* to trap unexpected errors, but change the enabled error handler immediately before the line that could cause the expected error. After you have handled the expected error, include an *On Error GoTo* statement to enable the main error handler again.

When you write code to trap an expected error, be sure to document the code thoroughly. State specifically why you are using *On Error Resume Next*—such as what error you expect and why.

Incorrect:

```
Private Sub cmdCoverLetter_Click()
    '* Purpose  :  Allow the user to browse and select a cover
    '*               page for faxing.
    On Error Resume Next

    Const c_CancelChosen = 32755
```

```
'* Use the common dialog control to allow the user to
'* select a file.
With dlgOpenFile
    .fileName = "*.cvp"
    .DefaultExt = "cvp"
    .DialogTitle = "Select Cover Page"
    .Filter = "All Files (*.*)|*.*|Cover Pages (*.cvp)"
    .FilterIndex = 2
    .InitDir = App.Path

    '* Tell the control to generate an error if Cancel is clicked.
    .CancelError = True

    '* Show the Open File dialog box and wait for the user to
    '* select a file or click Cancel.
    .ShowOpen

    '* See if an error was generated as the result of the
    '* user clicking Cancel.
    If Err.Number = c_CancelChosen Then
        '* Cancel was clicked; get out.
        GoTo PROC_EXIT
    End If

    txtCoverpage.Text = .fileName

End With

PROC_EXIT:
    Exit Sub

End Sub
```

Correct:
```
Private Sub cmdCoverLetter_Click()
    '* Purpose  :  Allow the user to browse and select a cover
    '*               page for faxing.
    On Error GoTo PROC_ERR

    Const c_CancelChosen = 32755

    '* Use the common dialog control to allow the user to
    '* select a file.
    With dlgOpenFile
        .fileName = "*.cvp"
        .DefaultExt = "cvp"
        .DialogTitle = "Select Cover Page"
```

(continued)

```
                .Filter = "All Files (*.*)|*.*|Cover Pages (*.cvp)"
                .FilterIndex = 2
                .InitDir = App.Path

                '* Tell the control to generate an error if Cancel is clicked.
                .CancelError = True
                '* If the user clicks Cancel, a run-time error occurs.
                '* Trap for this error.
                On Error Resume Next
                    '* Show the Open File dialog box and wait for the user to
                    '* select a file or click Cancel.
                    .ShowOpen

                    '* See if an error was generated as the result of the
                    '* user clicking Cancel.
                    If Err.Number = c_CancelChosen Then
                        '* Cancel was clicked; get out.
                        GoTo PROC_EXIT
                    End If

                '* Enable the main error handler.
                On Error GoTo PROC_ERR
                txtCoverpage.Text = .fileName

            End With

    PROC_EXIT:
        Exit Sub

    PROC_ERR:
        Call ShowError(Me.Name, "cmdCoverLetter_Click" , Err.Number , _
                    Err.Description)
        Resume Next

    End Sub
```

7.3   Create consistent error handler blocks.

When you use *On Error GoTo*, it's important to use consistent error blocks. *It's definitely best to use a central error handler,* but if you don't use one, create error handlers like this typical error block:

```
PROC_ERR:
    MsgBox "ModuleName | ProcedureName" & vbcrlf & "Error: " & _
        Err.Number & vbCrLf & Err.Description, vbCritical
    '* cleanup code such as a rollback
    Resume Next    '* or Resume, or GoTo PROC_EXIT
```

If you're going to alert the user to the error, which is usually the best approach, the *MsgBox* statement should be the first statement of the error block. If the *MsgBox* statement is not the first statement, the *Err* object might be reset and the *MsgBox* statement won't return the proper error number and/or description—for instance, if you branch to another procedure that enables an error handler. The only parts of the *MsgBox* statement that should be modified for each procedure are the procedure name and possibly the module name.

You can add code to the error block at your discretion, such as invoking a rollback on a database transaction. Of course, the necessary code will vary from procedure to procedure.

If you don't want to terminate a procedure as a result of an error, you must end the error block with *Resume, Resume Next, or Resume <line>*. To continue executing code starting at the line after the statement that caused the error, use *Resume Next*. If you believe the offending statement might now properly execute (such as when your error handler has corrected the problem), use *Resume* to send execution back to the statement that caused the error.

 OTE If you use *Resume* at the end of an error block without correcting the offending error, you risk creating an endless loop in your code! The error will cause the error block to execute, which will return to the offending statement, which will cause the error, and so forth.

Creating a central error handler eliminates the necessity to micromanage the error handler in every procedure. However, if you don't use a central error handler, you must handle and display errors in a consistent manner.

Incorrect:

```
PROC_ERR:
   MsgBox "Error!: " & Err.Number & vbCrLf & Err.Description
   GoTo PROC_EXIT

PROC_ERR:
   MsgBox Err.Number & vbCrLf & Err.Description
   GoTo PROC_EXIT
```

Correct:
```
PROC_ERR:
    MsgBox Me.Name & " | MyProcedure" & vbCrLf & Err.Number & vbCrLf & _
            Err.Description
    GoTo PROC_EXIT

PROC_ERR:
    MsgBox "MyModule  | MyProcedure" & vbCrLf & Err.Number & vbCrLf & _
            Err.Description
    GoTo PROC_EXIT
```

Practical Application

7.3.1 Don't let code fall through to *End Sub*, *End Function*, or *End Property*. Generally, the error block should be the last section of code in a procedure. However, if you want the procedure to terminate at the end of the error block, don't just let the code run through to *End Sub*, *End Function*, or *End Property*. Remember that it's vitally important that each procedure have only one exit point—see Chapter 3—so to terminate a procedure from the error block you should branch to the *PROC_EXIT* label.

Incorrect:
```
Private Sub otToolbox_ToolSelected(Tool As Toolbox.cTool)
    '* Purpose  :  When a new tool is selected from the toolbox,
    '*               select the corresponding tool of the Canvas object.
    On Error GoTo PROC_ERR

    '* If the selected tool is the same as the current tool, get out.
    If Tool.Index = objCanvas.ToolIndex Then GoTo PROC_EXIT

    '* If the selected tool of the Canvas is the marquee and an
    '* area is selected, redisplay the marquee.
    If objCanvas.ToolIndex = bdMarquee Then

        '* If the user has selected an area with the marquee,
        '* trigger a reset (repaint) of the marquee rectangle.
        If objCanvas.AreaSelected Then
            objCanvas.ResetMarquee
        End If

    End If

    '* Set the Canvas object to the new tool.
    objCanvas.ToolIndex = Tool.Index
```

```
PROC_EXIT:
    Exit Sub

PROC_ERR:
    Call ShowError(Me.Name, "otToolbox_ToolSelected", Err.Number, _
                Err.Description)
End Sub
```

Correct:

```
Private Sub otToolbox_ToolSelected(Tool As Toolbox.cTool)
    '* Purpose  :  When a new tool is selected from the toolbox,
    '*               select the corresponding tool of the Canvas object.
    On Error GoTo PROC_ERR

    '* If the selected tool is the same as the current tool, get out.
    If Tool.Index = objCanvas.ToolIndex Then GoTo PROC_EXIT

    '* If the selected tool of the Canvas is the marquee and an
    '* area is selected, redisplay the marquee.
    If objCanvas.ToolIndex = bdMarquee Then

        '* If the user has selected an area with the marquee,
        '* trigger a reset (repaint) of the marquee rectangle.
        If objCanvas.AreaSelected Then
            objCanvas.ResetMarquee
        End If

    End If

    '* Set the Canvas object to the new tool.
    objCanvas.ToolIndex = Tool.Index

PROC_EXIT:
    Exit Sub

PROC_ERR:
    Call ShowError(Me.Name, "otToolbox_ToolSelected", Err.Number, _
                Err.Description)
    GoTo PROC_EXIT

End Sub
```

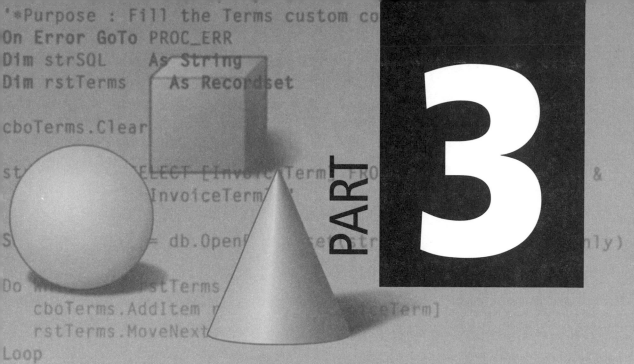

```
'*Purpose : Fill the Terms custom co
On Error GoTo PROC_ERR
Dim strSQL      As String
Dim rstTerms    As Recordset

cboTerms.Clear

st                SELECT [InvoiceTerm  FR                    &
                  InvoiceTerm

S            = db.Open                              ly)

Do W            stTerms
    cboTerms.AddItem                    ceTerm]
    rstTerms.MoveNext
Loop

C_EXIT
rstTerms.Close
Set rstTerms = Nothing
```

Coding Constructs

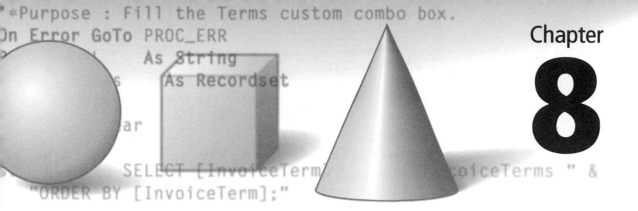

Formatting Code

No professional writer would forgo the use of punctuation or capitalization, and no professional developer should write unformatted or poorly formatted code. Consider the formatting of words, which is more than an exercise to keep English teachers busy. Language standards serve the reader and the writer to an equal degree. When you encounter a question mark at the end of an English sentence, you instantly know that the sentence is a question, not a statement or a declaration. That single little punctuation mark makes all the difference in the world, as illustrated in this short dialog:

> *Jayson: The dog ate it.*
> *Mike: The dog ate it?*
> *Jayson: The dog ate it!*

The same sentence is presented three times, but thanks to the use of standardized punctuation elements, it takes on very different meanings each time. Without these simple symbols, you would have to change the sentences to convey the same conversation:

> *Jayson: The dog ate it*
> *Mike: You're kidding me; are you saying the dog ate it*
> *Jayson: You must be dense; I said the dog ate it*

Even if the words aren't very well written, the simple act of applying the correct formatting (punctuation and spelling) makes a huge difference in the readability of the words. Words written in all capital letters or in phonetic form are understandable and can be used to communicate, but they make the communication process unnecessarily difficult. TRY TO READ A DOCUMENT WRITTEN IN ALL UPPERCASE LETTERS, or perhapz reed a letr riten solee uzing fonikz, and you'll see what I mean.

The consistent application of accepted formatting standards combined with uniform sentence construction (use of verbs, nouns, and so on) empowers writers to focus on the subtleties of what they're trying to say rather than the mechanics of what they're writing. It also allows the reader to focus on the message conveyed by the writer rather than having to work to decipher the words and sentences.

Words that are formatted according to the rules and constructs of a language often have more impact and are almost always easier to understand. The same is true of formatted code. Code that is consistently formatted according to a set of rules is easier to read, easier to understand, and often more reliable. By applying formatting techniques to your code, you'll create much more professional code that people might even enjoy reading, as opposed to code that causes others to reach for a bottle of aspirin when asked to perform a code review.

Consider the following two procedures. They are identical in content and perform exactly the same task because they are written with the same code. Note the two <?> notations in the first example. These indicate code statements that are so long that the lines can't be read on a typical display without scrolling across the code window.

Unformatted code:

```
Public Sub RequeryAccountPhone()
On Error GoTo PROC_ERR
Dim rstPhones As Recordset
Dim strSQL As String
'* Clear the phone list.
lvwPhones.ListItems.Clear
'* Retrieve the phone number information for this account.
strSQL = "SELECT * FROM tblPhoneNumbers WHERE [AccountNumber] = " M<?>
Set rstPhones = dbContacts.OpenRecordset(strSQL, dbOpenForwardOnly)
Do While Not rstPhones.EOF
```

```
      Call AddPhoneToList(rstPhones![FormattedPhoneNumber], rstPhones![Ph<?>
      rstPhones.MoveNext
Loop
rstPhones.Close
PROC_EXIT:
Set rstPhones = Nothing: Exit Sub
PROC_ERR:
MsgBox "Error: " & Err.Number & vbCrLf & Err.Description
GoTo PROC_EXIT
End Sub
```

Correctly formatted code:

```
Public Sub RequeryAccountPhone()
    '* Purpose  :  Fill a ListView control with all of the phone
    '*               numbers belonging to the current account.
    On Error GoTo PROC_ERR
    Dim rstPhones As Recordset
    Dim strSQL As String

    '* Clear the phone list.
    lvwPhones.ListItems.Clear

    '* Retrieve the phone number information for this account.
    strSQL = "SELECT * FROM tblPhoneNumbers " & _
            "WHERE [AccountNumber] = " & Me.AccountNumber & " " & _
            "AND [ContactNumber] Is Null " & _
            "ORDER BY [Primary];"

    Set rstPhones = dbContacts.OpenRecordset(strSQL, dbOpenForwardOnly)

    '* Add each record in the Recordset to the ListView.
    Do While Not rstPhones.EOF
        Call AddPhoneToList(rstPhones![FormattedPhoneNumber], _
                            rstPhones![PhoneLocation], _
                            rstPhones![Primary])
        rstPhones.MoveNext
    Loop

    rstPhones.Close

PROC_EXIT:
    Set rstPhones = Nothing
    Exit Sub

PROC_ERR:
    MsgBox "Error: " & Err.Number & vbCrLf & Err.Description
    GoTo PROC_EXIT

End Sub
```

While these procedures are identical in function and content, there's clearly a difference between them. If these procedures were written by another person and you had to maintain them, which one would you prefer to work with? If you were the author of these procedures and had to have the code pass a peer review, which procedure would you prefer to have written?

Steve McConnell in *Code Complete* (Microsoft Press, 1993) states the following: "The Fundamental Theorem of Formatting is that good visual layout shows the logical structure of a program." This is a powerful statement. Even if a procedure's algorithms border on genius, sloppy code is sloppy code. Formatting isn't just about making code look nice, it's about making it more readable and understandable. When you format your code, you should

- Make code easy to read and to understand. Readers should be able to follow the flow of code much as they would follow sentences and paragraphs within a document.

- Reduce the work necessary to understand structural constructs. Complicated constructs consisting of nested (one inside of another) loops or *If...Then* blocks can be terribly difficult to follow when indentation and white space aren't applied.

- Organize code into functional pieces and understandable fragments, much like paragraphs in a document. The first step is to create many specialized procedures rather than one large procedure that performs dozens of tasks—much like splitting a large document into chapters. Organizing the code within procedures is akin to breaking a logical argument into paragraphs.

- Avoid forcing the reader to make assumptions. When you reference an object's default property without explicitly naming the property (for example, *Text1 = "Shiny Object"* as opposed to *Text1.Text = "Shiny Object"*), you force the reader to make an assumption.

- Make the structure of code as self-documenting as possible. You can often make code self-documenting simply by applying correct indentation.

Every company, team, and developer has an opinion about code formatting (and if they don't, they should). Unfortunately, many developers appear to not give code formatting even a passing thought. Their goal is to write code that works, and that's that. You might decide to alter some of the suggestions you find in this chapter based on your own opinions, but if you choose not to follow these directives, think carefully before doing so. If you decide to adopt your own variations of code formatting, make sure that the standards you choose are well documented within your organization and that all programmers adhere to them strictly and consistently.

When code is correctly formatted, it appears "finished," even elegant. You can often tell which programmers take the most pride in their work by how well their code is formatted. Code formatting is not polish that you can apply after the fact. Like code commenting, formatting is rarely done after the code is written. You must adopt a set of formatting standards and apply the techniques as you write code. It might seem like extra effort to remember the various formatting elements and how and when to apply them, but after a while it will become second nature. After all, do you really have to think about putting a period, a question mark, or an exclamation point at the end of a sentence?

 OTE   This chapter does not discuss the writing or formatting of comments. See Chapter 9, "Commenting Code," for information on that topic.

➤ | ### Goals of Formatting Code

When you format your code, your goals should include

- Making your code easier to read and understand by organizing it into functional pieces and understandable fragments

- Reducing the work necessary to understand structural constructs

- Freeing the reader of your code from having to make assumptions

- Making the structure of your code as self-documenting as possible

Directives

8.1 Do not place multiple statements on a single line.

Microsoft Visual Basic is a robust language whose roots run deep. Many of its current features originate from early forms of Basic such as BASICA and GW-BASIC. While many of these "features" have survived a long time, it's time for some of them to die. One of these features is the ability to use the colon (:) to place multiple statements on a single line.

In the old days of Basic, code was often written on a screen that supported only about 80 characters (across) by 24 lines (down). Frequently, this meant that programmers had to pack as much information as possible into the tiny screen space. Some languages even restricted the number of characters or lines in a program. Whatever the reasons, many programmers adopted the technique of placing multiple statements on a single line. The truly cruel developers didn't just stop at placing two statements on a line, but would often include three or four! What's the harm, you say? Take a look at this procedure:

```
Dim intXLeg As Integer
Dim intYLeg As Integer
Dim udtCircle As typeCircle

'* Retrieve the length of the X leg of the rectangle.
intXLeg = Abs(m_rectBound.Right - m_rectBound.Left): intYLeg = _
Abs(m_rectBound.Bottom - m_rectBound.Top)
If (intXLeg = 0) Or (intYLeg = 0) Then GoTo PROC_EXIT

With udtCircle
    .Aspect = Abs(intYLeg / intXLeg): .xCenter = m_rectBound.Left + _
    (m_rectBound.Right - m_rectBound.Left) / 2: .yCenter = _
    m_rectBound.Top +  (m_rectBound.Bottom - m_rectBound.Top) /2

    '* Calculate the radius based on the longer leg of the rectangle.
    If intXLeg > intYLeg Then
        .Radius = intXLeg / 2
    Else
        .Radius = intYLeg / 2: End If
End With
```

This procedure is inherently complicated. It takes a rectangle and determines, based on the rectangle's coordinates, whether it bounds a valid circle. If so, the specific circle information is stored in the variable *udtCircle.* When multiple statements appear on the same line separated by a colon, it becomes difficult to determine where one statement ends and another begins; complexity is added for no valid reason. Notice the final *End If* in the procedure. It's tacked onto the same line as the *Else* clause's code statement. Why? Because it saves vertical space. Not a very good reason in this example, and not a good reason in any other situation. Look at the same code sample with each statement having its own line:

```
Dim intXLeg As Integer
Dim intYLeg As Integer
Dim udtCircle As typeCircle

'* Retrieve the length of the X leg of the rectangle.
intXLeg = Abs(m_rectBound.Right - m_rectBound.Left)
intYLeg = Abs(m_rectBound.Bottom - m_rectBound.Top)

If (intXLeg = 0) Or (intYLeg = 0) Then GoTo PROC_EXIT

With udtCircle
    .Aspect = Abs(intYLeg / intXLeg)
    .xCenter = Bound.Left + (m_rectBound.Right - m_rectBound.Left) / 2
    .yCenter = Bound.Top + (m_rectBound.Bottom - m_rectBound.Top) / 2

    '* Calculate the radius based on the longer leg of the rectangle.
    If intXLeg > intYLeg Then
        .Radius = intXLeg / 2
    Else
        .Radius = intYLeg / 2
    End If

End With
```

The code is still complex, but it is not nearly as difficult to read. When you let each statement assert itself and give each all the space it requires, you write what I call *territorial statements.* Territorial statements stake their ground and don't give an inch. They don't share a line with any other statement, and they consume as many lines as they need.

8.2   Use the line continuation character.

While many programmers create territorially weak statements by making statements share lines, even more developers create territorially weak statements by not giving them enough lines. One reason for this is that Visual Basic didn't always support the use of the line continuation character (_) to break long statements into smaller fragments on multiple lines. Many programmers did not adopt the line continuation character when it showed up, and they're still writing mile-long statements that wear out your mouse as you scroll through the statement. If you're still writing these supertanker lines of code, here's a chance to introduce a small change into your programming style that will make your code much easier to read and maintain.

Using the line continuation character is simple. You simply select an appropriate spot in a statement and place the character in that location, preceded by a space. The line continuation character denotes that the next line of code is part of the current code statement. The benefits of using this character are evident when you use it to break very long SQL statements into multiple lines, as shown here:

```
strSQL = "SELECT tblAssemblyDetail.*, tblInventory.Description, " & _
         "tblInventory.Serials FROM tblInventory RIGHT JOIN " & _
         "tblAssemblyDetail ON tblInventory.ItemID = " & _
         "tblAssemblyDetail.ItemID WHERE ((tblAssemblyDetail." & _
         "Assembly) = """ & Me.ItemID & """) ORDER BY " & _
         "tblAssemblyDetail.LineNumber;"
```

Without the use of the line continuation character, all you'd see in a typical code window is the text that appears on the first line. Thanks to the use of the line continuation character, all six lines displayed here actually compose a single code statement; it's a very territorial statement indeed.

When you deal with statements that contain large strings, if you don't enclose the string on each line with quotes, Visual Basic interprets the line continuation character as part of the string and you get a compile error. For instance, the following statement incorrectly uses the line continuation character:

```
strMessage = "The clouds moved swiftly over the valley, churning _
              and rumbling as they threatened the villagers."
```

This statement simply won't compile. To properly place the statement on multiple lines, you have to concatenate (by using the ampersand) pieces of the string, like this:

```
strMessage = "The clouds moved swiftly over the valley, churning " & _
             "and rumbling as they threatened the villagers."
```

 OTE   Since the line continuation character denotes a continuation, you can't place end-of-line comments after it.

Practical Applications

8.2.1   Do not exceed 90 characters on a line. In MS-DOS, you typically had columns of about 80 characters to work with—that was it. In Visual Basic, the number of visible characters on a line is determined by the font size and monitor resolution of the developer's machine. Strictly limiting the number of characters on a line to 80 is not necessarily appropriate, nor is writing statements that can be viewed in their entirety only on monitors set to a resolution of 1280 × 1024.

 OTE   If you're developing on a machine at a resolution of 800 × 600 or less, consider buying a larger monitor and increasing your resolution. Your productivity will increase at a resolution of 1024 × 768 if you have a large enough monitor. A 17-inch monitor is perfect for 1024 × 768 for many developers, although you might consider a 19-inch monitor if you have vision problems.

At 800 × 600, with a code window sized to pretty much fill the screen horizontally, you can fit about 90 characters on a line. At 1024 × 768 under the same circumstances, you can fit quite a bit more, but you shouldn't. Generally, it's best to work with a code window sized smaller than the screen so that you still have access to windows such as the Properties window and, more important, the Project Explorer. Add the fact that many people are still using 800 × 600, and you've got a strong case for using about 90 characters as a line length. Depending on the optimum locations to split a statement, you might go slightly over 90 characters or way under 90 characters. It's OK to fall short of 90 characters by 10 or even 20 characters if it makes sense, but you should try to not exceed 90 characters. It would be nice if Visual Basic had an option to place a light gray vertical line in the code window at a specified column so that you could easily see when you approach the maximum length for a statement. Perhaps in a future release…

8.2.2 Do not right-align multiple-line statements; always split a statement after a space. It isn't necessary and it's generally not a good idea to break statements so that each successive code line aligns with the right edge of the first line. When you break statements in this fashion, the breaks usually come in inferior locations. In addition, it becomes almost impossible to keep such rigid formatting when you modify a statement. When you break a statement into multiple lines, first find the general location where it would be best to break the statement. Then try to break the statement between reserved words or keywords. If you must break the statement in the middle of a string, try to place the break between words and after a space. By consistently breaking strings after spaces, you reduce the possibility of introducing problems when you modify the string.

 OTE   There are some places that you cannot break a statement, such as the middle of a reserved word. If you attempt to split the statement in such a place, you receive a syntax error.

Take a look at the statements below. Notice that an effort was made to line up the right sides of the lines. Although it looks pretty, this style is not practical and is prone to error. Notice that the words *serial* and *designated* are split. If you make any modifications to the text of this statement, you have to be careful to not leave orphaned letters or sentence fragments. Also, if you make changes and want to preserve the uniformity of the right side, you probably have to reformat some or all of the lines.

Incorrect:

```
strMessage = "Serial number " & strSerialNumber & "for item """ & _
             strItemID & """" is in location " & rstSerials![Location] & _
             "." & vbCrLf & "If you continue, the location of this s" & _
             "erial number will be changed to the location designate" & _
             "d in the transfer."
```

Correct:

```
strMessage = "Serial number " & strSerialNumber & "for item """ & _
             strItemID & """" is in location " & _
             rstSerials![Location] & "." & vbCrLf & "If you " &  _
             "continue, the location of this serial number will " & _
             "be changed to the location designated in the transfer."
```

If you make a spelling or syntax error in the text of a string, the worst that will probably happen is that you'll be embarrassed when the user sees the text displayed. If you accidentally corrupt the text of a SQL statement, your code might actually fail. Therefore, when you break up long SQL statements (a common task in database applications), you should maintain clear break points for ease of reading and maintenance. This is where the rule of always splitting after spaces gives you the most benefit. Consider the following code statement:

Statement with an error:
```
strSQL = "SELECT tblAccounts.*, tblCustomAccount.* FROM" & _
"(tblAccounts INNER JOIN tblAssignedAccGroups ON tblAccounts." & _
"AccountNumber = tblAssignedAccGroups.AccountNumber) " & _
"LEFT JOIN tblCustomAccount ON tblAccounts.AccountNumber = " & _
"tblCustomAccount.AccountNumber WHERE (((" & _
"tblAssignedAccGroups.Group) = """" & _
frmGroups.SelectedGroup & """"));"
```

Notice that there is no space at the end of the string at the end of the first line. When concatenated with the second line, the text "…FROM(tblAccounts…" is created—a definite syntax error, but not necessarily an obvious one to spot. Also note how the text on each line starts with a character and not a space. This consistency helps you spot errors and makes it easier to insert new code.

8.2.3   Break between expressions a statement that performs complicated expression evaluations. Breaking such statements between expressions doesn't just make your code easier to digest (because the entire statement is visible), it can actually make the expression easier for the reader to understand. Consider the following *If* statement:

```
If blnMoving And recStart.X = Int(X / intMag) And recStart.Y = _
Int(Y / intMag) Then
    ⋮
End If
```

This statement is split at an acceptable location, which allows the reader to view the entire statement without scrolling, but the statement doesn't make clear exactly what it is evaluating. A more logical place to break the line is between two conditions, as shown below. Note the variation as well. You can place the Boolean operators at the end of each line, but I believe that placing them at the beginning of each line improves clarity. Choose the style that you are most comfortable with and use it consistently.

Correct:
```
If blnMoving And recStart.X = Int(X / intMag) _
    And recStart.Y = Int(Y / intMag) Then
    ⋮
End If
```

Perhaps even better:
```
If blnMoving _
    And recStart.X = Int(X / intMag) _
    And recStart.Y = Int(Y / intMag) Then
    ⋮
End If
```

Variation:
```
If blnMoving And _
    recStart.X = Int(X / intMag) And _
    recStart.Y = Int(Y / intMag) Then
    ⋮
End If
```

8.3   Indent continuation lines.

There is no hard-and-fast rule for the number of characters to indent continuation lines; you must make a judgment based on the first line of the statement. Some general guidelines are:

■ When you set a variable to a value, make all continuation lines start at the same indentation as the value portion of the first line.

■ When you split a long procedure heading, indent all continuation lines two tab stops (generally six characters).

■ When you call a procedure, indent continuation lines to the start of the first argument.

■ When you set a variable or property equal to the result of an expression, break the statement just after the equal sign to ensure that as much as possible of the expression remains on one line.

■ When you split a long *If* statement, indent continuation lines two tab stops (six characters).

Formatting is visual, so think of these indentation guidelines visually. By comparing good and bad indentation in the following Practical Applications, you'll gain a better understanding of these indentation guidelines.

Practical Applications

8.3.1 When you set a variable to a value, make all continuation lines start at the same indentation as the value portion of the first line. If you are setting the variable to the result of a complicated expression, it might make more sense to break a line between subexpressions.

Incorrect:

```
strSQL = "SELECT tblAssemblyDetail.*, tblInventory.Description, " & _
"tblInventory.Serials FROM tblInventory RIGHT JOIN " & _
"tblAssemblyDetail ON tblInventory.ItemID = " & _
"tblAssemblyDetail.ItemID WHERE ((tblAssemblyDetail.Assembly) = " & _
"'Package A') ORDER BY tblAssemblyDetail.LineNumber;"
```

Also incorrect:

```
strSQL = "SELECT tblAssemblyDetail.*, tblInventory.Description, " & _
    "tblInventory.Serials FROM tblInventory RIGHT JOIN " & _
    "tblAssemblyDetail ON tblInventory.ItemID = tblAssemblyDetail." & _
    "ItemID WHERE ((tblAssemblyDetail.Assembly) = 'Package A') " & _
    "ORDER BY tblAssemblyDetail.LineNumber;"
```

Correct:

```
strSQL = "SELECT tblAssemblyDetail.*, tblInventory.Description, " & _
         "tblInventory.Serials FROM tblInventory RIGHT JOIN " & _
         "tblAssemblyDetail ON tblInventory.ItemID = " & _
         "tblAssemblyDetail.ItemID WHERE ((tblAssemblyDetail." & _
         "Assembly) = 'Package A') ORDER BY " & _
         "tblAssemblyDetail.LineNumber;"
```

8.3.2 When you split a long procedure heading, indent all continuation lines two tab stops (generally six characters). Alternatively, you can indent all lines after the first line to the start of the first parameter. Either style is acceptable. Choose the one you're most comfortable with and use it consistently.

Incorrect:

```
Public Sub CreateNewNote(lngAccountNumber As Long, _
strDate As String, strStartTime As String, strNote As String, _
lngContactNumber As Long, lngRepNumber As Long)
    On Error GoTo PROC_ERR
```

Also incorrect:

```
Public Sub CreateNewNote(lngAccountNumber As Long, _
    strDate As String, strStartTime As String, strNote As String, _
    lngContactNumber As Long, lngRepNumber As Long)
    On Error GoTo PROC_ERR
```

Correct:
```
Public Sub CreateNewNote(lngAccountNumber As Long, _
    strDate As String, strStartTime As String, strNote As String, _
    lngContactNumber As Long, lngRepNumber As Long)
  On Error GoTo PROC_ERR
```

Alternate:
```
Public Sub CreateNewNote(lngAccountNumber As Long, _
                         strDate As String, strStartTime As String, _
                         strNote As String, lngContactNumber _
                         As Long, lngRepNumber As Long)
  On Error GoTo PROC_ERR
```

8.3.3 **When you call a procedure, indent all continuation lines to the start of the first argument.** The name of the procedure being called will clearly stand out from the arguments being passed to it. When you split a statement that calls a very long procedure name that accepts many arguments, it might be impractical to indent to the first argument. In this case, indent two tab stops.

Incorrect:
```
Call CreateNewNote (rstAccount![AccountNumber], VBA.Date, VBA.Time, _
strNote, lngContactNumber, rstAccount![RepNumber])
```

Also incorrect:
```
Call CreateNewNote (rstAccount![AccountNumber], VBA.Date, VBA.Time, _
    strNote, lngContactNumber, rstAccount![RepNumber])
```

Correct:
```
Call CreateNewNote (rstAccount![AccountNumber], VBA.Date, VBA.Time, _
                    strNote, lngContactNumber, rstAccount![RepNumber])
```

8.3.4 **When you set a variable or property equal to the result of an expression, break the statement just after the equal sign to ensure that as much of the expression as possible remains on one line.** If the statement consists of many expressions, it might be better to break the statement between expressions, as discussed earlier.

Incorrect:
```
grdDetail.Columns(c_grdCanBuild).Text = lngQuantityLocation / _
    Val(grdDetail.Columns(c_grdNeeded).Text)
```

Correct:

```
grdDetail.Columns(c_grdCanBuild).Text = _
    lngQuantityLocation / Val(grdDetail.Columns(c_grdNeeded).Text)
```

8.3.5 When you split a long *If* statement, indent continuation lines two tab stops (six characters). Statements within the *If* construct are indented a single tab stop, so using two tab stops for the continuation lines offers visual clarity. Notice the use of a blank line after the *If* statement to separate the subordinate lines from the actual block of statements within the *If...End If* construct.

Incorrect:

```
If (lngCanBuild < lngMaxCanBuild) Or _
(lngMaxCanBuild < 0) Then

    lngMaxCanBuild = lngCanBuild

End If
```

Also incorrect:

```
If (lngCanBuild < lngMaxCanBuild) Or _
    (lngMaxCanBuild < 0) Then

    lngMaxCanBuild = lngCanBuild

End If
```

Correct:

```
If (lngCanBuild < lngMaxCanBuild) Or _
        (lngMaxCanBuild < 0) Then

    lngMaxCanBuild = lngCanBuild

End If
```

Splitting long statements to fit on multiple lines is an easy way to make your code easier to read and maintain. When a long statement appears on multiple lines, you can see the entire statement without any scrolling. When a statement is left on a single line, like a long freight train whose locomotive and caboose you can't see at the same time, making changes to the line is overly difficult; you can't see the full statement, nor can you see the previous or the next statement.

8.4 Use indentation to show organizational structure.

If you want to make a complicated procedure more difficult to comprehend, don't indent anything. Conversely, to make a complex procedure easier to understand, indent appropriately. Indentation gives the reader a visual representation of the organization of statements that perform unified tasks, much like a flowchart is a visual representation of a series of events. Indentation of code closely mimics the behavior of indentation in an outline or a table of contents because elements are placed into an ordered hierarchy.

While you might reject certain programming standards for reasons such as the number of developers working on a project and the size of the program, correct indentation is always required. Visual Basic makes it easy to indent code using predefined tab stops. These tab stops show the organizational structure of a procedure by visually outlining subordinate statements and the nesting of loops and decision blocks. Although Visual Basic lets you set your tab stops to any number of characters, the accepted standard is three characters. If you use fewer than three characters, visual definition is reduced. Using more than three wastes too much space, especially in complicated code with many nested constructs.

You define the number of characters in a tab stop by using Visual Basic's Options dialog box. Choose Options from the Tools menu, and then specify the number of characters in the Tab Width field, as shown in Figure 8-1.

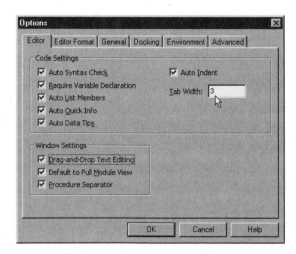

Figure 8-1.   *Use the Options dialog box to set the number of characters in a tab stop.*

Generally, the outer level of code (that is, the leftmost code, which is the highest in the hierarchy) should be indented one tab stop from the left side of the code window. This allows the heading of the procedure and its termination statement (such as *End Sub* or *End Function*) to clearly define the skeleton of the procedure, as shown here:

```
Function NoZeroLengthString(ByVal strText As Variant) As Variant
    '* Purpose  :  Convert a zero-length string to a Null.
    '* Accepts  :  strText - the text that may or may not be a zero-
    '*                       length string.
    '* Returns  :  If strText is a zero-length string, returns Null.
    '*             Otherwise, returns the starting string.
    On Error GoTo PROC_ERR

    '* Check to see whether the received string is a
    '* zero-length string.
    If strText = "" Then
        NoZeroLengthString = Null
    Else
        NoZeroLengthString = strText
    End If

PROC_EXIT:
    Exit Function

PROC_ERR:
    MsgBox "mdlUtilities | NoZeroLengthString" & vbCrLf & _
            Err.Number & vbCrLf & Err.Description
    GoTo PROC_EXIT

End Function
```

Each successive nested construct should be indented a single tab stop beyond the preceding level. An end-of-construct statement such as *End If, Loop,* or *Next* should be at the same indentation level as its beginning-of-construct statement, as shown here:

```
For intCounter = 0 To Forms.Count - 1

    '* Check the name of each form in the Forms collection.
    If Forms(intCounter).Name = strFormName Then
        m_blnIsFormLoaded = True
        GoTo PROC_EXIT
    End If

Next intCounter
```

Below is a list of situations in which you should indent. This list is not all-inclusive, but it catalogs most of the situations in which indentation is necessary. As important as it is to know when and how to indent, it's equally important to understand why you should indent at these locations so that you can make judgment calls in other circumstances. I'll illustrate these reasons in the following Practical Applications. You should indent

- After an *If* statement when an *End If* is used.

- After an *Else* statement.

- After a *Select Case* statement.

- After a *Case* statement.

- After a *Do* statement.

- Successive lines of a statement that has been split with the line continuation character.

- After a *With* statement.

- After calling an *Edit* or *AddNew* method of a Recordset object. The *Update* or *CancelUpdate* method should appear at the same level of indentation as the *Edit* or *AddNew* statement.

- After a *BeginTrans* method call.

Practical Applications

8.4.1 Indent after an *If* statement when an *End If* is used. The body of an *If...End If* block is perhaps the most common place for indentation. Since the body statements are subordinate to the *If* statement itself, they are indented. All end-of-construct statements such as *End If* appear at the same level of indentation as the statement that begins the construct.

Incorrect:

```
If Left$(txtLocation.Text, 4) = "Fax:" Then
MAPIMess.RecipAddress = "FAX:" & txtRecipient.Text & "@" & _
                        strFaxNumber
End If
```

Correct:

```
If Left$(txtLocation.Text, 4) = "Fax:" Then
    MAPIMess.RecipAddress = "FAX:" & txtRecipient.Text & "@" & _
                            strFaxNumber
End If
```

8.4.2 Indent after an *Else* statement. Since the *Else* statement has the same level of importance as the *If* and *End If* statements, it has the same level in the hierarchy and therefore the same level of indentation. The following code shows the statements that are subordinate to the *Else* statement, just as the statements following the *If* statement are subordinate to the *If* statement itself.

Incorrect:

```
If InStr(txtLocation.Text, "@") Then
MAPIMess.RecipAddress = "SMTP:" & txtLocation.Text
Else
MAPIMess.RecipAddress = "MS:" & strServer & "/" & txtLocation.Text
End If
```

Correct:

```
If InStr(txtLocation.Text, "@") Then
    MAPIMess.RecipAddress = "SMTP:" & txtLocation.Text
Else
    MAPIMess.RecipAddress = "MS:" & strServer & "/" & txtLocation.Text
End If
```

8.4.3 Indent after a *Select Case* statement. A *Select Case* construct has a beginning-of-construct statement and an end-of-construct statement. When two statements are used to begin and end a construct, the code block between the two statements should be indented.

Incorrect:

```
Select Case objTool.Name
Case Is = "Save"
Case Is = "Exit"
End Select
```

Correct:

```
Select Case objTool.Name
    Case Is = "Save"
    Case Is = "Exit"
End Select
```

8.4.4 Indent after a *Case* statement. It's not enough to indent the *Case* statements themselves in a *Select Case* construct. While the *Case* statements are subordinate to the *Select Case* statement, the block of statements that form the body of a *Case* statement are subordinate to the *Case* statement itself, and therefore should be indented.

Incorrect:

```
Select Case objTool.Name
   Case Is = "Save"
   Call SaveDocument
   Case Is = "Exit"
   Unload Me
End Select
```

Correct:

```
Select Case objTool.Name
   Case Is = "Save"
      Call SaveDocument

   Case Is = "Exit"
      Unload Me
End Select
```

8.4.5 Indent after a *Do* statement. The *Do...Loop* structure has both a beginning-of-construct and an end-of-construct statement, so its body of statements must be indented. Correctly indenting the body of statements within a loop construct clearly shows the reader the flow of execution produced by the loop.

Incorrect:

```
Do While Not rstSales.EOF
lstCategories.AddItem rstSales![Category]
rstSales.MoveNext
Loop
```

Correct:

```
Do While Not rstSales.EOF
   lstCategories.AddItem rstSales![Category]
   rstSales.MoveNext
Loop
```

8.4.6 Indent successive lines of a statement that has been split with the line continuation character. No single rule applies to the indentation of continuation lines. The amount of indentation is determined by the statement itself, as I described earlier in this chapter.

Incorrect:

```
strSQL = "SELECT tblAssemblyDetail.*, tblInventory.Description, " & _
"tblInventory.Serials FROM tblInventory RIGHT JOIN " & _
"tblAssemblyDetail ON tblInventory.ItemID = " & _
"tblAssemblyDetail.ItemID WHERE ((tblAssemblyDetail.Assembly) = " & _
"'Package A') ORDER BY tblAssemblyDetail.LineNumber;"
```

Also incorrect:

```
strSQL = "SELECT tblAssemblyDetail.*, tblInventory.Description, " & _
   "tblInventory.Serials FROM tblInventory RIGHT JOIN " & _
   "tblAssemblyDetail ON tblInventory.ItemID = tblAssemblyDetail." & _
   "ItemID WHERE ((tblAssemblyDetail.Assembly) = 'Package A') " & _
   "ORDER BY tblAssemblyDetail.LineNumber;"
```

Correct:

```
strSQL = "SELECT tblAssemblyDetail.*, tblInventory.Description, " & _
         "tblInventory.Serials FROM tblInventory RIGHT JOIN " & _
         "tblAssemblyDetail ON tblInventory.ItemID = " & _
         "tblAssemblyDetail.ItemID WHERE ((tblAssemblyDetail." & _
         "Assembly) = 'Package A') ORDER BY " &_
         "tblAssemblyDetail.LineNumber;"
```

8.4.7 Indent after a *With* statement. *With* statements reduce the amount of code necessary to access multiple members of an object. Using *With* blocks to access many members of an object improves readability and can increase the speed of the application. All statements between *With* and *End With* are indented a single tab stop from the level of indentation of the beginning *With* statement.

Incorrect:

```
With lstSortOrder
.Clear
.AddItem "Ascending"
.AddItem "Descending"
End With
```

Correct:

```
With lstSortOrder
   .Clear
   .AddItem "Ascending"
   .AddItem "Descending"
End With
```

8.4.8 Indent after calling an *Edit* or *AddNew* method of a Recordset. The *Update* or *CancelUpdate* method should appear at the same level of indentation as the *Edit* statement. It isn't always apparent, but calls to the *AddNew* and *Edit* methods of a Recordset act as beginning-of-construct statements because they must be followed with an *Update* or *Cancel-Update* method call. Calls to the *Update* and *CancelUpdate* methods act as end-of-construct statements and appear at the same level of indentation as the *AddNew* and *Edit* method calls. All code in between is indented a single tab stop.

Incorrect:
```
rstAccounts.Edit
rstAccounts![Name] = strName
rstAccounts![Address] = strAddress
rstAccounts.Update
```

Correct:
```
rstAccounts.Edit
    rstAccounts![Name] = strName
    rstAccounts![Address] = strAddress
rstAccounts.Update
```

8.4.9 Indent after a *BeginTrans* method call. A call to the *BeginTrans* method (beginning-of-construct) is always followed by a call to the *CommitTrans* method or the *RollBack* method (end-of-construct). The call to *BeginTrans* should have the same level of indentation as the call to the *CommitTrans* or *RollBack* method, with everything in between indented one tab stop.

Incorrect:
```
Workspaces(0).BeginTrans
Do While Not rstAccounts.EOF
    intCounter = intCounter + 1
    rstAccounts.Edit
        rstAccounts![RepNumber] = lngToRepNumber
    rstAccounts.Update
    rstAccounts.MoveNext
Loop
Workspaces(0).CommitTrans
```

Correct:

```
Workspaces(0).BeginTrans

    '* Update each record in the Recordset.
    Do While Not rstAccounts.EOF
        intCounter = intCounter + 1

        rstAccounts.Edit
            rstAccounts![RepNumber] = lngToRepNumber
        rstAccounts.Update

        rstAccounts.MoveNext
    Loop

Workspaces(0).CommitTrans
```

8.4.10   Indent code that is subordinate to a line label. Chapter 11, "Controlling Code Flow," discusses keeping *GoTo* statements to a minimum, but if you add error trapping and single exit points to all of your procedures, as you should, you'll always have at least two code labels in every procedure. Visual Basic doesn't allow you to indent labels, and this works to your advantage. If you indent all of your highest-level code one tab stop from the left side of the code window, the labels within the procedure will stand out because they will be flush left with the code window, as shown in the code below. Treat code under each label as top-level code by indenting a single tab stop, and indent subordinate statements according to the other Practical Applications in this section.

```
Function NoZeroLengthString(ByVal strText As Variant) As Variant
    '* Purpose  :  Convert a zero-length string to a Null.
    '* Accepts  :  strText - the text that may or may not be a zero-
    '*                       length string.
    '* Returns  :  If strText is a zero-length string, returns Null.
    '*             Otherwise, returns the starting string.
    On Error GoTo PROC_ERR

    '* Check to see whether the received string is a
    '* zero-length string.
    If strText = "" Then
        NoZeroLengthString = Null
    Else
        NoZeroLengthString = strText
    End If
```

(continued)

```
PROC_EXIT:
    Exit Function

PROC_ERR:
    MsgBox "mdlUtilities | NoZeroLengthString" & vbCrLf & _
           Err.Number & vbCrLf & Err.Description
    GoTo PROC_EXIT

End Function
```

 N OTE The indentation of code comments has its own set of directives and is discussed in Chapter 9.

8.5 Indent code within the Declarations section of a module to show subordination.

Code written in the Declarations section of a module is treated differently from procedure code. Code within a Declarations section is considered to be at the same level in the hierarchy as procedure definitions. Consequently, such code is not indented one tab stop from the left side of the code window; it is flush left. However, the indenting of code to show subordination is still applicable. The most notable circumstances are the declarations of enumerations and user-defined data types. The statements that make up the body of these declarations should be indented a single tab stop from the beginning and ending statements, as shown in the following Practical Applications.

Practical Applications

8.5.1 Indent the bodies of all user-defined data type declarations. User-defined data type declarations are similar in structure to procedures. They appear in the Declarations section of a module, so they do not have any initial indentation. However, just as the body of a procedure is indented a single tab stop, so is the body of a user-defined data type declaration.

Incorrect:
```
Private Type RECT
Left As Long
Top As Long
```

```
  Right As Long
  Bottom As Long
End Type
```

Correct:

```
Private Type RECT
   Left As Long
   Top As Long
   Right As Long
   Bottom As Long
End Type
```

8.5.2 **Indent the bodies of all enumeration declarations.** Enumeration declarations are similar to user-defined data type declarations and are formatted in the same way. Since enumeration declarations appear in the Declarations section of a module, they do not have initial indentation. However, the body of an enumeration declaration is indented a single tab stop.

Incorrect:

```
Option Explicit

Public Enum tpsAVI
tpsFileCopy = 0
tpsFileDelete = 1
tpsFileDeleteToRecycle = 2
tpsFileMove = 3
End Enum
```

Correct:

```
Option Explicit

Public Enum tpsAVI
   tpsFileCopy = 0
   tpsFileDelete = 1
   tpsFileDeleteToRecycle = 2
   tpsFileMove = 3
End Enum
```

8.6 Use white space to group related statements.

White space is not evil. In earlier days of programming, you had to make your code physically as small as possible. This generally meant eliminating all but the absolutely necessary white space. Those days are gone, and strategically placed blank lines make code much easier to follow and should be used appropriately.

Constructing procedures is not unlike writing a document. When you write a document, you group related sentences into paragraphs. If a sentence doesn't make sense within a paragraph, it's moved to a different paragraph or placed in a bulleted or numbered list. Code within a procedure is similar in that related statements generally appear in groups. Frequently, a code statement stands somewhat autonomously between two groups or other autonomous statements. Using blank lines to separate groups of related statements and autonomous statements makes the code easier to read and to analyze.

Many programmers use blank lines sporadically, placing them in somewhat random locations. Blank lines should clearly exhibit their purpose by appearing in logical locations.

In general, you should insert a blank line

- Before and after each *If…Then* construct (specifically, before the comment in front of the *If* statement)

- Before and after each *Select Case* construct

- Before and after each loop

- After declaring a block of variables

- Between groups of statements that perform unified tasks

You should insert two blank lines between procedures.

I'll discuss each of these situations in detail in the following Practical Applications.

Practical Applications

8.6.1   Insert a blank line before and after each *If…Then* construct (specifically, before the comment in front of the *If* statement).   The *If…Then* construct signifies that a decision is being made that affects the flow of execution. This decision is very much an independent thought even though it might be related to the processes surrounding it. When you debug code, you often scan the code for *If* statements to determine where the flow of execution changed unexpectedly. If you don't use blank lines before an *If* statement, it's not as apparent to the reader that a decision is being made.

Incorrect:

```
Private Sub cmdReplaceDoubleQuotes_Click()
   Dim intLocation As Integer
   '* If the user hasn't entered any text, get out.
   If Len(Text1.Text) = 0 Then GoTo PROC_EXIT
   '* Determine whether a double-quote (") appears in the string.
   intLocation = InStr(1, Text1.Text, Chr$(34))
   '* If intLocation > 0 there is a double-quote. Replace with
   '* two single quotes.
   If intLocation > 0 Then
      Text1.Text = Left$(Text1.Text, intLocation - 1) & "'" & _
                   Mid$(Text1.Text, intLocation + 1)
   End If
PROC_EXIT:
   Exit Sub
End Sub
```

Correct:

```
Private Sub cmdReplaceDoubleQuotes_Click()

   Dim intLocation As Integer
   Const c_DoubleQuote = """"

   '* If the user hasn't entered any text, get out.
   If Len(Text1.Text) = 0 Then GoTo PROC_EXIT

   '* Determine whether a double-quote (") appears in the string.
   intLocation = InStr(1, Text1.Text, c_DoubleQuote)

   '* If intLocation > 0 there is a double-quote. Replace with
   '* two single quotes.
   If intLocation > 0 Then
      Text1.Text = Left$(Text1.Text, intLocation - 1) & "'" & _
                   Mid$(Text1.Text, intLocation + 1)
   End If

PROC_EXIT:
   Exit Sub

End Sub
```

8.6.2   Insert a blank line before and after each *Select Case* construct. Like the *If* statement discussed above, *Select Case* statements adjust the flow of execution. Blank lines help isolate the decision and make the code more readable. To further increase clarity, place a blank line before every *Case* statement except the first one.

Incorrect:

```
Private Sub cmd_Click(Index As Integer)
    Const c_cmdOK = 0
    Const c_cmdCancel = 1
    '* Determine which button was clicked.
    Select Case Index
        Case Is = c_cmdOK
            Call SaveDocument
            Unload Me
        Case Is = c_cmdCancel
            Unload Me
    End Select
PROC_EXIT:
    Exit Sub
End Sub
```

Correct:

```
Private Sub cmd_Click(Index As Integer)

    Const c_cmdOK = 0
    Const c_cmdCancel = 1

    '* Determine which button was clicked.
    Select Case Index
        Case Is = c_cmdOK
            Call SaveDocument
            Unload Me

        Case Is = c_cmdCancel
            Unload Me
    End Select

PROC_EXIT:
    Exit Sub

End Sub
```

8.6.3 **Insert a blank line before and after each loop.** Loops can be difficult to understand. When you debug a procedure that has one or more loops, it's imperative that the loops be easy to spot in code. Placing a blank line in front of and after each looping construct clearly distinguishes the loop from surrounding code.

Incorrect:

```
Private Sub FillSecurityGroupList()
    Dim rstSecurity As Recordset
    Dim strSQL As String
    lstSecurityGroup.Clear
    Set rstSecurity = dbContacts.OpenRecordset("tblSecurityGroups", _
                    dbOpenForwardOnly)
    '* Add all the security groups in the Recordset to the list.
    Do While Not rstSecurity.EOF
        lstSecurityGroup.AddItem rstSecurity![SecurityGroup]
        rstSecurity.MoveNext
    Loop
PROC_EXIT:
    Exit Sub
End Sub
```

Correct:

```
Private Sub FillSecurityGroupList()

    Dim rstSecurity As Recordset
    Dim strSQL As String

    lstSecurityGroup.Clear

    Set rstSecurity = dbContacts.OpenRecordset("tblSecurityGroups", _
                    dbOpenForwardOnly)

    '* Add all the security groups in the Recordset to the list.
    Do While Not rstSecurity.EOF
        lstSecurityGroup.AddItem rstSecurity![SecurityGroup]
        rstSecurity.MoveNext
    Loop

PROC_EXIT:
    Exit Sub

End Sub
```

8.6.4 Insert a blank line after declaring a block of variables. If many variables are declared in a procedure or a module, consider using a blank line to separate each group of variables that are declared as the same data type.

Incorrect:

```
Private Sub SampleProcedure()
    Dim strLabelFile As String
    Dim strSQL As String
    Dim strOutput As String
    Dim strHeader As String
    Dim intFieldIndex As Integer
    Dim intFileNumber As Integer
    Dim lngAccountsDumped As Long
    Dim rstRepInfo As Recordset
    Dim rstReps As Recordset
    Dim rstContacts As Recordset
    Dim rstAccounts As Recordset
PROC_EXIT:
    Exit Sub
End Sub
```

Correct:

```
Private Sub SampleProcedure()

    Dim strLabelFile As String
    Dim strSQL As String
    Dim strOutput As String
    Dim strHeader As String
    Dim intFieldIndex As Integer
    Dim intFileNumber As Integer
    Dim lngAccountsDumped As Long
    Dim rstRepInfo As Recordset
    Dim rstReps As Recordset
    Dim rstContacts As Recordset
    Dim rstAccounts As Recordset

PROC_EXIT:
    Exit Sub
End Sub
```

Also correct:

```
Private Sub SampleProcedure()

    Dim strLabelFile As String
    Dim strSQL As String
```

```
      Dim strOutput As String
      Dim strHeader As String

      Dim intFieldIndex As Integer
      Dim intFileNumber As Integer

      Dim lngAccountsDumped As Long

      Dim rstRepInfo  As Recordset
      Dim rstReps     As Recordset
      Dim rstContacts As Recordset
      Dim rstAccounts As Recordset

PROC_EXIT:
   Exit Sub
End Sub
```

8.6.5   Insert a blank line between groups of statements that perform unified tasks. Good code should consist of logically sequenced processes or groups of related statements. These sections should be immediately visible to the reader.

Incorrect:

```
Public Function DeleteToRecycleBin(ByVal strFileName As String) _
      As Boolean
   '* Purpose  :  Delete a file, and send it to the Recycle Bin.
   On Error GoTo PROC_ERR
   Dim FileOperation As SHFILEOPSTRUCT
   Dim lngResult As Long
   '* Set up the parameters for deleting the file.
   With FileOperation
      .wFunc = FO_DELETE
      .pFrom = strFileName
      .fFlags = FOF_ALLOWUNDO + FOF_CREATEPROGRESSDLG
   End With
   '* Delete the file.
   lngResult = SHFileOperation(FileOperation)
   '* Return True if successful; otherwise return False.
   If lngResult <> 0 Then
      DeleteToRecycleBin = False
   Else
      DeleteToRecycleBin = True
   End If
PROC_EXIT:
   Exit Function
```

(continued)

175

```
PROC_ERR:
    MsgBox "Error: " & Err.Number & vbCrLf & Err.Description
    GoTo PROC_EXIT
End Function
```

Correct:

```
Public Function DeleteToRecycleBin(ByVal strFileName As String) _
    As Boolean
    '* Purpose  :  Delete a file, and send it to the Recycle Bin.
    On Error GoTo PROC_ERR
    Dim FileOperation As SHFILEOPSTRUCT
    Dim lngResult As Long

    '* Set up the parameters for deleting the file.
    With FileOperation
        .wFunc = FO_DELETE
        .pFrom = strFileName
        .fFlags = FOF_ALLOWUNDO + FOF_CREATEPROGRESSDLG
    End With

    '* Delete the file.
    lngResult = SHFileOperation(FileOperation)

    '* Return True if successful; otherwise return False.
    If lngResult <> 0 Then
        DeleteToRecycleBin = False
    Else
        DeleteToRecycleBin = True
    End If

PROC_EXIT:
    Exit Function

PROC_ERR:
    MsgBox "Error: " & Err.Number & vbCrLf & Err.Description
    GoTo PROC_EXIT

End Function
```

8.6.6   Insert two blank lines between procedures. If you still have Visual Basic configured to display only a single procedure at a time in the code window, you should consider changing your settings so that you can view multiple procedures in the code window. (See Figure 8-2.) This will increase your productivity. To enable this feature, choose Options from the Tools menu and select Default To Full Module View.

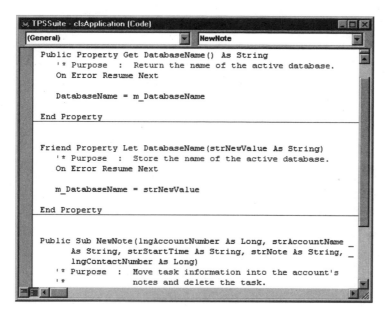

```
TPSSuite - clsApplication (Code)                          _ □ ×
(General)                    ▼   NewNote                        ▼

Public Property Get DatabaseName() As String              ▲
    '* Purpose  :  Return the name of the active database.
    On Error Resume Next

    DatabaseName = m_DatabaseName

End Property


Friend Property Let DatabaseName(strNewValue As String)
    '* Purpose  :  Store the name of the active database.
    On Error Resume Next

    m_DatabaseName = strNewValue

End Property


Public Sub NewNote(lngAccountNumber As Long, strAccountName _
        As String, strStartTime As String, strNote As String, _
        lngContactNumber As Long)
    '* Purpose  :  Move task information into the account's
    '*               notes and delete the task.               ▼
```

Figure 8-2. *Viewing multiple procedures in the code window makes it easier to work with
longer modules.*

Blank lines are sometimes considered a minor detail because their appearance does not directly affect the behavior of compiled code. When
Visual Basic compiles a project, all unnecessary white space is stripped
by the compiler, so Visual Basic couldn't care less whether you use white
space in your procedures. But white space isn't for Visual Basic's benefit—it's for your benefit and for the benefit of those who have to review
and maintain your code.

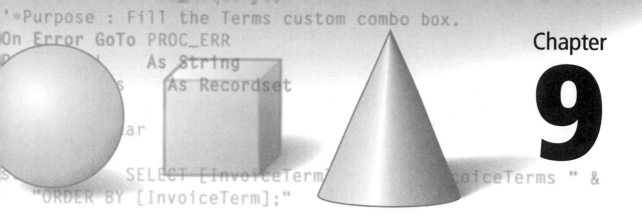

```
'*Purpose : Fill the Terms custom combo box.
On Error GoTo PROC_ERR
                As String
            As Recordset

                SELECT [InvoiceTerm]           oiceTerms " &
  "ORDER BY [InvoiceTerm];"

Set rstTerms = db.OpenRecordset(strSQL, dbOpenForwardOnly)

Do WHile Not rstTerms.EOF
    boTerms.AddItem rstTerms![InvoiceTerm]

Loop

C_EXIT:
rstTerms.C
Set rstTerm
```

Commenting Code

Have you ever purchased an item requiring some assembly, such as a bicycle, only to find that the instruction manual was missing from the box? It's bad enough trying to assemble an item when you actually have the often less-than-adequate instructions. (*Why does slot A in the picture look like it's on Part C, not Part D? Is this drawing to scale? That scribbling could be one of three different bolts. Argh!*) Trying to follow a procedure written without comments can be as difficult as putting together a bicycle without instructions. Trying to understand complicated or lengthy code without comments can be like trying to put together a bicycle blindfolded!

If you've ever had to revisit your own uncommented code after a year or so, you've almost assuredly started commenting your code since then. There are simply no good reasons for not commenting your code. Comments make code easier to understand and easier to follow. Good comments guide the reader through the twists and turns of your application like a good blueprint, explaining the expected results and possible exceptions to the desired outcome. If you give your variables and procedures good, descriptive names (as detailed in Chapter 6, "Variables"), much of your code becomes self-documenting. However, you still need comments. For the most part, it's hard to have too many comments, but it is possible to have ineffective comments. You must understand and apply all the different types of comments correctly to ensure that your code can be understood by other developers—or by you when you revisit the code.

A common excuse programmers give for not writing comments is that they take too much time to write. In reality, it doesn't take much time at all to comment as you write code. Some developers say that some of their procedures are difficult to comment. A good rule of thumb is that if a section of code is hard to comment, it's even harder for someone else to understand without comments. Tricky, hard-to-comment code is probably bad code. If you find yourself having a difficult time documenting all or part of a procedure, step back and take a good look at the code; you'll probably find a better approach.

Creating the right mix of different types of comments can be challenging because each procedure poses a unique set of considerations. But by following the guidelines in this chapter, you'll be able to improve your commenting noticeably.

> **Goals of Using Code Comments**
>
> Your goals when using code comments should include
>
> - Documenting the purpose of the code (the *why*, not the *how*)
> - Clearly indicating the thinking and logic behind the code
> - Calling attention to important turning points in the code
> - Reducing the need for readers to run a simulation of code execution in their heads

Directives

9.1 Document the purpose of the code.

It's not enough just to add comments to a procedure; you need to write good comments. Comments that simply reiterate what the code does add almost nothing to the code. In fact, if you're using good naming techniques to create self-documenting code, these types of comments add absolutely nothing. For instance, look at the comment in the following procedure. It simply reiterates the code itself; the variable names are even used within the comment. This comment documents the mechanics of the code rather than the purpose of the code or the reasoning behind it.

```
Private Sub cmdStartSale_Click()

    Dim intAge As Integer
    Const c_LegalAge = 21

    intAge = txtAge.Text

    '* If intAge >= c_legalAge then process the sale.
    If intAge >= c_LegalAge Then
        Call ProcessSale
    End If

End Sub
```

When you find yourself writing a comment that includes the literal name of a variable, stop and rethink the comment. Unless you're documenting the variable itself or reminding the reader of the purpose of an obscure variable, you should refrain from using variable names directly within a comment. When a variable name is used in a comment, the comment probably reiterates the code. Instead, you should document the purpose of the code or the reasoning behind it. The following procedure is identical to the previous one, but in this case the comment correctly annotates the code:

```
Private Sub cmdStartSale_Click()

    Dim intAge As Integer
    Const c_LegalAge = 21

    intAge = txtAge.Text

    '* If the buyer is of legal age to purchase alcohol,
    '* process the sale.
    If intAge >= c_LegalAge Then
        Call ProcessSale
    End If

End Sub
```

OTE Comments should describe the purpose of a section of code, not the mechanics of how it accomplishes that purpose—the *why* rather than the *how*.

9.2 If you need to violate good programming style, explain why.

At times it might be necessary to violate good coding principles. When you encounter such a situation, document what you are doing and why, using an inline comment. For instance, say you are unable to write your own sort routine or are under severe time constraints (laziness doesn't count), so you use a hidden list box control to sort a set of values. You place the list box on a form and set its *Sorted* property to True and its *Visible* property to False. You then populate the list box with all the elements to sort using the list box's *AddItem* method. Finally, you retrieve the newly sorted values from the list by using a loop to reference the list box's *List* property. This is clearly a hack, but it works. In cases such as this, it is imperative that you document what you are doing and why. The following code shows how you might document such a process.

```
'* Add the names in the name array to the lstSort
'* list box. It has its Sorted property set to True,
'* so looping through the list items will return
'* the values in the array in sorted order.
For intIndex = 1 To UBound(a_strNames)
    lstSort.AddItem a_strNames(intIndex)
Next intIndex
```

9.3 Document when an error is expected and why.

Due to the nature of Microsoft Visual Basic, some errors are unavoidable and others are absolutely necessary. For instance, you might decide that rather than attempting to see whether a record exists in a database before trying to save a new record (to avoid creating duplicates) it would be quicker to attempt to save the record and trap the error if the record is a duplicate. The following code shows this situation. When you expect an error in code and you deliberately trap for it, fully document why you're trapping the error and what error you expect. If more than one error might occur, document the others as well. (See Chapter 7, "Error Handling," for more information on trapping errors.)

```
'* Trap the error in case the user is attempting to save a
'* duplicate record.
On Error Resume Next
Err.Clear
dbSales.Execute strSQL, dbFailOnError

Const c_DuplicateRecord = 3022

'* If an error occurred, determine whether it was because of
'* trying to save a duplicate record.
If Err.Number <> 0 Then

    '* See whether the error was expected.
    If Err.Number = c_DuplicateRecord Then
        '* The user attempted to save a duplicate record.
        '* Tell the user and get out.
        MsgBox "The item '" & txtItem.Text & "' already exists " & _
                "in the database.", vbInformation
        GoTo PROC_EXIT
    Else
        '* This is an unexpected error; notify the user.
        Call ShowError(Me.Name, "ChangeCode", Err.Number, _
                    Err.Description)
        GoTo PROC_EXIT
    End If

End If

'* Turn regular error trapping back on.
On Error GoTo PROC_ERR
```

Sometimes, a statement might cause an error that is always benign. This can happen with Visual Basic's venerable *SetFocus* method. This method, which places the cursor into a specific control, has many applications. For example, you can use *SetFocus* when the user switches among tabs in a dialog box to ensure that when a new tab is displayed the first control on the tab has the focus. You can also use *SetFocus* when you validate data to put the cursor in a text box with invalid data so that the user can quickly correct the problem. While *SetFocus* is used liberally in most applications, many developers fail to precede each call with *On Error Resume Next*. You should do this because if a form or a parent control hasn't fully painted itself, *SetFocus* might fail with an Error 5. This error doesn't hurt anything, and in most cases it's perfectly acceptable to ignore the error. Since this particular situation happens frequently, it's probably not advisable to document each occurrence, but when you do want to document it you can use a comment such as the one shown here:

```
'* Ignore any errors that occur because the form is not ready for the
'* control to receive the focus.
On Error Resume Next
txtName.SetFocus

'* Turn regular error trapping back on.
On Error GoTo PROC_ERR
```

9.4   Comment before writing code.

One approach to commenting code is to start a procedure by writing the comments first. You can write full sentence comments or pseudocode if you prefer. Once you outline the code with comments, you can write code between the comments. As you write the procedure, you might have to adjust your comments. After you write the procedure, convert all pseudocode comments to standard sentences. The following is a shell of a procedure that consists of comments only:

```
Public Sub FloodFill(X As Single, Y As Single)
    '* Purpose  :  Fill an area on the bitmap with a color.
    '* Accepts  :  X and Y - coordinates on the bitmap where
    '*               the fill should begin.

    '* Set the FillStyle of the picture box to solid and the
    '* FillColor to the current drawing color.

    '* Get the boundary color for the fill. This is the current color
    '* at the specified coordinates.

    '* Use the ExtFloodFill API call to perform a fast flood fill,
    '* changing all adjacent pixels that have the boundary color
    '* to the current drawing color.

End Sub
```

The initial comments are like an outline. After you write them, you can fill in the outline with the necessary code. The following is the finished procedure with code inserted between the comments. The comments do not simply repeat the code; they explain what is occurring. In this example, the comments did not need to be changed or moved, but that won't always be the case.

```
Public Sub FloodFill(X As Single, Y As Single)
    '* Purpose  :  Fill an area on the bitmap with a color.
    '* Accepts  :  X and Y - coordinates on the bitmap where
    '*               the fill should begin.

    On Error GoTo PROC_ERR
    Dim lngResult As Long
    Dim lngBoundaryColor As Long

    '* Set the FillStyle of the picture box to solid and
    '* the FillColor to the current drawing color.
    picPreview.FillStyle = vbFSSolid
    picPreview.FillColor = m_lngDrawColor

    '* Get the boundary color for the fill. This is the current color
    '* at the specified coordinates.
    lngBoundaryColor = picPreview.POINT(X, Y)

    '* Use the ExtFloodFill API call to perform a fast flood fill,
    '* changing all adjacent pixels that have the boundary color
    '* to the current drawing color.
    lngResult = ExtFloodFill(picPreview.hdc, X, Y, _
                             m_lngBoundaryColor, FLOODFILLSURFACE)

PROC_EXIT:
    Exit Sub

PROC_ERR:
    MsgBox "Error: " & Err.Number & vbCrLf & Err.Description
    Resume Next

End Sub
```

9.5 Use solid-character comment lines only for major comments.

Some developers adopt formatting styles for comments that, while attractive, hinder the development process. It can be tempting to go overboard with comment formatting. A common example of such overzealousness is the use of formatting characters to create a line before or after comments. I call these comment lines *solid-character comment lines*. For instance, the asterisk (*)—one of the most common formatting characters and my personal favorite—is often overused in this way. Consider the comments in the following code fragment:

```
'*********************************************************
'* Retrieve the lengths of the legs of the rectangle.
'*********************************************************
sngXLeg = Abs(rectBound.Right - rectBound.Left)
sngYLeg = Abs(rectBound.Bottom - rectBound.Top)


'*********************************************************
'* Make sure the rectangle is a valid rectangle.
'*********************************************************
If (sngXLeg = 0) Or (sngYLeg = 0) Then
    '*********************************************************
    '* This is not a valid rectangle, so get out.
    '*********************************************************
    GoTo PROC_EXIT
End If


'*********************************************************
'* Populate the circle structure with the data that defines
'* the circle.
'*********************************************************
With udtCircle
    .Aspect = Abs(sngYLeg / sngXLeg)
    .xCenter = rectBound.Left + (rectBound.Right - rectBound.Left) / 2
    .yCenter = rectBound.Top + (rectBound.Bottom - rectBound.Top) / 2

    '*********************************************************
    '* Determine the radius using the longer leg of the rectangle.
    '*********************************************************
    If sngXLeg > sngYLeg Then
        .Radius = sngXLeg / 2
    Else
        .Radius = sngYLeg / 2
    End If

End With
```

Wow—all of those asterisks can give you a headache. If you leave your Visual Basic settings at their defaults, you'll see green all over the code window.

The color coding of comments is one of my favorite Visual Basic features. It seems so simple as to be almost silly, but if you've ever coded complex applications in Microsoft Access 2.0, which doesn't include a color-coded editor, you know where I'm coming from. I'd sooner quit developing than give up the color-coded editor. When scanning a procedure, it's great to be able to distinguish the comments in green text. But unnecessary comment lines decrease the ratio of usable green text to total green text.

In his book *The Visual Display of Quantitative Information* (Graphics Press, 1992), Edward Tufte discusses what he calls *data ink,* "the nonerasable core of a graphic." Nondata ink includes such elements as elaborate grid lines and detailed labels. Tufte discusses the necessity of a high data ink to total ink ratio. You can think of comments in much the same way.

Sometimes it makes sense to call attention to a comment by using solid-character comment lines, but in such cases they should be reserved for major comments, never minor comments. The solid-character comment lines in the following code are still overkill, but at least they make more sense by calling attention to the major elements of the procedure.

```
'****************************************************************
'* Retrieve the lengths of the legs of the rectangle.
'****************************************************************
sngXLeg = Abs(rectBound.Right - rectBound.Left)
sngYLeg = Abs(rectBound.Bottom - rectBound.Top)


'****************************************************************
'* Make sure the rectangle is a valid rectangle.
'****************************************************************
If (sngXLeg = 0) Or (sngYLeg = 0) Then
    '* This is not a valid rectangle, so get out.
    GoTo PROC_EXIT
End If


'****************************************************************
'* Populate the circle structure with the data that defines
'* the circle.
'****************************************************************
With udtCircle
    .Aspect = Abs(sngYLeg / sngXLeg)
    .xCenter = rectBound.Left + (rectBound.Right - rectBound.Left) / 2
    .yCenter = rectBound.Top + (rectBound.Bottom - rectBound.Top) / 2
```

(continued)

```
'* Determine the radius using the longer leg of the rectangle.
If sngXLeg > sngYLeg Then
    .Radius = sngXLeg / 2
Else
    .Radius = sngYLeg / 2
End If
```

```
End With
```

Solid-character comment lines pose additional problems. How many characters should the solid-character comment line contain? There's no doubt that they look better when they all contain the same number of characters, but what about when they're used before or after a short comment line? Or, more important, what about when they surround a longer comment, as they do in the previous example? Trying to maintain a consistent and attractive appearance with these solid-character comment lines quickly becomes tedious. Also, if you manually type each line, you're wasting time. The only alternatives to typing each line individually are to copy and paste the lines—also tedious—or to use some sort of code-formatting add-in.

9.6 Avoid creating comment boxes.

Far worse than solid-character comment lines are formatting characters on the right side of comments that create comment blocks or boxes. You've probably seen such comments, and you might have written a few. If you've ever maintained code that has these sorts of comments, chances are you've given up on them—and for good reason. Take a look at this comment:

```
'*****************************************************************
'* If the user clicks the left button, get the color at the    *
'* current coordinates and assign it as the ForeColor. If       *
'* the right button has been clicked, get the color under       *
'* the pointer and assign it as the BackColor.                  *
'*****************************************************************
```

Sure, the asterisks on the right look nice, but do they add anything to the comment? Actually, yes—more work for the person writing or editing the comments. Notice the white space after the last word on the second line.

As I was writing this comment, I typed the next word *the,* only to discover that it would run into the last asterisk. I was then faced with a decision and had to consider the following options:

- Adding an additional asterisk to the first line (the header) and another space in front of the last asterisk on the second line to realign it with the header.

- Backspacing over the word *the,* adding the necessary spaces and asterisk, and then resuming on the next line.

- Moving the cursor in front of the word *the,* adding the necessary spaces and asterisk, and then pressing Enter to move *the* to the next line.

After I decided to put the word *the* on the next line and resume typing, I encountered the exact same problem—oddly enough, with the exact same word. Isn't this fun? I added tedium to what many already call a tedious process. If writing comments was always this much work, I can see why some would choose to skip it altogether. Although the use of formatted lines in front of or after a comment can be justified to call attention to major events in code, the use of end-line formatting characters to create comment blocks is never justified. It does nothing but add extra work.

9.7   Use an apostrophe to denote comments.

In the old days of Basic, you denoted a comment by starting a line with the word *REM* (for Remark). Visual Basic still supports the use of *REM,* but you shouldn't use it. Using *REM* clutters the comment, creates wasted green space, necessitates more typing, can confuse add-in code formatters, and in general just looks bad. Instead of *REM,* use the apostrophe (')—and, perhaps, as I do, an asterisk (*)—to denote a comment:

```
'* If this is a new account, set up the necessary
'* default information. If the account exists, place
'* the record in edit mode.
If blnAddNew Then
    :
End If
```

Practical Application

9.7.1 Use special characters to identify a comment's author or indicate its temporary status. In a multiple-developer environment, it's often desirable to know which developer wrote a specific comment. While you could store revision information in the procedure comment header, this is a cumbersome process and doesn't help when different developers work on different pieces of the same procedure.

A great solution to the problem of identifying a comment author is to assign a unique formatting character to each developer and to have the developer follow each remark character (') with his or her assigned formatting character. Once you get into the habit of doing this, it becomes second nature. This approach is useful only in departments with a small number of programmers. When you use a scheme like this, you should create a key of the users and their formatting characters in a global module. It might be a good idea to keep the authors' contact information there as well.

Correct:
```
'* Purpose  :  Create tab stops in a list box.
'* Accepts  :  lstControl - the list box in which to set the tab stops
'*             lngTabs - the number of tab stops to set
'*             strStops - a string containing the character
'*             positions of the tab stops
On Error GoTo PROC_ERR
```

Also correct:
```
'$ Purpose  :  Create tab stops in a list box.
'$ Accepts  :  lstControl - the list box in which to set the tab stops
'$             lngTabs - the number of tab stops to set
'$             strStops - a string containing the character
'$             positions of the tab stops
On Error GoTo PROC_ERR
```

You should also use a special character for temporary comments or notes. Temporary comments can be useful when you comment out a section of code while debugging or when you need to write more code later. In such cases, you should use a formatting character or a word to mark the comment as temporary. Use the comment designator consistently to make it easy to search a project for temporary comments. The character or word that you use is entirely up to you, but be sure that everyone working with the code uses the same format.

Correct:

```
'# SECURITY STILL NEEDS TO BE IMPLEMENTED!

strSQL = "DELETE * FROM tblContacts;"
dbContacts.Execute strSQL, dbFailOnError
```

Also correct:

```
'NOTE: SECURITY STILL NEEDS TO BE IMPLEMENTED!

strSQL = "DELETE * FROM tblContacts;"
dbContacts.Execute strSQL, dbFailOnError
```

 OTE When you use formatting characters to denote something about a comment, document exactly what your standards are and share them with all developers.

9.8   Make your comments readable.

Comments are meant to be read by humans, not computers. Strive to make your comments intelligible. Keep in mind that a comment that is hard to understand is not much better than no comment at all. Also, as I've said throughout this chapter, comments are documentation. Just as documentation for an application must be clearly written, code comments should also follow good writing guidelines.

Practical Applications

9.8.1   Use complete sentences. While it's not necessary (and probably not advisable) to write paragraphs of comments, you should strive to write your comments in complete sentences. When developers write comments in phrases or sentence fragments, what they consider necessary information often falls short of what readers want or need to see. When you write comments in complete sentences, you force yourself to fully analyze the comment. Remember that excellent comments explain the general flow and purpose of a procedure even when stripped from the code they accompany.

Incorrect:

```
'* Does user have rights?
If Not (objApplication.Security.CanDeleteAccounts) Then
    MsgBox "You do not have security rights to delete accounts.", _
           vbInformation
    GoTo PROC_EXIT
End If

'* Confirm
If MsgBox("Delete this account?", _
        vbYesNo Or vbCritical) = vbNo Then
    GoTo PROC_EXIT
End If
```

Correct:

```
'* If the user doesn't have security rights to delete an account,
'* say so and get out.
If Not (objApplication.Security.CanDeleteAccounts) Then
    MsgBox "You do not have security rights to delete accounts.", _
           vbInformation
    GoTo PROC_EXIT
End If

'* Ask for confirmation before deleting, and get out if the user
'* doesn't want to delete.
If MsgBox("Delete this account?", _
        vbYesNo Or vbCritical) = vbNo Then
    GoTo PROC_EXIT
End If
```

9.8. **Avoid using abbreviations.** Unless your organization defines a documented set of words to abbreviate, you should avoid abbreviating words in your comments. Abbreviations often make comments harder to read, and people often abbreviate the same words in different ways, which can lead to confusion. If you must abbreviate, be very, very consistent. Say you have a human resources application that manages employees. Because the word *employee* appears in so many places, you might choose to abbreviate it as Emp. If you must do this, make sure that you do it consistently and that all other members of your team use the same abbreviation.

Incorrect:

```
'* Enable the del Acct menu item.
ActiveBar.Tools("DeleteAccount").Enabled = True
```

Correct:

```
'* Enable the Delete Account menu item.
ActiveBar.Tools("DeleteAccount").Enabled = True
```

9.8.3 Capitalize entire words to indicate their importance. To call attention to a word or words within a comment, use all uppercase letters. You can't apply formatting such as bold or italics because these features aren't supported by the Visual Basic code editor.

Correct:

```
Private Sub UpdateDatabase()
    '* Purpose  :  Update the database structure.

    '* DO NOT USE ERROR TRAPPING! Let the errors cascade up the
    '* call stack.
    ⋮
End Sub
```

9.9 Indent comments to align them with the statements that follow.

Comments are generally positioned in front of the code they document. To visually reinforce the relationship between a comment and the code it relates to, indent the comment at the same level as the code. Some developers indent code lines a single tab stop from the comment they follow, but if you were to remove the comments from a procedure that used this indentation scheme, it would quickly become apparent that the indentation does not correctly reflect the structure of the procedure. The code is not subordinate to the comment; it coexists with the comment.

9.10 Give each procedure a comment header.

Each procedure should have a comment header. Procedure comment headers can contain documentation of items such as the input parameters, the return values, the original author, the last person who edited the procedure, the last date revised, copyright information, or even a programmer's favorite color.

You have to decide what's important in a procedure comment header in your environment. At the very least, the comment header should contain the purpose of the procedure. The purpose should be stated clearly and concisely. If a procedure needs a thorough explanation, give it one, but avoid excessive wordiness, as in, "The purpose of this function is to…" The Purpose heading itself tells the reader this much. A typical procedure comment header looks something like this:

```
Private Function ShowPrintDialog() As Boolean
    '* Purpose  :  Display the Print dialog box and get print
                   options from the user.
    ⋮
End Function
```

The next elements you should consider adding to your procedure comment header are the input (parameters) and output (return value) of the procedure. For example:

```
Public Function ConvertSQLtoCrystalFormat(strSQL As String) _
    As String
    '* Purpose  :  Convert a standard SQL statement into a valid
    '*               selection formula for use with the Crystal
    '*               print engine.
    '* Accepts  :  strSQL - a valid SQL statement.
    '* Returns  :  A Crystal selection formula that is equivalent
    '*               to the passed-in SQL string.
    ⋮
End Function
```

By including the purpose, accepted parameters, and return value comments in a procedure comment header, you create a much more understandable procedure. When you document the accepted parameters, be sure to note any special considerations or assumptions. For example, if the procedure expects a parameter to be formatted or within a certain range of values, include that information in the comments. Finally, if a procedure modifies any global data either directly or by changing the value of a parameter passed by reference, document this behavior in the procedure comment header as well.

All procedure comment headers should be formatted in the same way, and each piece of information should be clearly differentiated. The previous comment header has a highly recommended format; a reader can easily scan the header's components for the necessary information. The

format is shown below as a shell, with no information. This format is
used consistently throughout this book.

```
'* Purpose  :  xxx
'* Accepts  :  yyy
'* Returns  :  zzz
```

Each heading (*Purpose*, *Accepts*, or *Returns*) is followed by two spaces
(pressing the Tab key after typing the heading moves you to the proper
location), a colon, another two spaces, and then the text for the heading.
If multiple lines are required, you should indent subsequent lines to the
start of the text after the colon, as shown below:

```
Public Function ConvertSQLtoCrystalFormat(strSQL As String) _
    As String
    '* Purpose  :  Convert a standard SQL statement into a valid
    '*              selection formula for use with the Crystal
    '*              print engine.
    '* Accepts  :  strSQL - a valid SQL statement.
    '* Returns  :  A Crystal selection formula that is equivalent
    '*              to the passed-in SQL string.
    ⋮
End Function
```

In addition to documenting the purpose, parameters, and return value of
a procedure, you can also include the following elements in a procedure
comment header:

- The original author of the procedure. This information can be
  handy when you need to ask the developer a question about the
  procedure or when you want to drop an e-mail bomb on the author
  of some particularly insidious piece of code. When you document
  the author, use the heading *Created By*.

- The date the procedure was last modified, and who modified it. It's
  difficult to keep this information up to date, so if the information
  isn't so important to your organization, you might want to leave it
  out. For instance, if a developer modifies a variable name, he or she
  must update the last modified date and possibly the last modified
  name. Sometimes it takes more work to modify the date and the

name than to make the actual change in the code. But if this information is vital to your operations, by all means keep it in the header. When you document the person who last modified the code, use the heading *Last Modified By*. When you document the date the procedure was last modified, use the heading *Last Modified*.

- Changes to the procedure. If you're really a masochist, you can keep a revision history in the procedure comment header. This information can include the date of each revision and a description of what was done. In a multideveloper environment, you must also keep the name of the person who made the changes. Keeping such revision information takes considerable effort, so balance the pros and cons of doing so before adopting this strategy.

- Copyright information. If you distribute your code to developers outside your organization, perhaps by selling source code or posting code to the Internet, you might want to include copyright information in each procedure or in the Declarations section of each module. You must determine the value of this approach, since it's easy for others to remove the information when they paste the code into their application. Also, if someone compiles the code into an application, no one will ever see the copyright information anyway. Still, if it is important to you, place the copyright information in the procedure comment headers or in the Declarations section of each module.

 OTE   Although *Event* procedures are similar to the procedures that you actually write, you do not need to document the parameters of an *Event* procedure. You also don't need to document simple property procedures that encapsulate module-level variables. I have omitted the procedure comment header from some examples in this book when I've felt that it would convolute the topic being illustrated.

Practical Applications

Every procedure should have a procedure comment header, and every header should contain at least the purpose of the procedure, the parameters accepted by the procedure, and any return value.

9.10.1 Document the purpose of a procedure in the procedure comment header.

Incorrect:

```
Function IsFormLoaded(strFormName As String) As Boolean
    '* This function accepts a form name and returns
    '* True if the form is loaded and False if it is not.
    :
End Function
```

Correct:

```
Function IsFormLoaded(strFormName As String) As Boolean
    '* Purpose  :  Determine whether a specified form is loaded.
    :
End Function
```

9.10.2 Document the parameters of a procedure in the procedure comment header.

Incorrect:

```
Function IsFormLoaded(strFormName As String) As Boolean
    '* Purpose  :  Determine whether a specified form is loaded.
    '* Accepts  :  The name of a form.
    :
End Function
```

Also incorrect:

```
Function IsFormLoaded(strFormName As String) As Boolean
    '* Purpose  :  Determine whether a specified form is loaded.
    '* Accepts  :  strFormName.
    :
End Function
```

Correct:

```
Function IsFormLoaded(strFormName As String) As Boolean
    '* Purpose  :  Determine whether a specified form is loaded.
    '* Accepts  :  strFormName - the name of a form.
    :
End Function
```

9.10.3 Document the return value of a function in the procedure comment header.

Incorrect:

```
Function IsFormLoaded(strFormName As String) As Boolean
    '* Purpose   :  Determine whether a specified form is loaded.
    '* Accepts   :  strFormName - the name of a form.
    '* Returns   :  True or False.
    ⋮
End Function
```

Also incorrect:

```
Function IsFormLoaded(strFormName As String) As Boolean
    '* Purpose   :  Determine whether a specified form is loaded.
    '* Accepts   :  strFormName - the name of a form.
    '* Returns   :  Whether or not the form is loaded.
    ⋮
End Function
```

Correct:

```
Function IsFormLoaded(strFormName As String) As Boolean
    '* Purpose   :  Determine whether a specified form is loaded.
    '* Accepts   :  strFormName - the name of a form.
    '* Returns   :  True if the form is loaded, False if not.
    ⋮
End Function
```

9.11 Document code processes by using inline comments.

The most common type of comment is generally referred to as an inline comment. While the procedure comment header documents the basics of the procedure, inline comments document the code itself. The implementation details aren't described in the procedure comment header because they might change over time and they add unnecessary complexity to the header. The place to document the implementation of a procedure is within the procedure itself. Take a look at the following procedure, which determines whether a form is loaded:

```
Function IsFormLoaded(strFormName As String) As Boolean
    '* Purpose   :  Determine whether a specified form is loaded.
    '* Accepts   :  strFormName - the name of a form.
    '* Returns   :  True if the form is loaded, False if not.
    On Error GoTo PROC_ERR
    Dim intCounter As Integer
```

```
'* Since referring to a form loads the form, the proper
'* way to determine whether the form is loaded is to loop
'* through the forms collection, which contains only
'* loaded forms.
For intCounter = 0 To Forms.Count - 1

    '* If the current form is the specified form,
    '* return True and get out.
    If Forms(intCounter).Name = strFormName Then
        IsFormLoaded = True
        GoTo PROC_EXIT
    End If

Next intCounter

'* Form was not found; return False.
IsFormLoaded = False

PROC_EXIT:
    Exit Function

PROC ERR:
    MsgBox "basMain | IsFormLoaded" & vbCrLf & "Error: " & _
        Err.Number & vbCrLf & Err.Description
    Resume Next

End Function
```

Notice how each decision is commented. As you read the code, the comments explain the implementation details. Try to place an explanatory inline comment at each construct, such as loops and decision structures. You should strive to make these comments clear and concise, but if something needs a detailed explanation, give it one. Since inline comments appear in the same location as the code they're describing, they're fairly easy to maintain. If you change the code, change the comment.

Practical Applications

Inline comments are the most common and most important comments. Use them to document the implementation of procedures, walking the reader through the various twists and turns.

9.11.1   **Place a comment before every *If* statement.** *If* statements make decisions that affect the flow of execution. Document each *If* statement within your code.

199

Incorrect:

```
If Command$ <> "" Then
    intLocation = InStr(Command$, strSearchString)

If intLocation = 0 Then
        '* Use the default ini file, assuming it's in the application
        '* path.
        strINIFile = App.Path & "\tpssuite.ini"
    Else
        '* Extract the name of the designated ini file.
        strINIFile = Mid$(Command$, Len(strSearchString) + intLocation)

        If Dir$(strINIFile) = "" Then
            strINIFile = App.Path & "\tpssuite.ini"
        End If
    End If
End If
```

Correct:

```
'* Look for command line options.
If Command$ <> "" Then
    intLocation = InStr(Command$, strSearchString)

    '* If an ini parameter has been found, attempt to use it.
    If intLocation = 0 Then
        '* Use the default ini file, assuming it's in the application
        '* path.
        strINIFile = App.Path & "\tpssuite.ini"
    Else
        '* Extract the name of the designated ini file.
        strINIFile = Mid$(Command$, Len(strSearchString) + intLocation)

        '* If the specified file is not found, use
        '* the default ini file.
        If Dir$(strINIFile) = "" Then
            strINIFile = App.Path & "\tpssuite.ini"
        End If

    End If

End If
```

9.11.2   Place a comment before every *Select Case* statement. Like *If* statements, *Select Case* statements evaluate expressions that affect the flow of execution. They are often more complex than *If* statements. You should thoroughly document *Select Case* statements.

Incorrect:

```
Private Sub txtSearch_KeyDown(KeyCode As Integer, Shift As Integer)

    Select Case KeyCode
        Case Is = vbKeyPageDown
            '* Move forward in the list the number of visible rows.
            datPhones.Recordset.Move grdPhones.VisibleRows

        Case Is = vbKeyPageUp
            '* Move backward in the list the number of visible rows.
            datPhones.Recordset.Move -grdPhones.VisibleRows
    End Select

End Sub
```

Correct:

```
Private Sub txtSearch_KeyDown(KeyCode As Integer, Shift As Integer)

    '* If the user pressed a navigation key, adjust the list
    '* accordingly.
    Select Case KeyCode
        Case Is = vbKeyPageDown
            '* Move forward in the list the number of visible rows.
            datPhones.Recordset.Move grdPhones.VisibleRows

        Case Is = vbKeyPageUp
            '* Move backward in the list the number of visible rows.
            datPhones.Recordset.Move -grdPhones.VisibleRows
    End Select

End Sub
```

9.11.3 **Place a comment before every loop, including** *For...Next* **loops and** *Do* **loops.** Every loop has a purpose, and often that purpose is not intuitively clear. Regardless of the complexity of the loop, document it with a comment preceding the loop.

Incorrect:

```
For intIndex = 1 To lvwReleasedItems.ListItems.Count
    '* Get the serial number from the list item.
    strSerial = lvwReleasedItems.ListItems(intIndex).Text

    '* Delete the serial number from the transfer table.
    strSQL = "DELETE * FROM tblTransferSerials " & _
            "WHERE [TransferNumber] = " & _
```

(continued)

```
                    m_lngTransferNumber & " AND [SerialNumber] = """ & _
                    strSerial & """;"

        dbTransfers.Execute strSQL, dbFailOnError

Next intIndex
```

Correct:

```
'* Loop through the selected serial numbers, and release each one.
For intIndex = 1 To lvwReleasedItems.ListItems.Count
    '* Get the serial number from the list item.
    strSerial = lvwReleasedItems.ListItems(intIndex).Text

    '* Delete the serial number from the transfer table.
    strSQL = "DELETE * FROM tblTransferSerials " & _
             "WHERE [TransferNumber] = " & _
             m_lngTransferNumber & " AND [SerialNumber] = """ & _
             strSerial & """;"

    dbTransfers.Execute strSQL, dbFailOnError

Next intIndex
```

9.11.4 Place a comment before every statement in which a global variable is changed. As I discussed in Chapter 6, global variables are evil! However, if you absolutely need to use a global variable, document why you are changing it. This will make debugging a bit simpler.

Incorrect:

```
Private Sub clsConnector_Terminate()
    '* Purpose  :  Keep track of the number of automation
    '*               clients holding references to the suite.
    On Error GoTo PROC_ERR

    g_lngAutomationInstances = g_lngAutomationInstances - 1

PROC_EXIT:
    Exit Sub

PROC_ERR:
    Call ShowError("clsConnector", "Class_Terminate", Err.Number, _
                   Err.Description)
    GoTo PROC_EXIT

End Sub
```

Correct:

```
Private Sub clsConnector_Terminate()
    '* Purpose  :  Keep track of the number of automation
    '*               clients holding references to the suite.
    On Error GoTo PROC_ERR

    '* Decrement the count of clients holding references to this
    '* connector object.
    g_lngAutomationInstances = g_lngAutomationInstances - 1

PROC_EXIT:
    Exit Sub

PROC_ERR:
    Call ShowError("clsConnector", "Class_Terminate", Err.Number, _
                Err.Description)
    GoTo PROC_EXIT

End Sub
```

9.12 Use end-of-line comments to document variables.

Some developers use end-of-line comments, which appear at the end of a code statement and can extend for multiple lines. Try to use these comments for short descriptions only. If a longer description is necessary, use an inline comment instead. End-of-line comments were used more frequently in the past; most developers now choose (and rightly so) to use inline comments instead. The following is an example of an end-of-line comment:

```
Do While intLocation > 0      '* Do while a space is found.
    ⋮
Loop
```

End-of-line comments tend to make the code more difficult to read when they are used in constructs such as the code snippet above. However, a good use of an end-of-line comment is for documenting the declaration of a variable whose purpose might not be clear, as shown here:

```
Dim objTaxReporter As Object    '* May hold an Employee object or an
                                 '* Employer object.
```

When you use multiple end-of-line comments (such as for multiple variable declarations at the top of a procedure), attempt to align them. This makes them a little easier to read.

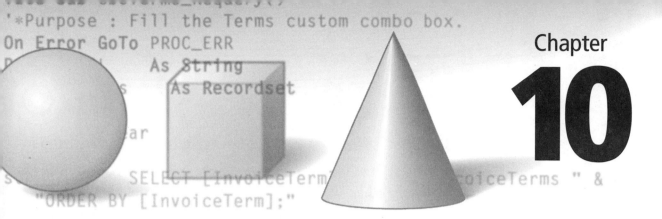

Looping Structures

If you couldn't create loops, you'd often have to write hundreds or thousands of lines of code instead. The basic idea of all types of loops is the same—to reduce the number of code statements needed to repeatedly perform a task. Loops come in a number of different types, and you should use the appropriate type in each situation. Some loops execute a specific number of times, while others execute as long as a certain condition is met. Using the correct loop for a job can mean more solid, efficient, and readable code.

OTE One key to writing efficient code is to eliminate redundancy. If you find yourself typing the same (or similar) lines of code repeatedly, chances are good that you should create a loop.

> **Goals of Using Looping Structures**
>
> Looping structures are great for
>
> - Reducing repetitive code
> - Iterating over an array or a collection
> - Increasing the speed and efficiency of your code

Directives

10.1   Use *For...Next* to loop a specific number of times.

The most basic type of loop is the *For...Next* loop, which loops a specific number of times. When the maximum number of iterations is reached, execution continues with the statement following the *Next* statement. When you create a *For...Next* loop, you designate the starting number to use for counting as well as the ending number. You can also specify an increment by using the *Step* keyword.

The *For...Next* construct has the following syntax:

```
For counter = start To end [Step step]

    [statements]

    [Exit For]

    [statements]

Next [counter]
```

The *For...Next* construct has these parameters:

■   *counter*   A required numeric variable used as a loop counter. The variable can't be a Boolean or an array element.

■   *start*   A required initial value of *counter.*

■   *end*   A required final value of *counter.* When *counter* reaches the *end* number, the statements within the loop are executed one last time and then execution continues with the line following the *Next* statement. If *counter* exceeds the *end* number, execution continues with the line following the *Next* statement.

■   *step*   An optional number that specifies the amount *counter* is incremented each time through the loop. If you omit *step*, the *counter* variable is incremented by 1.

Most of the programming work in a *For...Next* loop is done in the *For* statement that starts the loop. The majority of *For...Next* loops are fairly simple—the loop counter proceeds from one number to another by a step of 1. When you want a step of 1, you should omit the *Step* component. For instance, the following statement loops from 1 to 10 with a step of 1:

```
Dim intCounter As Integer

For intCounter = 1 To 10
    ⋮
Next intCounter
```

To increment the counter by a step other than 1, you must supply the *Step* component in the *For* statement. For example, to loop from 1 to 10 with a step of 2, you can use this *For* statement:

```
Dim intCounter As Integer

For intCounter = 1 To 10 Step 2
    Debug.Print intCounter
Next intCounter
```

To create loops that perform as you expect them to, you must fully understand the *Step* component. If you were asked to count to 10 by 2s, you'd probably count as follows:

```
2, 4, 6, 8, 10
```

However, the code shown above actually prints the following in the debug window:

```
1, 3, 5, 7, 9
```

When you start a loop with a *For* statement, the counter variable is initialized to the start value. In this example, the start value is 1. Once the loop executes, the counter variable is incremented (or decremented, in the case of a negative step value) by the value of *step*. This continues until the value of the counter variable exceeds the end value. When the counter variable reaches 9 and the loop completes, the counter variable is incremented to 11. Since 11 exceeds the end value of 10, the loop does not repeat again. Some developers don't understand this behavior. For example, what value is printed to the debug window when the following code executes?

```
Dim intCounter As Integer

'* Loop 10 times.
For intCounter = 1 To 10
    ⋮
Next intCounter

Debug.Print intCounter
```

If your first instinct is to say 10, you're mistaken but you're not alone. When the *Next* statement is reached and *intCounter* is 9, *intCounter* is incremented to 10 and the loop executes again. When the *Next* statement is encountered while *intCounter* has a value of 10, the loop does not immediately terminate. Instead, *intCounter* is incremented to 11 and execution again returns to the *For* statement. When the *For* statement evaluates *intCounter* and finds that it exceeds the end value, code execution moves to the statement immediately following the *Next* statement, which prints the value of *intCounter*. The value of *intCounter* that prints is 11.

 OTE In Chapter 5, "Using Constants and Enumerations," I discussed why you should eliminate magic (hard-coded) numbers in favor of constants. Loops are good places to look for opportunities to use constants.

Practical Application 10.1.1 shows how a procedure is more readable when you replace hard-coded numbers in a *For* statement with constants. In addition to magic numbers and constants, you can also use variables or control values for the start and end parameters. For instance, the following code uses the value of a variable for the upper limit:

```
Dim intCounter      As Integer
Dim intUpperLimit   As Integer

'* Initialize upper limit. This value can come from anywhere,
'* such as from a control on a form or from a text file.
intUpperLimit = 100

For intCounter = 1 To intUpperLimit
    ⋮
Next intCounter
```

When you use variable data for the start and end values in a *For...Next* loop, you must use valid values. For instance, the following procedure is the same as the previous one, with one small but important change: *intUpperLimit* is set to −5.

```
Dim intCounter      As Integer
Dim intUpperLimit   As Integer

'* Initialize upper limit. This value can come from anywhere,
'* such as from a control on a form or from a text file.
intUpperLimit = -5

For intCounter = 1 To intUpperLimit
    ⋮
Next intCounter
```

This loop doesn't execute at all. When the *For* statement is first encountered, *intCounter* is initialized to 1 and compared to *intUpperLimit*. Since it has a value greater than that of *intUpperLimit*, code execution moves to the statement immediately following the *Next* statement. In some processes, this might be acceptable behavior; in others, it might not.

Every *For* statement must have a corresponding *Next* statement. You technically don't have to include the counter variable in the *Next* statement, but you should. Omitting the counter variable isn't much of a problem in a simple procedure with only one loop. But as a procedure grows in size and complexity or as nested loops are created, it becomes much more important that the counter variable be used. For example, look at these nested loops:

```
Dim intCounter      As Integer
Dim intSecondCounter As Integer

'* Create the outer loop.
For intCounter = 1 To 100

    '* Create a nested loop along with a new counter.
    For intSecondCounter = 1 To 100
       '* Print the value of the second counter.
       Debug.Print intSecondCounter
    Next

Next
```

This example has a loop within a loop. Because the counter variables are omitted from the *Next* statements, it's less clear which *Next* statement is closing which loop. If there were many statements between the *For* and *Next* statements, it would be even more difficult to discern the closing of the loops.

You should indent all statements between the *For* and *Next* statements at least one tab stop to make the structure of the code apparent. (Chapter 8, "Formatting Code," discusses indentation in detail, but it's also worthwhile describing its importance here.) Indentation helps to display the flow or structure of code. Loops have a definite structure—a beginning, a body, and an end. The beginning and end statements appear at the same level in the hierarchy, with the body statements subordinate. The first statement after a *For* statement must be indented one tab stop. The indentation of the rest of the body statements depends on their relationship to this first statement.

While most *For...Next* loops are designed to loop a designated number of times, sometimes you need to end a *For...Next* loop prematurely. Many developers make the mistake of using *GoTo* and a label to exit a loop, as shown in Practical Application 10.1.5. The correct method of leaving a *For...Next* loop is to use the *Exit For* statement:

```
Dim intCounter As Integer

'* Loop through the possible days of the month.
For intCounter = 1 To 31
    '* If the counter is equal to the current day of the month,
    '* exit the loop.
    If intCounter = Format(Date, "d") Then Exit For
    Debug.Print intCounter
Next intCounter
```

The preceding code is not particularly functional, but it illustrates a point. If you must exit the loop early, do it with the *Exit For* statement.

Incorrect:

```
Private Function RawNumber(strNumber As String) As String
    '* Purpose  :  Strips an alphanumeric string down to just
    '*               its numeric component to be used for faxing.
    '* Accepts  :  strNumber  -  a string containing a phone number,
    '*               e.g., (402) 555-1212.
    '* Returns  :  The string with all nonnumeric elements removed.
    On Error GoTo PROC_ERR
```

```
   Dim strRaw       As String
   Dim intLocation  As Integer

   intLocation = 1

   '* Loop through all the characters in the string.
   Do While intLocation <= Len(strNumber)

      '* Determine whether the current character is numeric.
      If IsNumeric(Mid$(strNumber, intLocation, 1)) Then
         strRaw = strRaw & Mid$(strNumber, intLocation, 1)
      End If

      intLocation = intLocation + 1
   Loop

   RawNumber = strRaw

PROC_EXIT:
   Exit Function

PROC_ERR:
   Call ShowError(Me.Name, "RawNumber", Err.Number, Err.Description)
   GoTo PROC_EXIT

End Function
```

Correct:

```
Private Function RawNumber(strNumber As String) As String
   '* Purpose  :  Strips an alphanumeric string down to just
   '*               its numeric component to be used for faxing.
   '* Accepts  :  strNumber  -  a string containing a phone number,
   '*               e.g., (402) 555-1212.
   '* Returns  :  The string with all nonnumeric elements removed.
   On Error GoTo PROC_ERR
   Dim strRaw       As String
   Dim intLocation  As Integer

   '* Loop through all the characters in the string.
   For intLocation = 1 To Len(strNumber)

      '* Determine whether the current character is numeric.
      If IsNumeric(Mid$(strNumber, intLocation, 1)) Then
         strRaw = strRaw & Mid$(strNumber, intLocation, 1)
      End If

   Next intLocation
```

(continued)

```
        RawNumber = strRaw

PROC_EXIT:
    Exit Function

PROC_ERR:
    Call ShowError(Me.Name, "RawNumber", Err.Number, Err.Description)
    GoTo PROC_EXIT

End Function
```

Practical Applications

10.1.1 Use a constant for *step* whenever possible. Since the value of *step* is always numeric and its meaning varies from process to process, you should use a named constant rather than a literal value.

Incorrect:

```
'* Draw vertical grid lines on the canvas.
For intCount = 0 To (intEditWidth + 1) Step 4
    '* Use the API to move the drawing pen.
    lngResult = MoveToEx(lngScratchPadDC, intCount, 0, ByVal 0&)
    '* Draw a straight line.
    lngResult = LineTo(lngScratchPadDC, intCount, intEditHeight)
Next intCount
```

Correct:

```
Const c_Magnification = 4

'* Draw vertical grid lines on the canvas.
For intCount = 0 To (intEditWidth + 1) Step c_Magnification
    '* Use the API to move the drawing pen.
    lngResult = MoveToEx(lngScratchPadDC, intCount, 0, ByVal 0&)
    '* Draw a straight line.
    lngResult = LineTo(lngScratchPadDC, intCount, intEditHeight)
Next intCount
```

10.1.2 Avoid referencing the counter variable after a loop ends. When a *For...Next* loop ends, the final value of the counter variable is not equal to the value of *end*—it's higher or lower based on the value of *step*. If you expect a loop to run its full number of times, don't use the counter variable after the loop ends.

Although the following procedure marked as incorrect appears acceptable, it contains a nasty bug. When this procedure executes, an error is generated on the statement that attempts to print in the debug window. The error is *Error 9, Subscript out of range*, and it occurs because *intCounter* is actually 11 when the loop terminates. (The last element in the array has an index of 10.)

Incorrect:

```
Private Sub FillArray()
    '* Purpose  :  Fill an array with values, and print the
    '*               value in the last element.
    On Error GoTo PROC_ERR
    Dim intCounter          As Integer
    Dim aintArray(1 To 10)  As Integer

    '* Initialize the random number generator.
    Randomize

    '* Populate the array elements with random numbers.
    For intCounter = 1 To 10
        aintArray(intCounter) = (10 * Rnd) + 1
    Next intCounter

    '* Print the value of the last element.
    Debug.Print aintArray(intCounter)

PROC_EXIT:
    Exit Sub

PROC_ERR:
    Call ShowError(Me.Name, "FillArray", Err.Number, Err.Description)
    GoTo PROC_EXIT

End Sub
```

Correct:

```
Private Sub FillArray()
    '* Purpose  :  Fill an array with values and print the
    '*               value in the last element.
    On Error GoTo PROC_ERR
    Dim intCounter     As Integer

    Const c_ArrayMax = 10
    Const c_ArrayMin = 1
    Dim aintArray(c_ArrayMin To c_ArrayMax)  As Integer

    '* Initialize the random number generator.
    Randomize
```

(continued)

```
'* Populate the array elements with random numbers.
For intCounter = c_ArrayMin To c_ArrayMax
    aintArray(intCounter) = (c_ArrayMax * Rnd) + 1
Next intCounter

'* Print the value of the last element.
Debug.Print aintArray(c_ArrayMax)
```

```
PROC_EXIT:
    Exit Sub

PROC_ERR:
    Call ShowError(Me.Name, "FillArray", Err.Number, Err.Description)
    GoTo PROC_EXIT

End Sub
```

10.1.3 Include the counter variable in all *Next* statements. Code will still execute if you omit the counter variable from the *Next* statement, but it will be less readable and therefore more difficult to maintain.

Incorrect:

```
Const c_MinPort = 1
Const c_MaxPort = 4

'* Set the Comm port based on the selected option button.
For intCounter = c_MinPort To c_MaxPort

    '* If a Comm port option button is selected, use that Comm port
    '* and exit the loop.
    If optCommPort(intCounter).value = True Then
        intCommPort = intCounter
        Exit For
    End If

Next
```

Correct:

```
Const c_MinPort = 1
Const c_MaxPort = 4

'* Set the Comm port based on the selected option button.
For intCounter = c_MinPort To c_MaxPort

    '* If a Comm port option button is selected, use that Comm port
    '* and exit the loop.
```

```
    If optCommPort(intCounter).value = True Then
        intCommPort = intCounter
        Exit For
    End If

Next intCounter
```

10.1.4 **Indent body statements in a *For…Next* loop for visual clarity.**
Whenever you have a code construct with a beginning and ending statement, you have a situation that calls for indentation.

Incorrect:
```
'* Fill the date selection combo box.
For intYear = 1969 To 2020
cboYear.AddItem Str(intYear)
Next intYear
```

Correct:
```
'* Fill the date selection combo box.
For intYear = 1969 To 2020
    cboYear.AddItem Str(intYear)
Next intYear
```

10.1.5 **If you must exit a *For…Next* loop early, use an *Exit For* statement.**
Avoid using *GoTo* and a label to exit a loop.

Incorrect:
```
'* Select the "unassigned" category node in the Tree view control.
For lngIndex = 1 To treCategory.Nodes.Count

    '* Check to see whether this is the "unassigned" node.
    If treCategory.Nodes(lngIndex).Text = c_strUnassigned Then
        treCategory.Nodes(lngIndex).Selected = True
        '* No need to keep looking; get out of the loop.
        GoTo END_OF_LOOP
    End If

Next lngIndex

END_OF_LOOP:
```

Correct:
```
'* Select the "unassigned" category node in the Tree view control.
For lngIndex = 1 To treCategory.Nodes.Count
```

(continued)

```
'* Check to see whether this is the "unassigned" node.
If treCategory.Nodes(lngIndex).Text = c_strUnassigned Then
    treCategory.Nodes(lngIndex).Selected = True
    '* No need to keep looking; get out of the loop.
    Exit For
End If

Next lngIndex
```

10.2   Use *Do...Loop* to loop an undetermined number of times.

Sometimes you don't know the exact number of times a loop needs to be executed when the loop starts. You can start a *For...Next* loop with an upper limit that you know is larger than the number of iterations needed (if you know that value), check for a condition within the loop, and exit the loop with an *Exit For* statement when the condition is met. However, this is extremely inefficient, often impractical, and just plain wrong. When you need to create a loop and you don't know how many times it needs to execute, use *Do...Loop*.

The *Do...Loop* construct comes in a number of flavors. In its most basic form, it has the following syntax:

```
Do
    [statements]
Loop
```

This particular loop is endless—there is no conditional clause to determine when to stop looping. You might need an endless loop on rare occasions—game programming comes to mind—but more often you'll want to exit a loop when certain conditions are met.

The evaluation of a condition to terminate a *Do* loop can happen at the beginning or the end of the loop. Also, you can specify that a loop continue when a condition is met or until a condition is met. These options allow you a great deal of flexibility when writing loops.

The following is the syntax of a *Do* loop that uses the *While* keyword:

```
Do While condition
    [statements]
Loop
```

Here's an example of a simple *Do* loop that uses this syntax:

```
'* Populate a Tree view control with items from the marketing
'* codes table.
Do While Not (rstCodes.EOF)
   Set vntNode = treMarketing.Nodes.Add(intNodeIndex, tvwChild, , _
               rstCodes![MarketingCode], "CodeImage")
   rstCodes.MoveNext
Loop
```

As long as *condition* evaluates to True—in this case, as long as the recordset's EOF (end-of-file) property is not True—the loop continues to execute. Note that if *condition* evaluates to False when the loop first starts, the code between the *Do* and the *Loop* statements never executes—not even once.

The *Until* keyword keeps a *Do* loop going until a condition is met. The following code shows the same loop rewritten using the *Until* keyword:

```
'* Populate a Tree view control with items from the marketing
'* codes table.
Do Until rstCodes.EOF
   Set vntNode = treMarketing.Nodes.Add(intNodeIndex, tvwChild, , _
               rstCodes![MarketingCode], "CodeImage")
   rstCodes.MoveNext
Loop
```

This code example works exactly like the previous one, but it offers a better solution because it eliminates the need to negate the value of *rstCodes.EOF*. To use the *Do While* loop, you have to use *Not*, which requires extra processing and is a little more difficult to understand.

You can use the *While* or *Until* keywords in the *Loop* statement (the closing statement of the loop) rather than as part of the *Do* statement. When you place them in the *Loop* statement, *condition* is evaluated at the end of the loop rather than at the start. This ensures that the loop always executes at least once. You must be careful when you create a loop that checks the exit condition at the end of the loop, as shown here:

```
'* Populate a Tree view control with items from the marketing
'* codes table.
```

(continued)

```
Do
    Set vntNode = treMarketing.Nodes.Add(intNodeIndex, tvwChild, , _
                    rstCodes![MarketingCode], "CodeImage")
    rstCodes.MoveNext
Loop Until rstCodes.EOF
```

Note that this code suffers from the extreme possibility of failure. It will execute at least once regardless of whether the recordset is at end-of-file. If the recordset is at end-of-file when the loop starts, an attempt to reference the *MarketingCode* field causes a run-time error.

As you design a loop, consider whether it needs to execute at least once. If it does, evaluate *condition* at the end of the loop.

As with the *For...Next* loop, you can exit a *Do* loop without using *GoTo* and a label. To exit a *Do* loop at any time, use *Exit Do*. The following procedure creates a loop that would be endless without the *Exit Do* statement. In each pass through the loop, the program looks in the list box for the string *"ContactNumber"*. If the string is found, it is removed from the list box. When no more occurrences of the string are found, the loop is exited. Note that using *Exit Do* is often inferior to placing an effective exit condition at the beginning or the end of the loop.

```
'* The value "ContactNumber" might appear multiple times in the list
'* box. Use a loop to remove all occurrences of this value.
'* SelectListItem uses the API to perform a quick search.
Do
    lngIndex = SelectListItem(lstAvailableFields, "ContactNumber")

    '* Check to see whether the value "ContactNumber" was found.
    If lngIndex > -1 Then
        '* The value was found; remove it from the list.
        lstAvailableFields.RemoveItem lngIndex
    Else
        '* Item not found. All occurrences have been removed, so
        '* exit the loop.
        Exit Do
    End If

Loop
```

Generally, the expression that determines when to exit a loop uses a variable that's modified somewhere within the *Do* loop. Obviously, if the expression never changes, the loop is never exited.

Practical Applications

10.2.1 **Evaluate the exit condition of a** *Do...Loop* **at the start of the loop unless you have a reason to do otherwise.** Often you can choose whether to place the exit condition at the beginning or at the end of a loop. However, loops whose exit conditions are evaluated at the beginning are a bit easier to understand, and they will not be executed even once if the condition is False.

Incorrect:

```
If Not (rstReports.EOF) Then

    '* Loop through the Recordset of reports, adding each report to the
    '* ListView control.
    Do
        Set objItem = lvwReports.ListItems.Add()

        objItem.Text = rstReports![Title]
        objItem.SmallIcon = "Report"

        rstReports.MoveNext
    Loop Until rstReports. EOF

End If
```

Correct:

```
'* Loop through the Recordset of reports, adding each report to the
'* ListView control.
Do Until rstReports.EOF
    Set objItem = lvwReports.ListItems.Add()

    objItem.Text = rstReports![Title]
    objItem.SmallIcon = "Report"

    rstReports.MoveNext
Loop
```

10.2.2 **When choosing between** *While* **and** *Until*, **use the one that allows the simplest exit condition.** You can use either *While* or *Until* in most loops. However, depending on the situation, one of them (and not the other) will require that you use the *Not* operator to evaluate the opposite of an expression. You should use the value of a simple expression (rather than its opposite) whenever possible.

Incorrect:

```
Private Sub cboContacts_Requery()
    '* Purpose  :  Fill the contacts combo box with all contacts
    '*               for the current account.
    On Error GoTo PROC_ERR
    Dim strSQL      As String
    Dim rstContact As Recordset

    '* Retrieve the name of all contacts for the account.
    strSQL = "SELECT [Contact Name] FROM tblContacts " & _
            "WHERE [AccountNumber] = " & m_lngAccountNumber & " " & _
            "ORDER BY [Contact Name];"

    cboContacts.Clear

    Set rstContact = dbSales.OpenRecordset(strSQL, dbOpenForwardOnly)

    '* Populate the combo box.
    Do While Not (rstContact.EOF)
        cboContacts.AddItem rstContact![Contact Name]
        rstContact.MoveNext
    Loop

PROC_EXIT:
    '* Check to see whether rstContact is set to an instance
    '* of a Recordset.
    If Not (rstContact Is Nothing) Then
        rstContact.Close
        Set rstContact = Nothing
    End If

    Exit Sub

PROC_ERR:
    Call ShowError(Me.Name, "cboContacts_Requery", Err.Number, _
                    Err.Description)
    Resume Next

End Sub
```

Correct:

```
Private Sub cboContacts_Requery()
    '* Purpose  :  Fill the contacts combo box with all contacts
    '*               for the current account.
    On Error GoTo PROC_ERR
    Dim strSQL      As String
    Dim rstContact As Recordset
```

```
'* Retrieve the name of all contacts for the account.
strSQL = "SELECT [Contact Name] FROM tblContacts " & _
         "WHERE [AccountNumber] = " & m_lngAccountNumber & " " & _
         "ORDER BY [Contact Name];"

cboContacts.Clear

Set rstContact = dbSales.OpenRecordset(strSQL, dbOpenForwardOnly)

'* Populate the combo box.
Do Until rstContact.EOF
   cboContacts.AddItem rstContact![Contact Name]
   rstContact.MoveNext
Loop

PROC_EXIT:
   '* Check to see whether rstContact is set to an instance
   '* of a Recordset.
   If Not (rstContact Is Nothing) Then
      rstContact.Close
      Set rstContact = Nothing
   End If

   Exit Sub

PROC_ERR:
   Call ShowError(Me.Name, "cboContacts_Requery", Err.Number, _
                  Err.Description)
   Resume Next

End Sub
```

10.2.3 Use a *Do* loop or a *For…Next* loop instead of *GoTo* and a label whenever possible. In many situations, it's tempting to create a loop by using *GoTo* and a label. But this technique creates code that is difficult to understand and often less efficient.

Incorrect:

```
Private Function StripDoubleQuotes(ByVal strString As String) _
    As String
   '* Purpose   :  Locate all double quotes within a string and change
   '*                them to single quotes.
   '* Accepts   :  strString - the string in which to search for
   '*                double quotes.
   '* Returns   :  The string passed here as strString, with double
   '*                quotes replaced by single quotes.
```

(continued)

221

```
      Const c_DoubleQuote = """"
      Const c_SingleQuote = "'"
      Dim intLocation As Integer

StartCheck:
      '* Look for a double quote.
      intLocation = InStr(strString, c_DoubleQuote)

'* If a double quote is found, replace it with a single quote.
      If intLocation > 0 Then
          '* A double quote has been found. Replace it with
          '* a single quote.
          Mid$(strString, intLocation, 1) = c_SingleQuote
          '* Look for another double quote.
          GoTo StartCheck
      Else
          '* No more double quotes were found. Return the new string.
          StripDoubleQuotes = strString
      End If

End Function
```

Correct:

```
Private Function StripDoubleQuotes(ByVal strString As String) _
      As String
      '* Purpose  :  Locate all double quotes within a string and change
      '*               them to single quotes.
      '* Accepts  :  strString - the string in which to search for
      '*               double quotes.
      '* Returns  :  The string passed here as strString, with double
      '*               quotes replaced by single quotes.
      Const c_DoubleQuote = """"
      Const c_SingleQuote = "'"
      Dim intLocation As Integer

      Do
          '* Look for a double quote.
          intLocation = InStr(strString, c_DoubleQuote)

          '* If a double quote is found, replace it with a single quote.
          If intLocation > 0 Then
              '* A double quote has been found. Replace it with
              '* a single quote.
              Mid$(strString, intLocation, 1) = c_SingleQuote
          End If

      Loop While intLocation > 0
```

```
'* Return the result.
StripDoubleQuotes = strString
```

End Function

10.3   Use *Do...Loop* in place of *While...Wend.*

The *While...Wend* loop has been around for a long time, and its retirement is long overdue. *Do...Loop* is more flexible, so you should use it instead. (Also, *Wend* just sounds ridiculous.) The *While...Wend* loop looks like this:

```
While condition
   [statements]
Wend
```

The *While...Wend* loop behaves exactly like the following *Do* loop:

```
Do While condition
   [statements]
Loop
```

There isn't much more to say about the *While...Wend* loop. The exit condition is evaluated when the loop is started, and if the condition evaluates to True the code within the *While...Wend* loop is executed. When the *Wend* statement (Middle English, anyone?) is reached, execution jumps back to the *While* statement and the exit condition is reevaluated.

10.4   Use *For Each...Next* to loop through all members of a collection.

A *For Each...Next* loop is a powerful loop that programmers often overlook. It loops through all the members of an array or a collection of objects. Many programmers who do use *For Each...Next* for collections don't realize that it works on arrays as well—this is fortunate, because using *For Each...Next* on arrays causes a noticeable decrease in performance.

For Each...Next is designed and optimized to loop through collections of objects. You create an *element variable,* whose data type must be Variant, Object, or some specific object type, and then initiate the loop. During each pass through the loop, your element variable is set to reference an element in the collection. Manipulating the element variable directly manipulates the element in the collection. Using a *For Each...Next* loop is often faster than using a *For...Next* loop that utilizes the indexes of the items in a collection.

The following is the syntax for a *For Each...Next* loop:

```
For Each element In group
    [statements]
    [Exit For]
    [statements]
Next [element]
```

The element variable, which you define, must have a Variant or Object (generic or specific) data type. You should use the specific object type that is most suitable for all objects in the group (collection). For instance, when you loop through the *Controls* collection on a form, you can use Variant, Object, or Control as the data type. However, you can't necessarily use the TextBox, ListBox, or ComboBox data types unless you are sure that only controls of the specified type are on the form. Therefore, the logical choice is the Control data type.

Incorrect:

```
Public Property Get SpecialIsFormDirty(frmForm As Form) As Boolean
    '* Purpose  :  Determine whether any of the data on the form has
    '*               changed.
    '* Accepts  :  frmForm - the name of the form to test.
    '* Returns  :  True if even one control's DataChanged property
    '*               is True; otherwise False.
    '* NOTE     :  Errors are trapped because attempting to access
    '*               the DataChanged property of a control that doesn't
    '*               have one (such as a Frame) causes a run-time error.
    On Error Resume Next
    Dim intIndex        As Integer
    Dim blnDataChanged  As Boolean

    Const c_NoSuchProperty = 438
    Const c_NoError = 0

    '* Assume that the form is dirty.
    SpecialIsFormDirty = True

    '* Loop through all controls on the form.
```

```
   For intIndex = 0 To frmForm.Controls.Count - 1
      Err.Clear
      blnDataChanged = frmForm.Controls(intIndex).DataChanged

      '* Determine the type of error (if any) that was generated.
      Select Case Err.Number
         Case Is = c_NoError
            '* This control has a DataChanged property.
            If blnDataChanged Then GoTo PROC_EXIT

         Case Is = c_NoSuchProperty
            '* This control does not have a DataChanged property.

         Case Else
            '* Legitimate error. Send to error handler.
            GoTo PROC_ERR
      End Select

   Next intIndex

   SpecialIsFormDirty = False

PROC_EXIT:
   Exit Property

PROC_ERR:
   Call ShowError("clsApplication", "Get_IsFormDirty", Err.Number, _
                  Err.Description)
   GoTo PROC_EXIT

End Property
```

Correct:

```
Public Property Get SpecialIsFormDirty(frmForm As Form) As Boolean
   '* Purpose  :  Determine whether any of the data on the form has
   '*               changed.
   '* Accepts  :  frmForm - the name of the form to test.
   '* Returns  :  True if even one control's DataChanged property
   '*               is True; otherwise False.
   '* NOTE     :  Errors are trapped because attempting to access
   '*               the DataChanged property of a control that doesn't
   '*               have one (such as a Frame) causes a run-time error.
   On Error Resume Next
   Dim ctl              As Control
   Dim blnDataChanged   As Boolean

   Const c_NoSuchProperty = 438
```

(continued)

```
Const c_NoError = 0

'* Assume that the form is dirty.
SpecialIsFormDirty = True

'* Loop through all controls on the form.
For Each ctl In frmForm.Controls
    '* Reset the error object.
    Err.Clear
    blnDataChanged = ctl.DataChanged

    '* Determine the type of error (if any) that was generated.
    Select Case Err.Number
        Case Is = c_NoError
            '* This control has a DataChanged property.
            If blnDataChanged Then GoTo PROC_EXIT

        Case Is = c_NoSuchProperty
            '* This control does not have a DataChanged property.

        Case Else
            '* Legitimate error. Send to error handler.
            GoTo PROC_ERR
    End Select

Next ctl

SpecialIsFormDirty = False

PROC_EXIT:
    Exit Property

PROC_ERR:
    Call ShowError("clsApplication", "Get_IsFormDirty", Err.Number, _
                    Err.Description)
    GoTo PROC_EXIT

End Property
```

Practical Applications

10.4.1 Don't use *For Each…Next* to loop through arrays. When you use a *For Each…Next* loop to manipulate the elements of an array, your element variable must have type Variant. If the elements of the array are not Variants, Visual Basic must coerce them to type Variant to use *For…Each*. The result is much slower code.

Incorrect:
```
Dim lngResult     As Long
Dim vntUndoBitMap As Variant

'* Populate all Undo memory bitmaps with the current image.
For Each vntUndoBitMap In m_alngUndo()
   With vntUndoBitMap
      .UndoDC = CreateCompatibleDC(frmEditor.picPreview.hdc)
      .UndoHandle = CreateCompatibleBitmap(Me.picPreview.hdc, _
                    c_ImageWidth, c_ImageHeight)
      lngResult = SelectObject(.UndoDC, .UndoHandle)
   End With
Next vntUndoBitMap
```

Correct:
```
Dim lngResult     As Long
Dim intCounter    As Integer

'* Populate all Undo memory bitmaps with the current image.
For intCounter = c_MinUndo To c_MaxUndo
   With m_alngUndo(intCounter)
      .UndoDC = CreateCompatibleDC(frmEditor.picPreview.hdc)
      .UndoHandle = CreateCompatibleBitmap(Me.picPreview.hdc, _
                    c_ImageWidth, c_ImageHeight)
      lngResult = SelectObject(.UndoDC, .UndoHandle)
   End With
Next intCounter
```

10.4.2 Use the most specific data type possible in a *For Each...Next* loop. The element variable in a *For Each...Next* loop must be a Variant or some type of Object (generic or specific) variable. Variants have many drawbacks (as discussed in Chapter 6, "Variables"). If you use a Variant or generic Object when a specific Object type would work, you prevent Visual Basic from determining errors at compile time (such as referencing properties that don't exist for that type).

Incorrect:
```
Dim vntControl As Variant

'* Force a refresh of all text boxes on the form.
For Each vntControl In Me.Controls

   '* Check to see whether this control is a text box.
   If TypeName(vntControl) = "TextBox" Then
```

(continued)

```
        vntControl.Refresh
    End If

Next vntControl
```

Also incorrect:

```
Dim objControl As Object

'* Force a refresh of all text boxes on the form.
For Each objControl In Me.Controls

    '* Check to see whether this control is a text box.
    If TypeName(objControl) = "TextBox" Then
       objControl.Refresh
    End If

Next objControl
```

Correct:

```
Dim ctl As Control

'* Force a refresh of all text boxes on the form.
For Each ctl In Me.Controls

    '* Check to see whether this control is a text box.
    If TypeName(ctl) = "TextBox" Then
       ctl.Refresh
    End If

Next ctl
```

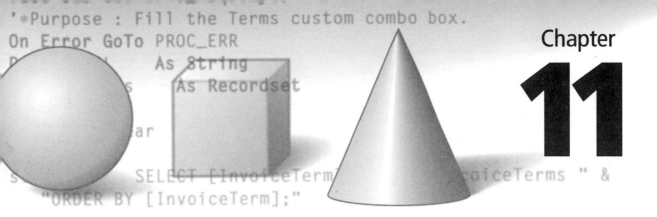

```
'*Purpose : Fill the Terms custom combo box.
On Error GoTo PROC_ERR
                As String
            As Recordset

      ar

        SELECT [InvoiceTerm                    oiceTerms " &
"ORDER BY [InvoiceTerm];"

Set restTerms = db.OpenRecordset(strSQL, dbOpenForwardOnly)

Do WHile Not rstTerms.EOF
    boTerms.AddItem rstTerms![InvoiceTerm]
```

Controlling Code Flow

```
Loop

OC_EXIT:
rstTerms.C
Set rstTer

Exit Sub
```

Rarely is a process within code accomplished with a single procedure that executes from the top down. Most processes are accomplished with multiple procedures, sometimes including more than one module. If you follow the execution path of a particular process, you'll usually experience many twists and turns, often spurred by decisions based on the evaluation of an expression. Initiating the given process a second time might cause an entirely different path of execution if even a single condition within the program has changed, such as the user entering new text in a text box. Frequently, the multiple paths of execution cause code to take on a rather labyrinthine appearance. Obviously, the ability to easily discern the changes in the execution path is important for being able to read the code and debug it.

As I've said, the decisions that create the twists and turns of an executing process are often made based on the evaluation of an expression or multiple expressions. Thus, it's important to make the decision points in the flow of code as understandable as possible. This involves knowing what branching structure to use in a situation, as well as when to use it. For instance, you need to know when using *Select Case* is more appropriate than using *If...Then...Else*. Using the proper construct in the proper place will make your code easier to read and make it easier to include additional expressions at a later time.

Regardless of the decision construct you implement in a given situation, you'll have to evaluate an expression. Most expressions can be written in many different ways; nevertheless, there's generally only one preferred way to write any given expression. Writing expressions correctly is critical, and I'll provide many Practical Applications in this chapter to help you create proper expressions. At best, poorly written expressions are difficult to read and understand. At worst, such expressions might cause the program to fail.

 OTE All decision constructs must follow strict indentation rules. See Chapter 8, "Formatting Code," for specific information on proper indentation.

Goals of Controlling Code Flow

Your goals when controlling code flow should include

- Using the correct decision structure in a given situation
- Reducing complexity so that code is easier to read and debug
- Minimizing the chance for errors in expression evaluations

Directives

11.1 Use *If...Then...Else* when the decision is based on one condition being True or False.

If...Then is well suited for making a decision based on the evaluation of a single condition, and it's the most commonly used decision construct. *If...Then* has the following syntax:

```
If condition Then statement
```

or

```
If condition Then
    [statements]
End If
```

If *condition* evaluates to True, the *statement* or *statements* are executed. If *condition* evaluates to False, the *statement* or *statements* are not executed. Expressions can be simple or complex. Regardless of complexity, the expression used for *condition* must evaluate to True or False. For instance, all the following expressions are valid for *condition*.

```
sngCoordinate >= 8
strFirstName = "Adam"
blnInHere
```

Although at first glance the last item doesn't appear to be a condition, remember that a condition always evaluates to either True or False. Since *blnInHere* refers to a Boolean variable (as denoted by its prefix), *blnInHere* inherently evaluates to True or False and is therefore a valid condition.

 OTE   If *condition* evaluates to a numerical value, Microsoft Visual Basic interprets the result as True or False; a zero value is considered False, and all nonzero numeric values are considered True.

To execute a statement or a set of statements when *condition* evaluates to False, use an *Else* statement. All statements between *Else* and *End If* are executed when *condition* evaluates to False. All statements between *If...Then* and *Else* execute only if *condition* evaluates to True; never do both sets of statements execute in a single pass through an *If...End If* construct.

Practical Applications

11.1.1   **Consider using *End If*, even if only one statement is executed.** If only one statement executes when *condition* evaluates to True, the statement can be put on the same line as *If* and *End If* can be omitted. However, to make the code more legible, you might consider placing the statement on its own line and closing the construct with *End If*.

Incorrect:
```
'* If locking conflicts were encountered, build this information
'* into the message string.
If lngLockingConflicts > 0 Then strMessage = strMessage & ", " & _
                               lngLockingConflicts & _
                               " contact(s) could not be added " & _
                               "due to locking conflicts!"
```

Correct:

```
'* If locking conflicts were encountered, build this information
'* into the message string.
If lngLockingConflicts > 0 Then
    strMessage = strMessage & ", " & lngLockingConflicts & _
                " contact(s) could not be added due to " & _
                "locking conflicts!"
End If
```

11.1.2 Don't assume that Visual Basic will short-circuit a compound condition. When creating an *If…Then* decision structure, it's possible to create a compound condition composed of multiple smaller conditions. Consider the following code:

```
If Not ((rstAlarms Is Nothing) Or (rstAlarms.EOF)) Then
    rstAlarms.Delete
End If
```

This decision structure attempts to delete a record if the Recordset's *EOF* (end-of-file) property is False. First, the *If* statement makes sure that the variable *rstAlarms* actually contains a Recordset, and then it makes sure that the *EOF* property is False. This code, however, has the potential to generate a run-time error.

If *rstAlarms* doesn't contain a Recordset (*rstAlarms Is Nothing* evaluates to True), you might think that Visual Basic wouldn't evaluate the second part of the condition, which is *rstAlarms.EOF*. With an *Or* compound condition, if either of the individual conditions evaluates to True, the entire condition evaluates to True. Therefore, with the first part of the compound condition being True (*rstAlarms Is Nothing*), there's really no need to evaluate the second part. Unfortunately, this is not how Visual Basic behaves: Visual Basic evaluates each component of a compound condition regardless of whether it's necessary. In this example, if *rstAlarms* indeed contains no Recordset, attempting to determine whether the Recordset's *EOF* property is True causes a run-time error. Some programming languages evaluate the individual conditions (from left to right) in a compound condition only until the value of the compound condition is clear. The remaining individual conditions are not evaluated and therefore cannot cause run-time errors. This behavior is called *short-circuiting*, and although it works nicely in some languages, relying on it in Visual Basic creates potential land mines in your code.

Incorrect:
```
Public Function FirstValidItemID() As String
    '* Purpose  :  Return the ItemID of the first item in
    '*              tblPhysicalInventory.
    '* Returns  :  The ItemID of the first item, if it has one.
    '*              Otherwise returns "<not valid>".
    Dim strSQL        As String
    Dim rstInventory  As Recordset

    Const c_NotValid = "<not valid>"


    '* Open tblPhysicalInventory.
    Set rstInventory = dbInventory.OpenRecordset _
                    ("tblPhysicalInventory", dbOpenForwardOnly)

    '* Since the Recordset is ForwardOnly, it will be positioned
    '* on the first record if there are any records.
    '* Check to see whether the first record has an ItemID.
    If Not (rstInventory.EOF) And rstInventory![ItemID] <> "" Then
        FirstValidItemID = rstInventory![ItemID]
    Else
        FirstValidItemID = c_NotValid
    End If

PROC_EXIT:
    Exit Function


End Function
```

Correct:
```
Public Function FirstValidItemID() As String
    '* Purpose  :  Return the ItemID of the first item in
    '*              tblPhysicalInventory.
    '* Returns  :  The ItemID of the first item, if it has one.
    '*              Otherwise returns "<not valid>".
    Dim strSQL        As String
    Dim rstInventory  As Recordset

    Const c_NotValid = "<not valid>"


    '* Open tblPhysicalInventory.
    Set rstInventory = dbInventory.OpenRecordset _
                    ("tblPhysicalInventory", dbOpenForwardOnly)
```

(continued)

```
'* Default the return value as "<not valid>".
FirstValidItemID = c_NotValid

'* Since the Recordset is ForwardOnly, it will be positioned
'* on the first record if there are any records.
'* Check to see whether there are any records.
If Not (rstInventory.EOF) Then

    '* There is a record; return the Item ID if it has one.
    If rstInventory![ItemID] <> "" Then
        FirstValidItemID = rstInventory![ItemID]
    End If

End If

PROC_EXIT:
    Exit Function

End Function
```

11.2   Use *Select Case* when comparing a non-Boolean expression to a variety of possible values.

When evaluating an expression that has only two possible values (True or False), *If...Then* is the best decision construct to use. If you must take some action when the expression evaluates to False as well as when it evaluates to True, add an *Else* clause. Because there's no easy way to use *If...Then* to compare an expression to more than two possible values, however, *Select Case* becomes the best choice in that situation. A typical *Select Case* construct has the following syntax:

```
Select Case testexpression
    [Case expressionlist1
        [statementblock-1]]
    [Case expressionlist2
        [statementblock-2]]
    ⋮
    [Case Else
        [statementblock-n]]
End Select
```

 OTE   *Select Case* can be used in many advanced ways, including putting multiple result values on a single *Case* line. My intent in this chapter is simply to show you when to use it and how to use it properly.

At times, you might find that you want to perform an action only when a given condition is True. If the condition evaluates to False, you want to evaluate a second condition and execute code based on the results of this new condition. You can create quite complex decision structures by using this method. The following shows a skeleton of just such a decision construct:

```
If condition1 Then
    ⋮
ElseIf condition2 Then
    ⋮
ElseIf condition3 Then
    ⋮
Else
    ⋮
End If
```

Notice that these conditions can be entirely unrelated. This is in contrast to the *Select Case* structure where the conditions are formed by successively comparing one (typically non-Boolean) test expression to each of the expressions in the *Case* statements. If you find that you are evaluating the same expression and comparing it to a variety of possible values, you should use *Select Case* rather than *If...Then...ElseIf...End If*.

Incorrect:
```
'* Set the pushed state of the proper option button in the control
'* array.
If rstTask![Type] = "Phone Call" Then
    optType(c_PhoneCall).Value = True

ElseIf rstTask![Type] = "Appointment" Then
    optType(c_Appointment).Value = True

ElseIf rstTask![Type] = "To-do" Then
    optType(c_Todo).Value = True

End If
```

Correct:
```
'* Set the pushed state of the proper option button in the control
'* array.
Select Case rstTask![Type]
    Case Is = "Phone Call"
        optType(c_PhoneCall).Value = True
```

(continued)

```
      Case Is = "Appointment"
         optType(c_Appointment).Value = True

      Case Is = "To-do"
         optType(c_Todo).Value = True

      Case Else
         '* No other values are expected.
   End Select
```

 OTE   You can use *Select Case* in ways that might not be immediately apparent. For instance, when you have a number of option buttons on a form, you often need to determine which of the option buttons is selected (*Value = True*). If you consider True as your test expression, you can create a fairly nifty construct to determine which option button is selected:

```
   '* Determine which option button is selected.
   Select Case True
      Case Is = optDragBehavior(c_CopyFile).Value
         ⋮
      Case Is = optDragBehavior(c_MoveFile).Value
         ⋮
      Case Is = optDragBehavior(c_CreateShortcut).Value
         ⋮
      Case Else
         '* There are no further option buttons in this array.
   End Select
```

Practical Applications

11.2.1   Always include a *Case Else* with every *Select Case* construct, even when it's not needed.   Generally, you design a *Select Case* construct such that it handles every possible value of *testexpression*. *Case Else* is useful for creating code to execute when none of your specifically expected results are encountered. However, many developers often leave out *Case Else* if they've included *Case* statements for all expected results. In general, it's a good idea to always include *Case Else*. If you want to ignore the results not specifically accounted for in the *Case* statements, simply note this in a comment in the *Case Else* clause. If you firmly believe that no value would cause *Case Else* to execute—that is, if all possible results are accounted for in the *Case* statements—consider raising an error in the

Case Else clause. That way, if a value slips through—which could happen if additional possible results are created during future development and the *Select Case* structure is not properly updated—you'll know about it. Always including a *Case Else* clause makes your code more self-documenting and you don't force other developers to guess your intentions for handling results not specifically accounted for in *Case* statements.

Incorrect:

```
Select Case m_intActiveSearchType
    Case Is = c_ListSearch
        txtSearch.Text = grdListFind.Columns(c_ListFindName)

    Case Is = c_PhoneSearch
        txtSearch.Text = grdPhones.Columns(c_PhoneFindName)

    Case Is = c_PriceBookSearch
        txtSearch.Text = grdPriceBook.Columns(c_PriceBookFindName)

End Select
```

Correct:

```
Select Case m_intActiveSearchType
    Case Is = c_ListSearch
        txtSearch.Text = grdListFind.Columns(c_ListFindName)

    Case Is = c_PhoneSearch
        txtSearch.Text = grdPhones.Columns(c_PhoneFindName)

    Case Is = c_PriceBookSearch
        txtSearch.Text = grdPriceBook.Columns(c_PriceBookFindName)

    Case Else
        '* All possible values should be covered, but just in case…
        MsgBox "Unexpected value encountered for " & _
            "m_intActiveSearchType in " & Me.Name & _
            " | txtSearch_KeyDown.", vbCritical
End Select
```

11.2.2   Use an intelligible ordering sequence for all *Case* statements.
The order of the various *Case* statements in a *Select Case* construct might seem superficial, but it's often quite important. When ordering the statements, consider speed and readability. When a *Select Case* statement is

encountered, the *Case* statements are evaluated in their listed order until a condition is found to be True. In a large list of items, and when speed is the primary concern, you might consider putting the most frequently expected values at the top of the *Case* list. More often than not, however, speed is second in importance to readability and ease of maintenance. In these cases, put the list of items in alphabetical or numerical order, which makes it easier to debug the code and to add new values to the *Case* list.

Incorrect:

```
Select Case rstBilling![Basis]
    Case Is = "Metered"
        Call ComputeMeteredContract

    Case Is = "Hourly"
        Call ComputeHourlyContract

    Case Is = "Units"
        Call ComputeUnitsContract

    Case Is = "Incidents"
        Call ComputeIncidentsContract

End Select
```

Correct:

```
Select Case rstBilling![Basis]
    Case Is = "Hourly"
        Call ComputeHourlyContract

    Case Is = "Incidents"
        Call ComputeIncidentsContract

    Case Is = "Metered"
        Call ComputeMeteredContract

    Case Is = "Units"
        Call ComputeUnitsContract

    Case Else
        '* No other values are expected.
End Select
```

11.2.3 **Don't create a *Case* statement that will never produce a True result.** When creating *Select Case* structures that evaluate a numeric value, you can create *Case* statements that never produce a True result. This usually occurs as a result of incorrectly ordering the *Case* statements, causing an earlier statement to evaluate to True before a later statement is encountered. Notice how the *Case Is <= 0* statement in the incorrect code below never evaluates to True. A value of less than 0 causes the preceding *Case* statement (*Case Is <= 5*) to evaluate to True, stopping all further evaluations.

Incorrect:

```
Select Case sngTaxRate
    Case Is <= 5

    Case Is <= 0

    Case Is <= 10

    Case Else

End Select
```

Correct:

```
Select Case sngTaxRate
    Case Is <= 0

    Case Is <= 5

    Case Is <= 10

    Case Else

End Select
```

11.3 Use end-of-line comments to add clarity to nested decision structures.

Chapter 9, "Commenting Code," describes the proper way to comment a program in great detail. Although Chapter 9 argues that in-line comments are superior to end-of-line comments, end-of-line comments are appropriate at times—for example, when nested decision structures significantly complicate code. In long procedures, it can be difficult to determine which end-of-construct statement (*End Select* or *End If*) corresponds to which beginning-of-construct statement. In these situations, use an end-of-line comment after the last statement of each decision structure to state which decision construct the closing statement belongs to.

OTE If you prefer, you can use end-of-line comments after the terminating statements of all your decision structures, regardless of whether they're part of a nested group.

Incorrect:

```
If otnumHours.Value <= 0 Then
    MsgBox "This is an hourly contract. You must enter a positive " & _
        "number of hours", vbExclamation
    otnumHours.SetFocus
Else
    '* Determine whether the user has entered a rate.
    If otnumRate.Value > 0 Then
        otnumPrice.Value = otnumHours.Value * otnumRate.Value
    Else
        If otnumPrice.Value > 0 Then
            '* No rate entered; check whether a contract price is set.
            '* If a contract price is set, figure the rate based on the
            '* hours entered.
            otnumRate.Value = otnumPrice.Value / otnumHours.Value
        End If
    End If
End If
```

Correct:

```
'* Make sure the user has entered a positive number of hours.
If otnumHours.Value <= 0 Then
    MsgBox "This is an hourly contract. You must enter a positive " & _
        "number of hours", vbExclamation
    otnumHours.SetFocus
Else

    '* Determine whether the user has entered a rate.
    If otnumRate.Value > 0 Then
        otnumPrice.Value = otnumHours.Value * otnumRate.Value
    Else

        '* There is no rate entered, see if there is a price.
        If otnumPrice.Value > 0 Then
            '* A contract price is set. Figure the rate based on the
            '* hours entered.
            otnumRate.Value = otnumPrice.Value / otnumHours.Value
        End If    '* otnumPrice.Value > 0

    End If    '* otnumRate.Value > 0

End If    '* otnumHours.Value <= 0
```

11.4 Format expressions for accurate evaluation and ease of understanding.

The evaluation of expressions is at the heart of creating decision structures. Most expressions can be written in multiple ways. Properly formatting an expression reduces the possibility of errors in your code and increases its readability. Since most expressions used in decision structures evaluate to a Boolean value (True or False), correctly working with Boolean expressions is crucial.

Practical Applications

11.4.1 Never compare a Boolean expression to True or False. This seems like a basic principle, but it's one that is often violated. Boolean values *are* True or False, so there's no need to compare them to True or False. The incorrect code below came from a well-respected Visual Basic magazine. Lack of a naming convention aside, this procedure suffers from a case of overcomplication. *BOF* and *EOF* are properties of the Recordset object that indicate that the Recordset is at beginning-of-file or end-of-file, respectively. Each can be either True or False. Since they are inherently Boolean values, comparing them directly to True or False makes the code cluttered and can decrease performance.

Incorrect:

```
Public Function IsEmptyRecordset(rs As Recordset) As Boolean
    IsEmptyRecordset = ((rs.BOF = True) And (rs.EOF = True))
End Function
```

Correct:

```
Public Function IsEmptyRecordset(rs As Recordset) As Boolean
    IsEmptyRecordset = rs.BOF And rs.EOF
End Function
```

11.4.2 Create Boolean variable names that reflect the positive rather than the negative. A classic case of overcomplicating a procedure is creating a Boolean variable name that reflects the negative of some condition. Basing decisions on such variables adds an unnecessary layer of complexity—for instance, why call a variable *blnNotLoaded* when *blnLoaded* works just as well and is easier for the mind to deal with? When you work with the negative, you increase the chances for errors in your code because you might not catch problems as you write them. This isn't not like using double negatives in a sentence—get it? If you must deal with the negative, use *Not* on the positive form of the variable rather than using the negative form of the variable.

Incorrect:

```
Dim blnInvalidTemplate As Boolean

'* Attempt to open the template. The function OpenTemplate returns
'* success or failure.
blnInvalidTemplate = Not (OpenTemplate(strTemplateName))

'* If the template is invalid, get out.
If blnInvalidTemplate Then
    GoTo PROC_EXIT
End If
```

Correct:

```
Dim blnValidTemplate As Boolean

'* Attempt to open the template. The function OpenTemplate returns
'* success or failure.
blnValidTemplate = OpenTemplate(strTemplateName)

'* If the template is invalid, get out.
If Not (blnValidTemplate) Then
    GoTo PROC_EXIT
End If
```

11.4.3 Use parentheses in expressions for clarity, even when they're not required. Parentheses are used in algebraic expressions to override the traditional order of operations. For instance, standard order of operations dictates that multiplication takes place before addition. So, the statement *Debug.Print 1 + 5 * 6* prints the value 31. To override this behavior, you use parentheses. Items in parentheses are evaluated first. For instance, *Debug.Print (1 + 5) * 6* prints 36. Although you don't have to provide parentheses if you want to use the traditional order of operations, you should use them anyway to add clarity to complicated expressions.

Incorrect:

```
'* Compute the height and width of the editable area.
m_sngEditWidth = m_sngImageWidth * m_intMagnification + 1
m_sngEditHeight = m_sngImageHeight * m_intMagnification + 1
```

Correct:

```
'* Compute the height and width of the editable area.
m_sngEditWidth = (m_sngImageWidth * m_intMagnification) + 1
m_sngEditHeight = (m_sngImageHeight * m_intMagnification) + 1
```

11.4.4 Make code flow obvious. When writing decision structures, make the flow of the code as obvious as possible. Pen and paper shouldn't be required for someone to figure out your intentions. The incorrect code below was also culled from a well-known Visual Basic publication. Can you easily tell exactly what's happening here? The code is setting the *Cancel* parameter equal to the result of the *MsgBox* function. No...the return value of the function is compared to *vbCancel*, and the result (True or False) is what's stored in the *Cancel* parameter. Why make the reader work so hard? The revised code performs the same function without any real loss of performance, and it's much easier to understand.

Incorrect:

```
Private Sub Form_Unload(Cancel As Integer)
    Cancel = (MsgBox("Quit Now?", vbOKCancel Or _
              vbQuestion, "Confirmation Demo") = vbCancel)
End Sub
```

Correct:

```
Private Sub Form_Unload(Cancel As Integer)

    '* Check to see whether the user clicked Cancel.
    If MsgBox("Quit Now?", vbOKCancel Or _
         vbQuestion, "Confirmation Demo") = vbCancel Then
       Cancel = True
    End If

End Sub
```

11.5 Refrain from using *GoSub* whenever possible.

The ability to use *GoSub* in code dates back to the early days of Basic, when code was linear rather than procedural. *GoSub* allows you to create a "pseudosubroutine." A *GoSub* <label> statement causes execution to jump to the specified label, which must be in the same procedure as the *GoSub* statement. A *Return* statement causes execution to return to the line following the *GoSub* statement. *GoSubs* make code difficult to read and debug. With the advent of procedure-based, event-driven code, a *GoSub* is rarely needed. If you find yourself writing a *GoSub*, ask yourself whether the code that you branch to could be handled in-line within the procedure. If not, determine whether it could be turned into a separate procedure. If it can, chances are good that creating a separate procedure is a better approach.

The one time *GoSub* really comes in handy is when the code in the pseudosubroutine works on a large number of variables local to the procedure. Under certain rare circumstances, the overhead and hassle of passing many local variables to another routine make *GoSub* a better proposition.

11.6 Use *GoTo* only when there are no other alternatives or when jumping to an error handler or single exit point.

Although the venerable *GoTo* statement has been used to force execution to a specific line in a procedure for quite some time, *GoTo* statements make code difficult to follow because they often redirect the execution path in unintuitive ways. *GoTo* is perfect, however, for jumping to a single exit point and for jumping to an error handler; otherwise, there's usually a better way to write a process than by using *GoTo*. Rarely, if ever, should a *GoTo* statement send code execution *back* in a procedure (using *GoTo PROC_EXIT* in an error handler comes to mind). Often, when a *GoTo* statement sends execution back, some sort of standard looping construct would be a better solution. The following code illustrates how code with a *GoTo* statement can be better written as a *Do* loop.

Incorrect:
```
Private Function StripDoubleQuotes(strString As String) As String
    '* Purpose  :  Double quotes cause errors in SQL statements.
    '*               This procedure strips them from the entered text
    '*               and replaces them with single quotes.
    '* Accepts  :  strString - the string in which to search for
    '*                           double quotes.
    '* Returns  :  The original string with all double quotes replaced
    '*               with single quotes.
    On Error GoTo PROC_ERR
    Dim intLocation As Integer

    Const c_DoubleQuote = """"
```

```
START_CHECK:
      intLocation = InStr(strString, c_DoubleQuote)

      '* Determine whether or not a double quote was found.
      If intLocation > 0 Then
        '* There is at least one double quote.
        Mid$(strString, intLocation, 1) = "'"
        GoTo START_CHECK
      Else
        StripDoubleQuotes = strString
      End If

PROC_EXIT:
  Exit Function

PROC ERR:
  Call ShowError(Me.Name, "StripDoubleQuotes", Err.Number, _
                Err.Description)
  GoTo PROC_EXIT

End Function
```

Correct:

```
Public Function StripDoubleQuotes(ByVal strString As String) As String
   '* Purpose  :  Double quotes cause errors in SQL statements.
   '*               This procedure strips them from the entered text
   '*               and replaces them with single quotes.
   '* Accepts  :  strString - the string in which to search for
   '*                          double quotes.
   '* Returns  :  The original string with all double quotes replaced
   '*               with single quotes.
   On Error GoTo PROC_EXIT
   Dim intLocation    As Integer
   Dim strText        As String
   Dim blnQuotesFound As Boolean

   Const c_DoubleQuote = """"

   blnQuotesFound = False

   '* Determine whether or not a double quote was found.
   Do
      intLocation = InStr(1, strString, c_DoubleQuote)

      '* See whether a double quote was found.
      If intLocation > 0 Then
         Mid$(strString, intLocation, 1) = "'"
         blnQuotesFound = True
```

(continued)

```
        Else
            blnQuotesFound = False
        End If

    '* Continue looking for double quotes until none are found.
    Loop While blnQuotesFound

    StripDoubleQuotes = strString

PROC_EXIT:
    Exit Function

PROC_ERR:
    Call ShowError(Me.Name, "StripDoubleQuotes", Err.Number, _
                   Err.Description)
    GoTo PROC_EXIT

End Function
```

Practical Application

11.6.1 Use all uppercase letters for *GoTo* labels. *GoTo* statements make code hard to read. Reduce the amount of effort required to scan a procedure for *GoTo* labels by using all uppercase letters for those labels.

Incorrect:

```
Private Sub lvwPhones_MouseDown(Button As Integer, Shift As Integer, _
    x As Single, y As Single)
    '* Purpose  :  Ensure that the item clicked is always selected,
    '*               even if clicked with the right mouse button.
    On Error GoTo proc_err

    '* Determine whether there is a list item where the user clicked.
    If lvwPhones.HitTest(x, y) Is Nothing Then
        Set lvwPhones.SelectedItem = Nothing
    Else
        '* There is a list item where the user clicked. Select it now.
        lvwPhones.SelectedItem = lvwPhones.HitTest(x, y)
    End If

proc_exit:
    Exit Sub

proc_err:
    Call ShowError(Me.Name, "lvwPhones_MouseDown", Err.Number, _
                   Err.Description)
    GoTo proc_exit

End Sub
```

Correct:

```
Private Sub lvwPhones_MouseDown(Button As Integer, Shift As Integer, _
    x As Single, y As Single)
    '* Purpose  :  Ensure that the item clicked is always selected,
    '*               even if clicked with the right mouse button.
    On Error GoTo PROC_ERR

    '* Determine whether there is a list item where the user clicked.
    If lvwPhones.HitTest(x, y) Is Nothing Then
        Set lvwPhones.SelectedItem = Nothing
    Else
        '* There is a list item where the user clicked. Select it now.
        lvwPhones.SelectedItem = lvwPhones.HitTest(x, y)
    End If

PROC_EXIT:
    Exit Sub

PROC_ERR:
    Call ShowError(Me.Name, "lvwPhones_MouseDown", Err.Number, _
                Err.Description)
    GoTo PROC_EXIT

End Sub
```

User Interaction

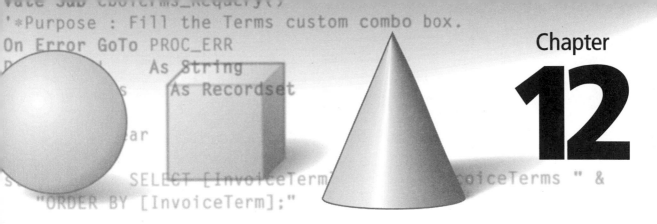

Interface Design

The primary purpose of this book is to provide a set of standards for writing professional and maintainable code. As I've repeatedly stressed, well-written code usually performs better than poorly written code and is almost always easier to maintain. But, regardless of how wonderful and productive your code is, users typically interact with your application's interface, not its code. Many books deal with the intricacies of interface design, and many are quite good, including *About Face: The Essentials of User Interface Design* (IDG Books Worldwide, 1995), *Developing User Interfaces for Microsoft Windows* (Microsoft Press, 1999), and *The Windows Interface Guidelines for Software Design* (Microsoft Press, 1995). These books don't just teach how to create good interfaces; they also get into theories of what makes a good interface and why.

This chapter and the next focus on the interface of your program and the interaction between the interface and the user. This chapter concentrates on the interface itself, and the next chapter deals with user interaction. Of course, this chapter can't completely cover the subject of designing interfaces with Microsoft Visual Basic. Instead, it's meant to give you specific, practical information on creating better interfaces. Its Directives and Practical Applications address some of the more common interface mistakes and will help you build tighter and more intuitive interfaces.

The Necessity of Consistent Interface Design

Developing for Microsoft Windows has many benefits. When creating a Windows application, you don't have to focus on the foundation of the interface design. For instance, Windows already contains the code for drawing forms, complete with menus, Minimize and Maximize buttons, and a border. Windows draws forms consistently, using system colors and standard sizes for common elements. DOS application developers, on the other hand, had to individually create their own interfaces, which led to a bewildering amount of variety. Switching from one DOS program to another was more than just a physical task (usually requiring that the first program be shut down before the second was started); it required a mental leap as well. The general behavior of each DOS program was often so unique that you couldn't apply techniques or skills learned in one program to a different program.

Over time, experience taught users and developers alike what worked well and what didn't. Eventually, common interface elements evolved. For instance, we take for granted that every application we run in Windows gives us a nice menu bar at the top of the program's main window. Not all DOS programs offered a menu bar (although most eventually did). When Windows came along, it freed programmers (somewhat) from the details of the basic interface. This sometimes means that developers must give up flexibility, but the trade-off is usually more than worth it.

Although developers benefited from the standardized approach of Windows, users gained the most from that approach. Users quickly became accustomed to the interface of Windows, and just as quickly they became intolerant of programs that didn't adhere to the Windows standards. For example, if a user could print in three of her favorite programs simply by pressing Ctrl+P, it became unacceptable to have to press Alt+P in other programs. As developers, we're always focusing on reusable code. Users want *reusable knowledge*.

Microsoft Office is a good example of the advantages of interface standardization. Whether you love it or hate it, you have to respect what the

Office interface offers users. Switching from one Office program to another, a user is empowered by the fact that commonality in features between the two programs equates to commonality in interaction. If you want to view or change the main options of a program, you look on the Tools menu for an Options item. Creating a new document is always performed from the File menu. If you're looking for the New, Save, or Print buttons on the toolbar, you always look to its left side; when you need to access Help, you look on the right side of the toolbar. If no toolbar button is available for Help, you look on the Help menu or simply press F1. Through such consistency, Office gives users the ability to leverage skills across applications.

Interface consistency spans many levels. At the highest level, all Windows programs have a common interface—the Windows interface. (For example, dialog boxes that allow users to close them have an X in the upper right corner, and all forms are drawn using common system colors and sizes.) The next level is application consistency. Office again serves as an excellent example. Toolbars have a similar appearance, including common icons and a common order of buttons. The location of menu items and the assignation of their associated shortcut keys are also standardized. The mechanics of shortcut key behavior is consistent among Windows applications. You have complete freedom to assign specific shortcut keys to different menu items in your own application; nevertheless, you should attempt to create shortcuts that are consistent with common Windows programs. Creating application consistency demands attention to detail and considerable effort.

The next layer, and the focus of this chapter, is general design consistency. When you look at two dialog boxes in two different programs, they should seem very similar, as though they could both be part of the same program even though their content and purpose might be very different. Windows handles much of this detail by performing all the drawing routines, such as drawing a form or a combo box. However, it's up to you to use a combo box where appropriate and to assign properties that make sense to forms and controls. For instance, why give a dialog box a sizeable border or a Maximize button if doesn't resize its contents? Why create a set of 12 option buttons when a single combo box can be used? In this chapter, you'll learn to avoid these mistakes and to apply a set of standards to your interfaces to give them an appearance and behavior consistent with popular Windows applications and Windows itself.

Goals of Consistency in Interface Design

The goals of consistency in interface design are

- Creating interfaces that are consistent within a program, as well as across applications

- Allowing users to leverage their existing skills (that is, to apply reusable knowledge)

- Reducing user confusion and frustration

- Producing visually attractive interfaces to build user confidence and satisfaction

Directives

12.1   Give forms a consistent appearance and behavior.

Forms are the building blocks of a program's interface; if an application has a user interface, it has at least one form. Although forms are very common, many developers design them poorly. When you add a new form to a project, Visual Basic creates an empty form from a template. Usually the properties of the new form are inappropriate for the type of form you want to create. By following the Practical Applications listed in this directive, you'll create better forms.

Practical Applications

12.1.1   **Assign the proper border style to every form.** When you add a new form to a project, Visual Basic automatically sets the form's

BorderStyle property to Sizable. More often than not, this setting is inappropriate. If a form doesn't resize its contents when the form's size is changed, chances are the border should not be sizeable. Forms are regularly used to create dialog boxes—windows that gather information from the user. Such dialog boxes aren't supposed to have resizeable borders. The following sections describe the possible values for *BorderStyle* and give recommendations for when to use each value.

Fixed Dialog   When *BorderStyle* is set to Fixed Dialog, the form has a solid border that can't be resized. (See Figure 12-1.) This is the most common border style for forms. A form with fixed borders can (and should) have a title bar and can have a control-menu box. However, you cannot put a Minimize or Maximize button on such a form; it stands to reason that if a form can't be resized, you shouldn't be able to maximize it. If you want to include a Minimize button on such a form, which is a valid idea, you must use the Fixed Single style, which I'll discuss in a moment.

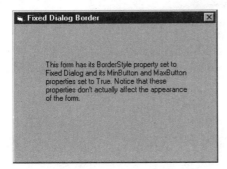

Figure 12-1.   *A form with its* BorderStyle *property set to Fixed Dialog makes an excellent dialog box. Such forms cannot be resized.*

 OTE   When a form's *BorderStyle* is set to Fixed Dialog, you can set its *MinButton* and *MaxButton* properties to True, but the corresponding buttons won't appear on the form.

None   In general, every form should have a border. When a form doesn't have a border, it also lacks a title bar and a control-menu box. As a result, a form without a border can't be resized or closed without special code. (See Figure 12-2.) Such deviation from standard behavior frustrates users. Most users run multiple applications at the same time—after all, this is a big reason to use Windows in the first place—and not having the ability to move a form out of the way of another program is more than a bit annoying. Unless you have an incredibly good reason to do otherwise, give all forms borders.

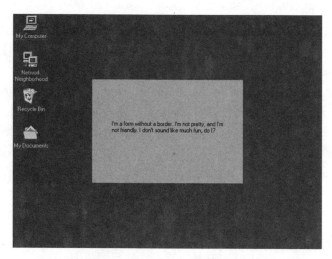

Figure 12-2. *Forms without borders violate good design principles. The valid occasions for using such forms are rare.*

Fixed Single   A form with *BorderStyle* set to Fixed Single has the same border as forms with *BorderStyle* set to Fixed Dialog. (See Figure 12-3.) The only real difference is that you can place Minimize and Maximize buttons on a Fixed Single form but not on a Fixed Dialog form. The ability to put a Maximize button on a form with a fixed border is not all that important. If you're not letting the user manually resize the form, you wouldn't let them make the form larger by maximizing it. However, sometimes the Minimize button is desirable. For instance, you might want to create a palette dialog box from which users can select a color or create their own, and you might decide to let users minimize the dialog box when they're not using it. When the dialog box is minimized rather than closed, all selections in the dialog box persist. When users restore the dialog box, all changes made previously, such as defining a custom color, remain just as they were left.

Figure 12-3.   *A form with* BorderStyle *set to Fixed Single can't have its size adjusted by dragging an edge, but it can contain Minimize and Maximize buttons.*

Sizable   Setting *BorderStyle* to Sizable creates a form with borders that the user can drag to change the size of the form. (See Figure 12-4.) This is the default style for new forms. In general, sizeable borders should be applied only to forms that resize their contents to match the new size designated by the user.

It might be argued that using sizeable borders even for a form that doesn't resize its contents is a good idea because it allows the user to force the form to take up less screen real estate, thereby letting the user get a better view of other screen elements. However, when you size a form smaller than the area needed to display its contents, you drastically reduce the form's effectiveness. (Likewise, if a user sizes a form larger than necessary and it doesn't resize its contents, you end up with a large gray area and a puzzled user. See Figure 12-5.) If you think a user will need to make a form smaller, consider making its border Fixed Single and giving the form a Minimize button.

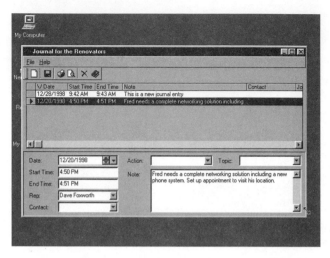

Figure 12-4. *The pointer changes when moved over the border of a sizeable form. The user can then drag the border to change the size of the form.*

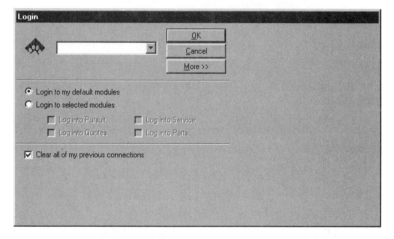

Figure 12-5. *If you let a user resize a form that doesn't adjust its contents accordingly, unpleasant results can occur.*

Fixed ToolWindow and Sizable ToolWindow   The Fixed ToolWindow and Sizable ToolWindow styles are unique, and you don't often run across forms that use these styles. Tool windows are generally small dialog boxes that float over main windows of a program. Tool windows usually host tools or actions that can be applied to the main window. For instance, CorelDraw allows you to open a number of tool windows that float over the program's main drawing surface. (See Figure 12-6.) Tool windows have thinner title bars and smaller title bar text than ordinary windows. The border of a tool window can be fixed or sizeable, and it always has a Close box.

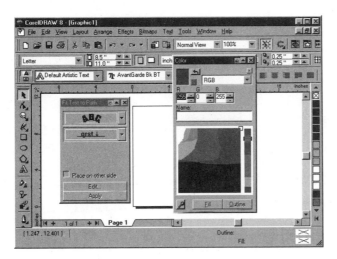

Figure 12-6.   *CorelDraw has many tool windows that float above the drawing surface, providing quick and easy access to various functions.*

 OTE   A form shouldn't be made a tool window arbitrarily, nor should a tool window be used to save screen real estate. The difference in height between a standard title bar and a tool window title bar is too small to make much of a difference.

Consider making a form a tool window if it meets the requirements below. (Note that a form meeting these requirements shouldn't necessarily be a tool window. And if a form doesn't meet these requirements, it's almost certainly not a good candidate for a tool window.)

- The form floats over a main form.

- The form is never displayed modally.

- The form contains tools or actions that affect the main form.

Incorrect:

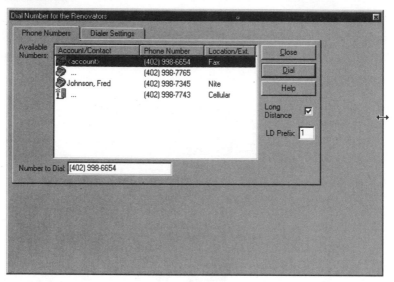

Figure 12-7. *This form doesn't resize its contents, so it should not have a sizeable border. Also, it's not a floating tool window and therefore should not have a tool window title bar.*

Correct:

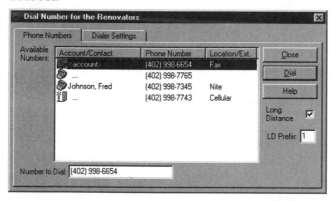

Figure 12-8. *Since this form doesn't resize its contents and is discarded when the user is finished with it, it's considered a dialog box and therefore has a fixed border.*

12.1.2 Give every form an intelligent and consistent startup position. The position you choose for your forms is important for many reasons. If a form doesn't appear in an expected position, the user might not even realize that it's displayed. This can easily occur if the user has multiple forms open. Also, if the user's display size is smaller than the display size of the computer used to create the project, it's possible that the form will appear off the screen!

When a form is first displayed, its position is determined by the value of its *StartUpPosition* property. The *StartUpPosition* property has four possible values:

- Manual
- Center Owner
- Center Screen
- Windows Default

Avoid setting *StartUpPosition* to Manual; unfortunately, it can be easy to inadvertently do this. If you are developing in Visual Basic's SDI (single-document interface) mode—see Figure 12-9—simply moving a form around your screen changes its *StartUpPosition* property to Manual. When that

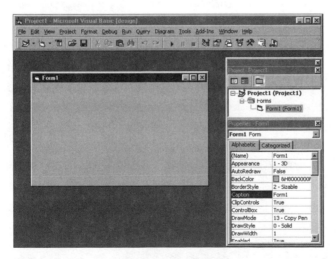

Figure 12-9. *In SDI mode, moving a form changes its* StartUpPosition *property to Manual, and at run time the form appears in the location where it was last saved.*

form displays at run time, it appears in the same location it occupied when the form was last saved. You don't want to do this. When developing in MDI (multiple-document interface) mode, each form is edited in a form designer. (See Figure 12-10.) Moving a form designer does not affect the *StartUpPosition* property of the form it contains. If you develop in

SDI mode (as I do), get in the habit of checking the *StartUpPosition* properties of forms after you've finished working with them to make sure they're as you want them.

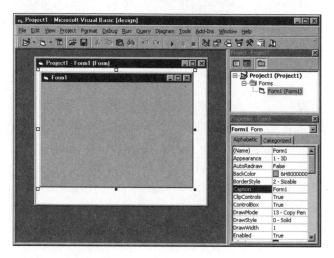

Figure 12-10. *In MDI mode, each form is edited in a form designer. Moving a designer does not affect the form's* StartUpPosition *property.*

The Windows Default value is actually a throwback to earlier days of Windows programming, and it's the default value of the *StartUpPosition* property of all new forms. Forms with this setting appear positioned in the upper left corner of the screen, as shown in Figure 12-11. This is an acceptable, but usually not ideal, location.

Figure 12-11. *Forms with* StartUpPosition *set to Windows Default display in the upper left corner.*

The Center Owner and Center Screen values are usually your best choices. When a form's *StartUpPosition* property is set to Center Screen, the form is displayed dead center on the user's screen, regardless of the screen resolution in effect. When a form's *StartUpPosition* property is set to Center Owner, the form appears centered on top of its owner form. You designate a form's owner when invoking its show method—the second parameter is the new owner:

```
frmMyForm.Show vbModal, Me
```

You can use any valid form reference in place of *Me*, or you can omit the owner assignment altogether. If you don't indicate a specific form as the owner, the desktop becomes the owner of the form and the new form is displayed centered on the desktop (just like with the Center Screen property value). The best approach is to set all of your form's *StartUpPosition* properties to Center Owner. That way forms that have no designated owner, such as the first form displayed by your program, appear centered on the user's screen and subsequent forms appear centered over their owner forms, regardless of where the owners are located. (See Figure 12-12.) Remember: users can drag your forms around—even to different monitors!

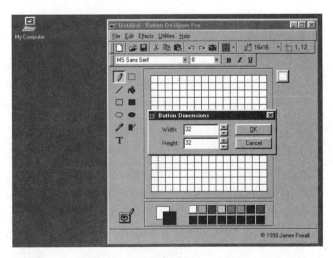

Figure 12-12.   *To make a form appear centered over another form, set the form's* StartUpPosition *property to Center Owner and assign the bottom form as the centered form's owner.*

When displaying a critical dialog box, such as a notification that the printer has run out of paper, display the dialog box centered on the screen so that the user will be more likely to notice it right away.

12.1.3 **Correctly unload forms and free the resources that they consume.** It's a common mistake to think that unloading a form completely destroys it. Actually, when a form is unloaded, only the displayed component is unloaded; the code associated with the form module remains in memory. This means that module-level variables are preserved and that reloading the form is not the same as reinitializing it. The only way to fully unload a form is to set it equal to Nothing:

```
Set frmMyForm = Nothing
```

 OTE   On the companion CD you'll find a project titled Form Unload Example. This simple project illustrates how modules are preserved when a form is unloaded but not set equal to Nothing.

Since you can unload a form from many places, and because a user can unload a form by clicking its Close button, you should set the form equal to Nothing in its *Unload* event. If *Set <form> = Nothing* is the only statement in the *Unload* event, it's relatively safe to use *On Error Resume Next* for the error handler. If you need to put additional statements in the *Unload* event, use a more robust error handler.

Unless a form is specifically designed to retain its values, set the form equal to Nothing in its Unload *event.* Your code will consume fewer resources, and it might perform more reliably and consistently (because each time a form is loaded, a "clean" version of the form will be created).

12.1.4 **Don't create morphing forms.** Morphing forms are forms that drastically change their appearance in response to some condition. Usually, the condition that causes the change is not obvious to the user, who is left completely befuddled. Imagine sitting in your living room watching television. You pop into the kitchen to have a snack. When you come back, the living room is full of different furniture, has different carpeting, and is painted a different color. All because you grabbed a Twinkie instead of a healthful vegetable. You'd be confused, right? This is exactly how a user feels when you start mucking with the appearance of a form.

When you are presenting a lot of information (or sets of information) to the user, consider using multiple specialized forms. If you need to present the information on a single form, use an advanced interface technique. These techniques include

- Tab controls to present categorized information.

- Tree view controls to present hierarchical lists. When the user selects a node, you can change the contents of an associated container control, such as a frame.

- A Microsoft Outlook–style navigation bar to present icons representing distinct items to view. When the user clicks an icon, you can change the contents of an associated container control.

These are not the only ways of presenting complicated data, but they give you a starting point. A form should behave much like a room in a house. In your house, a bathroom has one purpose and the kitchen another. Don't create a form that attempts to perform multiple duties; it will probably end up performing all of them less than adequately.

12.2 Present controls with a standard appearance.

Many programs are datacentric programs and therefore contain lots of text boxes, combo boxes, and label controls. You should follow a few guidelines when presenting these interface elements.

Practical Applications

12.2.1 Assign text boxes and other "single-line" controls the same height as a standard combo box. Since the height of a combo box can't be changed—it's a read-only property—you should always use it as your base height for other single-line controls, such as text boxes. At my company, we prefer to work in pixels, and as a rule we set the *ScaleMode* properties of all our forms to pixels. This makes it easier to remember common settings. For instance, the combo box control has a height of 21 pixels. The odd thing is, new text boxes placed on a form are given a height of 33 pixels—go figure! I don't believe I've ever used a 33-pixel-high text box, nor have I seen one in a commercial program. If the Visual Basic gurus would grant me the one wish of defaulting text box heights to the same height as a combo box, it would save a *lot* of time for everyone involved. Until I find a bottle with a genie in it, however, you'll have to make this change to your text boxes manually. Here's a shortcut I've found that works well:

1. Place all your text boxes and combo boxes on your form.

2. Select a combo box, and then extend the selection to include all the text boxes. Make sure that all controls are selected together by holding down the Ctrl key while selecting them, and *make sure* that a combo box is the first control selected.

3. Double-click the *Height* property in the Properties window. You'll receive the error shown in Figure 12-13, but that's OK. After you click OK, the selected controls will all have the same height as the combo box.

Figure 12-13. *Don't let this error bother you. When changing a property for a number of controls, Visual Basic will change that property for all controls that allow it.*

When you select a group of controls and double-click a property in the Properties window, that property's existing value in the first control you selected is copied to all the controls in the group. In this example, the first control selected was the combo box. When Visual Basic copies the property value to all controls in the group, it attempts to update the property for the combo box as well as for the text boxes. Since the combo box's *Height* property is read-only, the error occurs. This error is benign and only slows you down by a click—definitely worth it!

Incorrect:

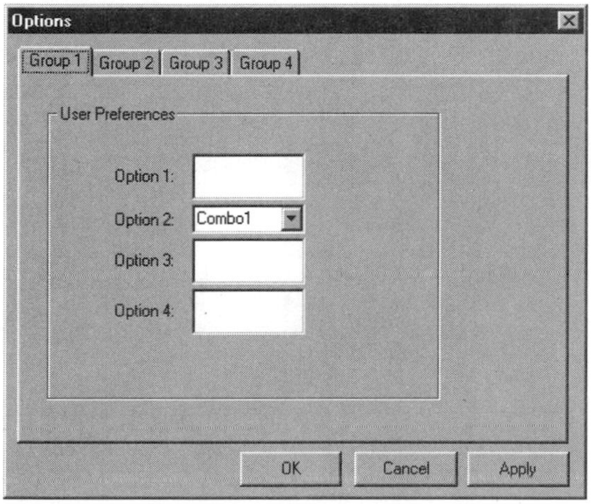

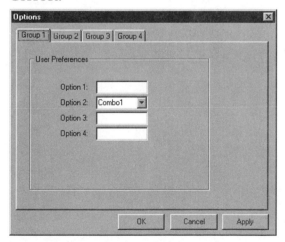

Figure 12-14. *The three text boxes and the combo box all have their default heights. It's pretty hard not to notice the problem.*

Correct:

Figure 12-15. *Give text boxes the same height as the standard combo box to create a visually appealing interface that optimizes the use of space.*

12.2.2   Place labels at the proper vertical location in relation to the controls with which they coincide. Watch out when you place label controls next to other controls such as text boxes and combo boxes. Often, the top of a label isn't properly set according to the top of the control to which it's related. In addition, label text is often given incorrect justification. Figure 12-16 shows a form with all of these problems. I'm sure you don't create forms as bad as this, but the form illustrates the problem.

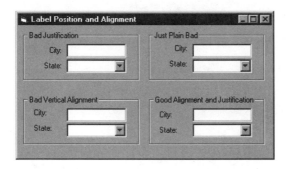

Figure 12-16.   *Properly aligning a label next to its corresponding control and setting the justification to Left Justify makes for a cleaner interface.*

Here are some guidelines to follow when using label controls:

■ Set each label's *Autosize* property to True unless you have a specific reason to do otherwise.

■ Set each label's *BackStyle* property to Transparent unless you have a specific reason to do otherwise.

■ Set the *Top* property of the label to four pixels greater than the *Top* property of the label's related control. This can be inconvenient to set up because the Visual Basic alignment tools won't do this for you. However, your form will have a better and more consistent appearance.

■ Label captions should end with a colon (:).

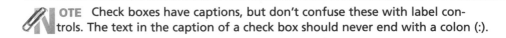 **OTE**   Check boxes have captions, but don't confuse these with label controls. The text in the caption of a check box should never end with a colon (:).

12.2.3   Give all label controls a transparent background unless you have a specific reason to do otherwise. By default, label controls are created with their *BackStyle* properties set to Opaque. This means that the label has a background. Fortunately, this background is the same color as the form on which it is placed. However, to ensure an appearance that is consistent with any color scheme used on the target computer, set the *BackStyle* property of all label controls to Transparent. (See Figure 12-17.)

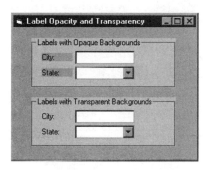

Figure 12-17.   *All of these label controls have their* BackColor *property set to the system color for* ButtonFace, *as they should. However, notice what happens when the frame controls have* BackColor *changed to a yellow. The label controls with a* BackStyle *of opaque don't look right; those with a* BackStyle *of transparent look fine.*

12.2.4   Disable items when they aren't available rather than hiding them. Practical Application 12.1.4 discusses morphing forms. (A morphing form alters its appearance in a drastic and not obvious way in response to an often unknown event.) Even if you don't intentionally create morphing forms, it's possible to inadvertently create minor morphing forms. One way to do this is by hiding items when they're not available instead of disabling them.

Most controls that can be placed on a form, as well as individual menu items, have *Enabled* and *Visible* properties. When you create minor morphing forms by hiding controls (that is, by setting their *Visible* properties to False) rather than disabling them when they're unavailable, you create an environment that is difficult for users to handle. A user can't always relate to the fact that a minute ago a menu item existed but now it's gone, or that since yesterday a form's text box for addresses has disappeared.

Another serious offense is hiding command buttons when they're temporarily unavailable. For instance, say that you have a Print button and before a user can print he must specify a file name in a text box on the form. When the text box is empty, you don't want the user to be able to click the Print button. You could (and should) place code in the command button's *Click* event to display a message to the user if the user tries to print without specifying a valid file name. However, this should not be the first line of defense against such an action.

If the user is not supposed to click a button, the user shouldn't be allowed to click it. However, hiding a command button is the wrong means to this end. A user might not grasp the idea that the button will appear (magically, it seems) when he enters a file name. He'll only be confused by the seeming lack of a print option. Disabling the Print button is the preferred method. When a command button is disabled, users realize that the function is present but unavailable. Most users are able to further reason that the current environment is preventing them from printing for some reason and that most likely some action on their part will enable the functionality.

Incorrect:

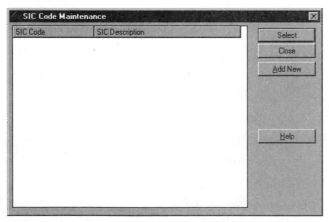

Figure 12-18.   *Where, o where, have my little buttons gone?*

Correct:

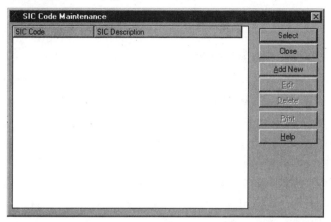

Figure 12-19. *Instead of hiding the buttons from the user, simply disable them to show that they are not applicable at the moment.*

12.2.5   Use *Tag* properties judiciously (if at all). Inexperienced programmers—and experienced programmers looking for shortcuts—often abuse the *Tag* property. (Warning: this particular item is one of my pet peeves.) Almost every control has a *Tag* property, which is nothing more than a String property that has no intrinsic functional link with the control to which it belongs. Rather, the *Tag* property is available for developers to use as an extra property in any way they see fit. Unfortunately, most uses of the *Tag* property would be better handled with variables in code.

Using *Tag* properties is often cumbersome for developers and almost always confusing to others reading the code. *Tag* properties don't allow for any validation, and because they're of type String they're poor places to keep numeric data. Some third-party controls require that you place specific information in a *Tag* property, and there's usually nothing you can do about this. However, if you're using the *Tag* property to store your own data and you want to use such a third-party control, you've got a problem.

A number of tricks-and-tips articles show nifty little routines that allow you to stuff delimited information into a *Tag* property, thereby allowing you to store multiple pieces of information in a single *Tag*. To extract a given piece of information, you must pass the value of a *Tag* property through a routine that parses the string and returns the desired piece of information. This is hardly intuitive. Another negative aspect of *Tag* properties is that they behave much like global variables in that they have global scope and can be changed by any piece of code within the application. Chapter 6, "Variables," discusses the evils of global variables, and many of the problems described there are inherent in the *Tag* property.

I wish I could tell you never to use the *Tag* property, but that just isn't practical. However, be judicious in your use of it. More than likely, there's a better approach to the problem. If you're going to let others see your code, consider the complexity involved with deciphering *Tag*-referenced code. Just because you *can* use a *Tag* property doesn't mean you *should*. If you must use this property, give a clear and concise comment on what you're doing *at every reference* to the *Tag* property. Never assume that a reader will know what your code is doing or what you're storing in a *Tag* property. If you're accomplishing something particularly complex with a *Tag* property (and you've chosen not to take a different approach), consider writing a few paragraphs of explanatory text in the Declarations section of a module. Then, at each *Tag* reference, point the user to the location of the information.

Incorrect:

```
Private Sub cmdPrint_Click()
    '* Purpose  :  Print the current purchase order.
    On Error GoTo PROC_ERR

    '* Prevent reentrancy due to a double-click.
    If cmdPrint.Tag = "InClick" Then GoTo PROC_EXIT

    cmdPrint.Tag = "InClick"

    '* Print the purchase order.
    Call PrintPurchaseOrder

    '* Clear the flag that indicates we're in here.
    cmdPrint.Tag = ""

PROC_EXIT:
    Exit Sub

PROC_ERR:
    Call ShowError(Me.Name, "cmdPrint_Click", Err.Number, _
                   Err.Description)
    Resume Next

End Sub
```

Correct:

```
Private Sub cmdPrint_Click()
    '* Purpose  :  Print the current purchase order.
    On Error GoTo PROC_ERR
    Static blnInHere As Boolean

    '* Prevent reentrancy due to a double-click.
    If blnInHere Then GoTo PROC_EXIT

    blnInHere = True

    '* Print the purchase order.
    Call PrintPurchaseOrder

    '* Clear the flag that indicates we're in here.
    blnInHere = False

PROC_EXIT:
    Exit Sub

PROC_ERR:
    Call ShowError(Me.Name, "cmdPrint_Click", Err.Number, _
                    Err.Description)
    Resume Next

End Sub
```

12.3 Use the best interface component for a given situation.

I know: that's a pretty obvious-sounding directive. Still, although selecting a component (a control) for use on a form seems easy or trivial, many developers choose poorly. Each of the standard controls in the Visual Basic toolbox is designed for a specific purpose. When you mistakenly use one control where you should use another, your interface becomes weak at its core. It's hard to build a solid house when the foundation is weak. Knowing which control works best in a particular situation is the first step to building a solid interface.

NOTE In many situations, an ActiveX control (such as the tree view control) is a much better choice than a standard control. This chapter, however, focuses on the correct use of the standard controls. At times, I will mention a specific ActiveX control that might be appropriate, but I won't generally discuss the details of using ActiveX controls.

Practical Applications

12.3.1   Use a text box control to display editable text. The text box, perhaps the most common of all controls, excels at displaying text that the user can edit. The text box can display small amounts or large amounts of text. The text box even adds its own scroll bars when its *MultiLine* property is set to True and the text box contains more text than it can display at one time.

If you're displaying text that the user can't edit, the text box might not be the best choice. Text boxes have a fair number of features. In the world of controls, more features frequently means more overhead (resources consumed). Label controls, the sole purpose of which is to display text that can't be edited, don't have near the functionality of text boxes, and therefore they use fewer resources.

In complex situations in which you have a number of pieces of text that the user can edit (text boxes) and you have one or more pieces of text for display only, you might consider using text boxes for all the pieces of text. While you can set the properties of a label control so that it looks similar to a text box, the label control will never be a perfect match. Figure 12-20 shows a text box and two label controls. If you look closely, you'll notice that the label controls display their captions one more pixel up and to the left than the text box displays its text. Although this difference is small, it's a difference nonetheless. If you have a number of static pieces of text and can get away with making them all labels, do so. If you have to mix static and editable text and all the text must look the same, you're better off using all text boxes.

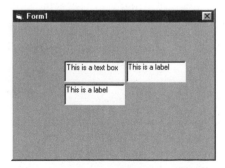

Figure 12-20.   *Labels and text boxes can be set to appear very similar but not exactly the same.*

12.3.2   Use option buttons to display static lists of five or fewer items.
Options buttons are good for letting a user select an item from a very
small list. In the early days of Basic, option buttons were called radio buttons because their behavior closely mimics that of the buttons on old AM/
FM radios. The buttons, usually located along the bottom of the frequency
display, allowed the user to select a preset listed station by pushing its
corresponding button. Only one button could be selected at a time, and
pushing a button caused the previously selected button to pop out. Option buttons allow the user to see all available options at one time and
quickly choose among them. (See Figure 12-21.)

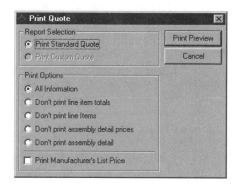

Figure 12-21.   *Option buttons work well for letting a user select a single item from a small
static list.*

Option buttons work only with small lists because of the amount of
screen real estate needed to display the options. Option buttons should be
reserved for static lists, since dynamic lists have the effect of creating
morphing forms when the option button captions (and thus the physical
appearance of the form) change. If you need to display dynamic lists or
lists with more than five items, use a combo box, a list box, or an ActiveX
control (such as the list view).

When several option buttons are placed on a form, only one button can be
selected at a time. (The buttons are said to be *mutually exclusive.*) If you
place a container control on a form and then place several option buttons
in the container, only one of the buttons in the container can be selected
at a time. Two option buttons can be selected at the same time as long as
they are in different containers. The frame control is the best choice of

container when you want to create independent sets of option buttons because it uses fewer resources than other alternatives, such as the picture box control.

Since the option buttons in a given container are closely tied to one another, it's best to make them into a control array. This makes your code easier to read, and it helps facilitate determining which button is selected. When using a set of option buttons, you eventually have to determine which button is selected. Although you can do this many ways, the best approach I've found is to add the following procedure to your project:

```
Private Function SelectedOptionIndex(vntOptionButtonArray _
    As Variant) As Integer
'* Purpose  :  Determine the selected option button in an
'*               option button array.
'* Accepts  :  vntOptionButtonArray - an option button array.
'* Returns  :  The index of the selected button in the array.
On Error GoTo PROC_ERR
Dim optOption  As OptionButton


'* Loop through the option button array looking
'* for a button with its Value property set to True.
For Each optOption In vntOptionButtonArray

    '* If the Value property of the control is True, return it's
    '* index and get out.
    If optOption.Value Then
        SelectedOptionIndex = optOption.Index
        GoTo PROC_EXIT
    End If

Next optOption

PROC_EXIT:
    Exit Function

PROC_ERR:
    Call ShowError(Me.Name, "cmdDisplaySelectedPrintMode_Click", _
                Err.Number, Err.Description)
    GoTo PROC_EXIT

End Function
```

Once this procedure exists in your project, you determine the selected option button in any option button array simply by calling this function and passing it the name of the array. The function returns the index of the selected option button, which you can use any way you see fit. For instance, to print the index of the selected option button in the array *optPrintMode—optPrintMode(0)*, *optPrintMode(1)*, and so forth—you could use the following statement:

Debug.Print SelectedOptionIndex(optPrintMode)

 OTE A *For...Each* loop is used rather than a *For...Next* loop because control arrays can have index numbers missing in their sequence. *For...Each* will test every control, regardless of any gaps in the sequence.

12.3.3 **Use a list box to display dynamic lists and static lists with over five items when space is not a concern or the user needs to see many values quickly.** The list box excels at displaying large lists, allowing the user to view many items simultaneously without user intervention (such as opening a drop-down combo box). When you want to let the user select multiple items at one time, the list box is really the only standard control you can use. (See Figure 12-22.)

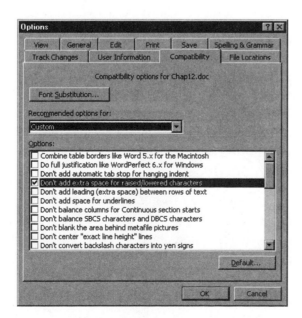

Figure 12-22. *Multiselection list boxes with check marks to denote selection are a great user interface tool.*

12.3.4 Use a combo box to display dynamic lists and static lists with over five items. The combo box is perhaps the best all-around control for letting users select items from a list. Although the combo box allows the user to select an item from both short and long lists, the amount of screen real estate required remains the same (when using the standard combo box styles).

 NOTE The combo box can be displayed in one of two ways, depending on the value of its *Style* property. (See Figure 12-23.) The preferred way is achieved with a *Style* of Dropdown Combo or Dropdown List. Although the combo box still supports the Simple Combo style, this style is generally considered antiquated, and you should avoid using it in your interfaces.

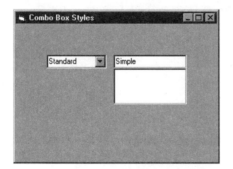

Figure 12-23. *Combo boxes can be either standard (dropdown style) or simple. You should avoid using the simple combo box in your programs.*

Unless screen real estate is particularly sparse, consider using a set of option buttons for static lists of five items or less. For static lists of three items or less, it's definitely best to use a set of option buttons.

12.3.5 Use check boxes to let users toggle options in small, static lists. When allowing users to select and deselect items (such as program options), use check boxes whenever possible. (See Figure 12-24.) Note that unlike option buttons, several check boxes in a group can be selected at the same time. The multiselection list box now supports check boxes—refer to Figure 12-22—but, in general, a set of dedicated check box controls is better, unless the list is quite large or is built from a dynamic list (such as being filled from a database table).

Figure 12-24. *Use check boxes to let the user toggle options.*

12.3.6   Use a picture box control only when absolutely necessary. Picture box controls consume more resources than most other standard controls, and they're often used unnecessarily. There's usually a control that is a better choice than the picture box. For instance, to display pictures loaded from a file—and nothing more—the image control is a far better choice than the picture box. The image control doesn't let you perform advanced actions, such as drawing shapes or printing text, but it does use considerably fewer resources (thus loading faster and using less memory) than the picture box.

Another common misuse of the picture box is as a parent or container control. To create independent sets of option buttons on a form, for example, you must place each set in a different container control. The picture box is usually the worst choice of container in these cases. If you don't need the unique functionality provided by the picture box control, such as the ability to draw or print on the control, you shouldn't consume the additional resources required by a picture box. Often, the simple frame control is the best choice as a parent control. (You can turn off the frame's border, if necessary.)

OTE The primary drawback of using frame controls as parent controls is that they don't have their own *ScaleMode* property, and therefore all coordinates in the frame are specified in twips, which are often harder to use than pixels. If you like to place controls by using pixels, add the controls to a picture box with its *ScaleMode* set to pixels. When you are happy with the arrangement, cut the controls from the picture box, paste them on a frame, and then delete the picture box control.

I blame the common misuse of the picture box on the way Visual Basic is taught in most classes and books. The picture box is used in most examples and lessons because of its amazing functionality and flexibility. Unfortunately, a caveat is rarely offered, and bad habits are born.

12.3.7   Use a scroll bar to indicate quantity or speed. Scroll bars are fairly common controls, but they usually appear as part of other controls, such as within combo boxes and list boxes. Rarely do you encounter a stand-alone scroll bar control. Scroll bars are good controls for indicating a speed or a quantity. To indicate speed, the value of the scroll bar is updated programmatically to keep it in sync with some time-related activity. More often, however, scroll bars are used to show quantity. The volume setting in a game is a good application of the scroll bar, as is allowing the user to scroll through a picture. (See Figure 12-25.) The scroll bar control can also be used to select from non-numeric yet sequential options. For

Figure 12-25.   *Using scroll bars in conjunction with a picture box, you can create image-view ports like the one shown here.*

instance, a game program might have a graphic detail option that can be set to Minimum, Sparse, Average, Busy, or Wow. Since these items form an increasing sequence, a scroll bar could be used to select among them. However, unless there are more than five such options, using option button controls is generally a better choice.

12.4 Provide comprehensive and sensible menus.

Although you might rely heavily on your mouse or another pointing device to perform design tasks while in Windows, many Windows users are keyboard users, using a mouse only when absolutely necessary. Data entry people, in particular, never take their hands off the keyboard. Many software companies receive support calls from angry customers because a commonly accessed function is accessible with a mouse only. Menus are the easiest way for a user who relies on the keyboard to navigate your program, and every program you create should make its features easily accessible through logical menus.

 OTE New users of an application often scan the menus before opening a manual. (Heck, most users never open the manual!) When you provide comprehensive menus, you make your program more intuitive and easier to learn and use.

Practical Applications

12.4.1 Format and organize menus in a manner consistent with other popular Windows applications. When designing your menus, look at some of the many popular Windows applications available and consider the similarities and differences between their menus and yours. Although your application might be quite unique and therefore have very different menus than other applications, there are probably similarities as well. When possible, make items in your application follow the same structure and design as similar items in the other programs. For example, almost every Windows program has at least a File menu and a Help menu. The File menu is always the first drop-down menu on a menu bar, and the Help menu is the last—you should never deviate from this organization.

Consistent menu organization goes much deeper than the order and presence of top-level menu items, however. If you take a look at a number of popular Windows programs (not just Microsoft's), you'll see many consistencies. For instance, if the program supports a New function, the corresponding menu item is always the first item on the File menu; you'll never see it on the Edit menu, for example.

When a menu command is used to display a dialog box in which the user must enter more information before the command can execute, the menu command is followed by an ellipsis (…). Don't use ellipses for menu commands that execute functions directly. People are accustomed to this, and you should oblige them by providing them with this information. It's easy, and there's no reason not to do it.

The tables appearing throughout the remainder of this chapter show the common commands of the most widespread drop-down menus. These tables aren't all-inclusive, but they should help you design great menus. The underlined letter in some of the commands denotes the key that you should assign as the access key. You create access keys by prefacing the desired letter with an ampersand in the menu editor, as shown in Figure 12-26.

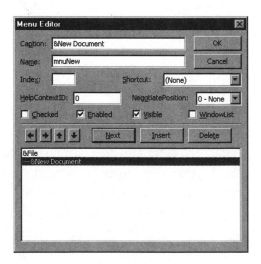

Figure 12-26. *Access keys are assigned much like accelerator keys in a label's caption—preface the letter with an ampersand.*

A number of items in the lists are labeled *Disable when appropriate*. Most of these are menu commands that perform an action based on an active file (a file that is opened by the user). If the user doesn't have a file open, disable the menu commands by using the *Enabled* property. Do not hide the menu item by setting its *Visible* property to False. Also, the items are listed in each table in the order in which they should appear on the menu.

File Menu: The Common Commands

Command	Description
New...	Creates a new file. (The type of file—that is, document, database and so on—is determined by the application.)
Open...	Displays the Open Dialog box from which the user can select a file to open.
Close	Closes the active window. (Disable when appropriate.)
Save	Save changes to the current (active file). (Disable when appropriate.)
Save As...	Displays the Save As dialog box so that the user can specify a file name, and then saves the current file under that name. (Disable when appropriate.)
Save All	Saves all the currently opened files. (Disable when appropriate.)
Find File...	Displays the Find File dialog box with which the user can locate a file.
Page Setup...	Displays the Page Setup dialog box. (Disable when appropriate.)
Print Preview	Displays the current file as it will look when printed. (Disable when appropriate.)
Most Recently Used List	Lists the most frequently accessed files in the order in which they were opened (newest to oldest). Selecting one of these items opens the corresponding file.
Exit	Terminates the application, closing all windows and files. Prompts the user to save changes when appropriate.

End Menu: Common Commands

Command	Description
Undo	Nullifies the last command performed by the user, restoring the document to the state it was in before the action was performed.
Repeat	Repeats the last command executed by the user.
Cut	Deletes the current selection and moves a copy of it to the Clipboard.
Copy	Copies the current selection to the Clipboard but leaves the selection unaffected.
Paste	Inserts a copy of the contents of the Clipboard at the current insertion point.
Clear	Deletes the current selection but does not move a copy to the Clipboard.
Select All	Selects the entire contents of the active file. This is most applicable in documentcentric programs.
Find...	Displays the Find dialog box, which the user can use to locate information (traditionally, text).
Replace...	Displays the Replace dialog box. The Replace dialog box is often the Find dialog box with a replace feature activated.

View Menu: Common Commands

Command	Description
Full Screen	Changes the view to fill the entire screen.
Toolbars...	Displays the Toolbars submenu, allowing the user to choose which toolbars to display.
Zoom...	Displays the Zoom dialog box. (This is mostly applicable to documentcentric programs.)

Insert Menu: Common Commands

Command	Description
General application items	Commands specific to the program should be placed at the top of the menu.
File...	Displays a variation of the Open dialog box from which the user can select a file to insert at the current insertion point.
Picture...	Displays a variation of the Open dialog box from which the user can select a picture file to insert at the current insertion point. Consider having this dialog box contain a clipart viewer.

Tools Menu: Common Commands

Command	Description
General application tools	Commands specific to the program should be placed at the top of the menu.
Macro...	Displays the Macro dialog box from which users can create and manage macros.
Options...	Displays the Options dialog box for the entire program.

Window Menu: Common Commands
(Mostly Applicable to MDI Applications)

Command	Description
New Window	Opens a new window, displaying the current file within it.
Arrange All	Arranges all currently opened windows in some predetermined format.
Split	Lets the user split the window into two parts.
Window list	Displays a numbered list of all currently opened files. Selecting an item in the list activates the window containing the file.

Help Menu: Common Commands

Command	Description
Product Name Help...	Displays the Windows Help program for the current application.
(Separator bar)	Used to separate the application Help from the rest of the Help commands.
Application-specific entries	Includes items such as tutorials, Web links, and customer support information.
About *product name*	Displays a standard About dialog box containing information about the program.

12.4.2   Assign shortcut keys to frequently used menu items. A shortcut key (also referred to as an accelerator key or a hot key) is a keyboard combination that causes a menu command to be invoked without the user having to access the menu. Never underestimate the importance that users place on shortcut keys. Chances are you're using some shortcut keys while developing with Visual Basic, and you'd probably be pretty unhappy to find them removed in a future version. I, for one, would be lost without the ability to press F5 to compile and run or Ctrl+F5 to start with a full compile.

Shortcut keys appear on drop-down menus to the right of menu items' captions. (See Figure 12-27.) Shortcut keys are defined using the Menu Editor dialog box. It's beyond the scope of this book to teach you how to build menus, so I won't go into details on creating shortcut keys. The important thing here is understanding the idea behind them and their importance so that you will use them constructively in your programs.

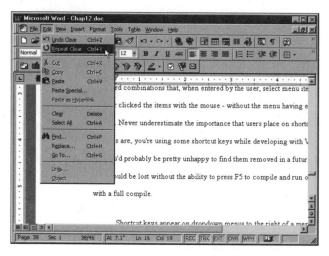

Figure 12-27. *Shortcut keys are usually displayed to the right of menu commands. Pressing the key combination triggers the command, and the menu doesn't even have to be opened.*

 OTE Although Visual Basic provides you with the Menu Editor dialog box to create menus, the tool is pretty weak. Each menu item must be defined as a single entity, menu items can't be automatically placed on toolbars, each uniquely named menu item fires its own event, and you can't even put pictures on the menus without resorting to some complicated API calls. This might be the first time I've mentioned a third-party product in one of my books, but I have to say that I use ActiveBar from Data Dynamics in all my applications. I won't say much more than that it allows you to create powerful menus and toolbars without touching Visual Basic's menu editor and that if you're interested in a seriously cool tool for building powerful menus and toolbars, you should check it out for yourself.

Shortcut keys are key combinations generally consisting of a Ctrl, Shift, or Alt key or some combination thereof being held while pressing a letter or a function key. Shortcut keys can also be function keys without modifiers (such as the shortcut key F7 in Microsoft Word used to run the spelling checker). Of course, the variations are finite, and you'll have to carefully consider how to assign them in your program. First consider the basic shortcut keys listed in the Basic Shortcut Keys table in this section, and apply them to your menu items if applicable. Next list the functions accessed by your menu items in the order that you expect them to be most frequently used, and start assigning shortcut keys to the items at the top of the list. Avoid using common shortcut keys found in the following table for uses different than those listed—users are probably accustomed to those keys having meanings other than yours.

Although it's not always possible, try to assign logical key combinations. Obviously, the meaning of, say, F6 is hardly logical, but when assigning modifiers such as Alt with another character you have some flexibility. For instance, the key combination of Ctrl+Q might be a more intuitive shortcut key for Quit Payroll than Ctrl+T.

There are essentially two types of shortcut keys: basic and extended. Basic shortcut keys are suitable in most applications, and you're encouraged to implement as many of them as possible in your programs. If you don't implement a particular basic shortcut key as defined in the coming table, don't use the shortcut key for something else in your program; most users are accustomed to these shortcut keys performing these functions.

The extended shortcut keys are completely optional, and they correspond to features that you might or might not have in your program. If your program supports a listed feature, you're strongly encouraged to use the associated shortcut key. If not, feel free to use the extended shortcut keys in your application as you see fit.

Basic Shortcut Keys

Shortcut	Menu/Command
Ctrl+N	File	New or its equivalent
Ctrl+O	File	Open
Ctrl+S	File	Save
Ctrl+P	File	Print
Ctrl+Z	Edit	Undo
Ctrl+Y	Edit	Repeat
Ctrl+X	Edit	Cut
Ctrl+C	Edit	Copy
Ctrl+V	Edit	Paste
Delete	Edit	Clear
Ctrl+A	Edit	Select All
F1	Context Help (Note: this is not displayed on the menu.)

Extended Shortcut Keys

Shortcut	Menu/Command
Ctrl+W	File	Close (Note: displaying this on the menu is optional.)
Ctrl+Alt+O	View	Outline
Ctrl+D	Format	Font
Ctrl+E	Format	Center align
Ctrl+J	Format	Justify align
Ctrl+L	Format	Left align
Ctrl+R	Format	Right align
Shift+F7	Tools	Thesaurus (Note: displaying this on the menu is optional.)
Ctrl+Alt+S	Window/Split (Note: do not display this on the menu.)
Shift+F1	Context-sensitive Help (Note: do not display this on the menu.)

12.4.3 Every toolbar button should have a corresponding menu item.

If a program has a menu (as most programs should), it should also have a toolbar. Visual Basic includes a toolbar ActiveX control, but it's fairly limited and you might want to consider a third-party tool. The actual toolbar items in your program will, of course, depend on the features supported.

The following list shows the standard toolbar items found in most Windows programs in the order they should appear from left to right. If you include any of these buttons on your toolbar, display them in this order.

New File
Open File
Save File
Print
Print Preview
Check Spelling
Cut
Copy
Paste
Paint Format
Undo
Redo
Help

Most likely, your program will have other buttons in addition to some or all of these. The place to put these application-specific buttons is to the left of the Help button, which is always the rightmost button on the toolbar, if provided.

12.5 Use system colors wherever possible.

If you've ever changed any of your Windows system colors, such as the active window or inactive title bar colors, you might have been pleasantly surprised to find that certain programs altered their display to match the new color settings. If a program didn't, it should have. You change your system colors by using the Display Properties dialog box accessed by right-clicking the desktop and selecting Properties. (See Figure 12-28.) Windows maintains a set of values for the user-selected colors or chosen color scheme. These values are available to you as a Visual Basic programmer, and you should use them.

Figure 12-28. *Users can change their various system colors to any colors they see fit by using the Display Properties dialog box.*

Each Windows system color has a specific constant in Visual Basic. Although the color referenced by a given constant might change, the value of the constant always remains the same. (Hence, it's a constant, not a variable.) When you assign a system color constant to a color property of an object, the current system color assigned to that constant is used. Visual Basic makes it easy to reference system colors by providing you a system color palette in the Properties window. This color palette is accessible from any color property of a selected object. (See Figure 12-29.)

If your program doesn't use system colors, it will stick out like a sore thumb when the user modifies her colors. It's also important to note that users don't just change their color settings for aesthetic reasons. I work with a programmer who's color-blind (or so he claims—there's a rumor floating around that this has been a running gag on us for about 10 years). He's modified his system colors (and the colors of his Visual Basic code editor as well) so that he can better see things. As I understand it, being

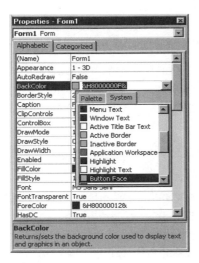

Figure 12-29. *You don't have to memorize color values or even constant names because you can select a system constant from the color palette.*

color-blind does not necessarily mean that you don't see colors, just that you don't see or distinguish them the same way as a person who is not color-blind. Certain colors can appear to be the same color, which can make it difficult or impossible to read text or see other information. If you cleverly hard-code color values where system colors would do, you can actually make using your program difficult or impossible! Using system colors is playing well with others.

The system colors are defined using rather cryptic hexadecimal numbers, making it pretty much impossible to memorize their numeric values. For instance, the system color for the face of buttons (battleship gray, in most cases) is &H8000000F&. I don't know about you, but I can't keep a dozen numbers like this organized in my head in any useful manner. Fortunately, Visual Basic has a set of constants for these system colors. Use them in your code whenever possible. The following table lists the system color constants, their values, and their basic descriptions.

System Color Constants

Constant	Value	Description
vbScrollBars	0x80000000	Scroll bar color
vbDesktop	0x80000001	Desktop color
vbActiveTitleBar	0x80000002	Color of the title bar for the active window
vbInactiveTitleBar	0x80000003	Color of the title bar for the inactive window
vbMenuBar	0x80000004	Menu background color
vbWindowBackground	0x80000005	Window background color
vbWindowFrame	0x80000006	Window frame color
vbMenuText	0x80000007	Color of text on menus
vbWindowText	0x80000008	Color of text in windows
vbTitleBarText	0x80000009	Color of text in caption, size box, and scroll arrow
vbActiveBorder	0x8000000A	Border color of active window
vbInactiveBorder	0x8000000B	Border color of inactive window
vbApplicationWorkspace	0x8000000C	Background color of MDI applications
vbHighlight	0x8000000D	Background color of items selected in a control
vbHighlightText	0x8000000E	Text color of items selected in a control
vbButtonFace	0x8000000F	Color of shading on the face of command buttons
vbButtonShadow	0x80000010	Color of shading on the edge of command buttons
vbGrayText	0x80000011	Grayed (disabled) text
vbButtonText	0x80000012	Text color on push buttons
vbInactiveCaptionText	0x80000013	Color of text in an inactive caption
vb3Dhighlight	0x80000014	Highlight color for 3-D display elements
vb3DDKShadow	0x80000015	Darkest shadow color for 3-D display elements
vb3Dlight	0x80000016	Second lightest 3-D color after vb3Dhighlight
vbInfoText	0x80000017	Color of text in ToolTips
vbInfoBackground	0x80000018	Background color of ToolTips

It's impossible to fully discuss interface design in a single chapter. However, the principles covered here are probably applicable to 99 percent of the applications you'll create. When you follow these guidelines, your programs won't suffer the fate of so many others. You'll have a cleaner, more intuitive, and more efficient interface that allows the user to work in harmony with your application and leverage skills already developed and nurtured.

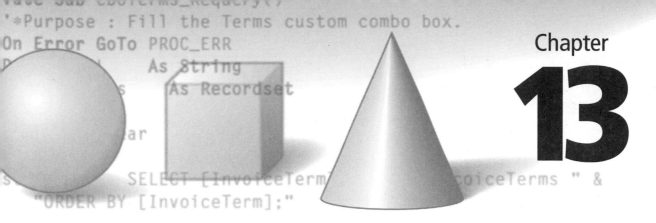

User Input and Notification

Users communicate with a program by way of keyboard and mouse input. Programs communicate with users by way of sounds, message boxes, dialog boxes, and other visual cues. This two-way communication allows users to work smoothly with an application, getting their jobs done as easily as possible.

> **NOTE** Many different pointing devices are used today, including touch pads, tablets, and trackballs. For the most part, the concepts presented in this chapter apply not only to the mouse but also to these other pointing devices. I'll refer to the mouse when discussing interaction with the user's pointing device in general, however, for simplicity and because the mouse is still the dominant pointing device in the market.

It's important to remember that a program is really just a tool. Unless you've written a game, most users aren't running your program simply for the sake of running it. Instead, each is using your program to accomplish some task more efficiently. When the two-way communication between the user and your program suffers from deficiencies in either direction, the effectiveness of the program as a tool is diminished. Users shouldn't have to think much about using your program, much like you don't have to think about the mechanics of using a butter knife to spread peanut butter on a slice of bread.

User Input

Obviously, not every program interacts with a user in the same manner. For instance, a paint program such as Adobe's PhotoShop is very much mouse-oriented; you perform the majority of the functions in PhotoShop by using the mouse or some other pointing device. The idea of allowing a user to perform each and every function in PhotoShop using only the keyboard is a pipe dream for sure, but the product's developers have provided ways for users to use the keyboard to accomplish certain tasks. Although it's best to accommodate both keyboard and mouse users—yes, these are often separate camps—the nature of an application itself might make this extremely difficult.

At the opposite end of the spectrum are data entry applications. Data entry people are primarily keyboard people. If you really want to make one of these folks mad, insert a mouse-only task in the middle of a data entry process. (Remember, even though your program is a shining jewel to you, it's just a tool to the user.) Interrupting the user's work flow this way complicates the process for the user by adding a change of work mode. Because that change of mode is likely to be perceived as unnecessary by the user, it quickly becomes tedious and frustrating with repetition. So, when considering the interaction between the user and your program, be mindful of your target market. Create a profile of the type of person you expect to run your program, and carefully consider *how* that person works.

Most applications fall somewhere between the mouse extreme and the keyboard extreme. Microsoft Visual Basic, for example, requires you to be proficient with both the mouse and the keyboard. You can't write code with the mouse, but try adding controls to a form, moving and aligning them, and setting properties to create a functional and attractive interface by using only the keyboard! Because in most cases a user must work with both the mouse and the keyboard, it's important to make the transitions between the two input devices as smooth as possible. Furthermore, it's vitally important that you provide mouse capability and keyboard capability whenever possible. When a function supports both the mouse and the keyboard, it has what I call *interactive duality*. Interactive duality ensures that users will be able to use your program in the manner that suits their needs best.

Say you're typing some code in the Visual Basic code editor and you now want to test your changes by running the project. What do you do? Because your hands are already positioned on the keyboard, the most efficient method is pressing F5. On the other hand, say you're dragging a control around on a form with the mouse, trying to find that perfect spot for the control. You have the control where you want it and now want to run the project to see how it looks in run mode. Of course, the most efficient method in this case is clicking the Run button on the toolbar. You're already using the mouse, so this is quick and easy. Whenever you have to switch between the keyboard and the mouse, a pause occurs in your work process as your mind switches gears and you reposition your hands. However slight that pause might be, it's a distraction that's often avoidable because most functions can be created with interactive duality.

A program's interface is both a barrier and a bridge. This chapter teaches you how to make interfaces that let users more easily meld with your program. A good interface lets users do their jobs without having to think about the mechanics of the process. This undoubtedly creates more satisfied users, which helps you enjoy reduced support costs, an increase in the number of users that purchase upgrades, and better word-of-mouth advertising.

Notifications

You'd be hard-pressed to write an application without at least one message box statement. Usually, a program has dozens of message box statements scattered throughout its code. Even though displaying notifications by using the *MsgBox* statement is common, many developers don't do it correctly. When you display a notification to a user, you're communicating with that person much the same as if you had called the user by phone.

Writing good notification messages is a task with many facets. The simplest aspect—determining whether a notification tells the user what the user needs to know—is just the beginning. You must also be conscious of tone, formality, grammar, spelling, format, and the amount of technical jargon. Creating a good notification message is a skill; however, even if you're not adept at writing prose, you can still create better notification messages by following the principles in this chapter.

> **Goals When Handling User Input and Notification**
>
> Your goals when handling user input and notification should include
>
> - Creating interactive duality for as many functions as possible
> - Supporting full keyboard navigation
> - Knowing your audience and anticipating the ways in which they'll use your program
> - Telling your users what they need to know in a professional, clear, and concise manner

Directives

13.1 Ensure thorough keyboard navigation and interaction.

Depending on the type of program you're creating, it might not be possible to provide keyboard accessibility for all functions that are accessible with the mouse. However, a user should be able to navigate your program without a mouse. This means that your menus should support shortcut keys and access keys. For more information on these methods of keyboard access, refer to Chapter 12, "Interface Design."

In addition to making your menus keyboard-friendly, you must also make it possible for users to use the keyboard to easily navigate the controls of every form and dialog box. Furthermore, it should be possible for a user to accept or reject changes in a dialog box via the keyboard. Enabling full keyboard access can be quite tedious, and chances are you won't account for all situations prior to releasing your product, but you can rest assured that your customers will be more than enthusiastic about letting you know the situations you forgot!

Practical Applications

13.1.1 Thoughtfully set the tab order of all of your forms. Even if a user loves using the mouse, it's inevitable that sooner or later he is going to want to progress forward or backward through the controls on a form by using the Tab key. The Tab key is the Microsoft Windows standard key for moving the focus forward (and backward using Shift+Tab) through the controls on a form. *Every one of your forms should allow complete forward and backward navigation by way of Tab and Shift+Tab.* There is simply no good excuse for not providing this.

The order in which the Tab key progresses through the controls on a form is known as the *tab order*. The tab order is determined by the *TabIndex* and *TabStop* properties of the controls on the form. All controls that can receive the focus have a *TabIndex* property, but not all controls have a *TabStop* property. Controls that have a *TabIndex* property but not a *TabStop* property are treated as though they have a *TabStop* property always set to True. When a user presses the Tab key, the focus is moved from the control that currently has the focus to the control that has the next highest *TabIndex* property value. If the control with the next highest *TabIndex* value is not visible or has its *TabStop* property set to False, the search continues until a visible control is found that has its *TabStop* property set to True.

To define a tab order for a form, simply assign the first control to receive the focus a *TabIndex* of 0, the next control a *TabIndex* of 1, and so on. Although the concept is simple, it's an amazingly tedious process in Visual Basic.

As you add controls to a form, Visual Basic assigns values incrementally to the *TabIndex* properties. For instance, the first control placed on a form has a *TabIndex* of 0, the next control a *TabIndex* of 1, and so on. This is rarely the order you want by the time a form is finished being designed. As you develop the form, you usually add new controls, delete existing controls, and shuffle controls around so as to create that killer interface. As you perform these actions, the system-assigned *TabIndex* values become arbitrary. Thus, verifying the tab order of a form should be one of the last tasks you perform before a form is put into production (that is, compiled into a usable file). This isn't to say you shouldn't adjust your tab order as you work on a form, because you really should. However, regardless of how many times you've tweaked a form's tab order, when you're done working with a form and are ready to move onto another, verify the tab order.

Setting the tab order of the controls on a form should be a simple point-and-click process; after all, you have to do this with every form you create. However, Visual Basic does not include such functionality, and you have to change the *TabIndex* property value of each and every control individually. I've tried to come up with a more diplomatic way to say this, but I can't: *this sucks*. Let's hope that the Visual Basic team gives us this ability soon; it would save countless hours of development time for hundreds of thousands of developers.

When manually assigning values to the *TabIndex* properties of a form's controls, you can take two approaches. The first, and most obvious, method is selecting the control you want to be the first control in the tab order and assigning it a *TabIndex* of 0. Then select the next control in the order and give it a *TabIndex* of 1. Continue this process until all controls have the proper *TabIndex* setting. This is beyond tedious and will soon have you bashing your head against the keyboard; or, worse yet, you'll get tired of the process and give up. Fortunately, an easier (yet not as obvious) approach exists.

Instead of working from the first control to the last, work from the last to the first. The great thing about this approach is that you have to assign only a single value to all the *TabIndex* properties: the value 0. When you assign a control a *TabIndex* value, any control with the same value, as well as every control with a higher value, is automatically adjusted to preserve its place in the tab order. So, when you assign the last control in the tab order a *TabIndex* of 0, it becomes the first control in the tab order. However, when you assign the second-to-last control a *TabIndex* of 0, the last control's *TabIndex* is automatically set to 1. When the third-to-last control has its *TabIndex* property set to 0, the second-to-last control is assigned a *TabIndex* of 1 and the last control is assigned a *TabIndex* of 2. It's much easier to select the controls in reverse order and give them each a *TabIndex* of 0 rather than selecting them in forward order and explicitly entering their distinct *TabIndex* values.

 N OTE   When using a container control, such as the frame control, assign the container control a *TabIndex* value one less than that of the first control to receive the focus in the container.

Incorrect:

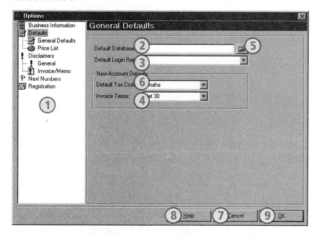

Figure 13-1.   *An incorrect tab order confuses and slows down the user. Often, the user has to reach for the mouse to get where he or she wants to go.*

Correct:

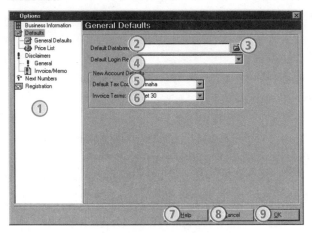

Figure 13-2. *The tab order shown here doesn't include the container controls. It's meant to show you the flow that the user would experience when pressing the tab key.*

13.1.2 Create a default command button and a cancel command button in dialog boxes when feasible. Most applications display modal dialog boxes. These dialog boxes are used to gather information from the user before they are closed. Generally, such dialog boxes include at least two command buttons: OK and Cancel. Clicking the OK button commits the user's settings and closes the dialog box; clicking the Cancel button closes the dialog box and discards the user's settings. You may have noticed that in most programs pressing the Esc key (Escape) has the same effect as clicking the Cancel button. You can (and should) duplicate this behavior in your applications.

To assign the Esc key to a command button, set the command button's *Cancel* property to True. When a command button's *Cancel* property is set to True, pressing Esc while any control on the form has the focus triggers that command button's *Click* event. Only one command button per form can have its *Cancel* property set to True. If you set one command button's *Cancel* property to True and then set the *Cancel* property of a second command button to True, the first button's *Cancel* property will be automatically set to False.

To assign the Enter key to a command button, you set the button's *Default* property to True. When a command button's *Default* property is set to

True, pressing Enter while any control on the form has the focus triggers that button's *Click* event. As in the case of the *Cancel* property, only one command button per form can have its *Default* property set to True and setting the *Default* property of a command button to True sets the *Default* property of all the other command buttons to False.

Although the *Cancel* property of every dialog box's Cancel button should be set to True, you'll have to determine whether to assign a default command button (by setting a certain command button's *Default* property to True) based on the nature of the dialog box. The main issue to consider when assigning a default command button is whether the dialog box includes any multiline text boxes. In a multiline text box, pressing Enter causes a new line of text to be created (such as when creating a new paragraph). Unfortunately, Visual Basic doesn't recognize this special situation and interprets the user pressing Enter as a clicking of the default button. This is extremely aggravating to a user. If you're including a multiline text box in a dialog box, you're better off not designating a command button as the default button for the form.

13.1.3 Assign access keys to commonly used command buttons. Almost everyone is familiar with menu access keys. When a letter in the name of a top-level menu is underlined (such as the *F* in *File*), pressing the Alt key in conjunction with the underlined letter opens the menu. What many developers are unaware of, however, is that you can assign access keys to command buttons.

How to go about assigning access keys to command buttons isn't obvious because of the lack of a dedicated access key property. You designate an access key by prefixing a character in the command button's *Caption* property with an ampersand (&). When Visual Basic displays a command button's caption, it looks for an ampersand. If one is found, the ampersand is not displayed. Instead, the character immediately following the ampersand is shown with an underscore, and that character becomes the access key for the command button. Pressing Alt in conjunction with a command button's access key triggers the command button's *Click* event just as though the user clicked the button with a mouse.

OTE To display an ampersand within the caption, use two ampersands. For instance, to display the caption *Print & Exit*, set the *Caption* property to *Print && Exit*.

Access keys are great because they give keyboard users an efficient means to trigger command buttons without clicking them—you should assign access keys to all commonly used command buttons on your forms. However, when assigning access keys, be aware of the following points:

■ Don't assign an access key to a command button that has either its *Default* or *Cancel* property set to True. When a command button has its *Default* or *Cancel* property set to True, it can be "clicked" by pressing Enter or Esc, respectively; there is simply no need to assign access keys in these situations.

■ Don't assign access keys that conflict with the access keys of menu items. For instance, if a form has a File menu, the *F* in *File* should be designated as the access key for the menu to be consistent with other programs. Don't assign the letter F as a button access key on a form that already has F as the access key of a menu; the menu always wins. Refer to Chapter 12 for more information on menus.

Incorrect:

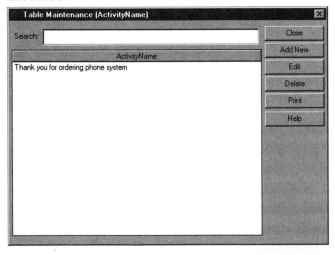

Figure 13-3. *Without access keys, a user is forced to tab to the desired command button or reach for the mouse.*

Correct:

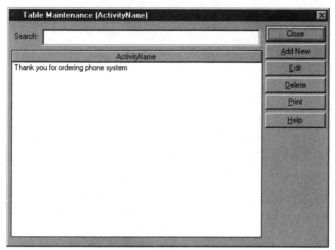

Figure 13-4. *Notice the use of logical access keys. The Close button doesn't have an access key because it is the default button.*

13.1.4 Set the *MaxLength* property of controls bound to data fields. When creating data forms, make the forms as easy to use as possible. This includes making functions and menus accessible via the keyboard, assigning access keys to command buttons, and creating default and cancel buttons when appropriate. Another helpful practice you can follow with data entry forms actually involves stopping the user from typing too much at the keyboard.

Most fields in a database table have a maximum number of characters that they can store. Attempting to store more characters in a field than allowed results in the error shown in Figure 13-5. When a user encounters this error, she's forced to stop working, determine which field on the screen is the culprit, and reduce the number of characters in her entry. Often, she'll shorten the entry and then try to save it again, only to find that the entry is still too long. This process is repeated until the user finally enters a string small enough to fit in the data field. But there's no good reason for making the user go through this.

Figure 13-5. *This is most certainly not a friendly way to treat a user.*

Text box controls include a *MaxLength* property. When a single line text box's *MaxLength* property is set to 0 (the default), the only constraint on the number of characters the text box can contain is the amount of memory on the user's computer. Multiline text boxes have a limit of 32 KB. Any value greater than 0 for *MaxLength* causes the text box to limit the number of characters it accepts. If the user attempts to enter more characters than the amount allowed by *MaxLength*, Visual Basic stops the characters from being entered in the text box and alerts the user with a beep. This situation is definitely preferable to being allowed to enter anything you like and then being shown an error when you attempt to save a record.

If you bind your text boxes to a data control, you might be under the assumption that Visual Basic automatically sets the *MaxLength* property when the control is bound. This is a great idea, but it doesn't actually work that way. Binding a text box control has no effect on the control's *MaxLength* property; the text box continues to have the same value in its *MaxLength* property as it had before it was bound to the data source. Therefore, to prevent the user from entering more data in a text box than can be saved in the underlying Recordset, you have to set the *MaxLength* property manually for each text box.

You can take two approaches to setting the *MaxLength* property: set the *MaxLength* property of a text box at design time, or retrieve the maximum number of characters allowed by a field in the Recordset and set the *MaxLength* property of the corresponding text box at run time (using the *Size* property of a DAO Field object, for example). The latter method gives you more flexibility in that if you change a field size you don't have to worry about making the change manually to all text boxes that access the field. Setting the properties at run time is a bit slower than having the properties set at design time, but the performance difference is probably negligible. Still, it's a consideration. Choose whichever method you think is best—just be sure to set the *MaxLength* properties.

Incorrect:

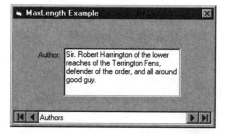

Figure 13-6. *If a very long text string can't be saved, why let the user enter it?*

Correct:

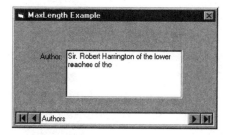

Figure 13-7. *Setting a text box's* MaxLength *property restricts the number of characters that can be entered.*

13.2   Provide consistent and intuitive mouse interaction.

For most users, the mouse is the primary device for interacting with the computer. Although keyboard users are often neglected, sometimes developers neglect mouse users as well.

Practical Applications

13.2.1   Provide pop-up menus whenever possible. A pop-up menu is a menu that appears when the user right-clicks an object that supports pop-up menus. (See Figure 13-8.) This section's focus is not on the organization of pop-up menus but rather on the proper ways to invoke pop-up menus. Microsoft Windows 95 started the era of pop-up menus, and now most users can't live without them.

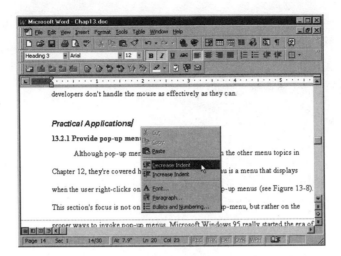

Figure 13-8. *Pop-up menus let users quickly access context-sensitive functions by right-clicking an object.*

Right-clicking an object is an easy way to explore an application. For instance, if you're not sure what you can do with a message item in Microsoft Outlook, you need only right-click an item to see a pop-up menu of commands related to the item. You should create pop-up menus for as many items as possible in your program. Windows displays standard pop-up menus for certain controls such as the text box, so don't go crazy and think you have to add a pop-up menu to every control on a form. Use your head, and try to put yourself in the user's place. In general, lists of items, whether in a list box, tree view, or list view control, are good candidates for pop-up menus.

When you display a pop-up menu for an item, the pop-up menu should contain items specifically related to the item that was right-clicked. For instance, when displaying a pop-up menu for a person's name in a contact list, it would be perfectly logical to show items such as Add New, Delete, Send Fax, and Dial Phone. However, items that aren't directly related to the object being clicked—such as Mark As Read or Save As in this example—shouldn't appear on the menu. Think of pop-up menus as being *context menus*. Just as pressing F1 displays context-sensitive help, right-clicking an object should display a context-sensitive menu.

Pop-up menus are displayed by using the *PopupMenu* method of a Form object. The *PopupMenu* method has the following syntax:

```
object.PopupMenu menuname, flags, x, y, boldcommand
```

The following table describes the *PopupMenu* method's syntax.

Part	Description
object	Optional. The form that displays the pop-up menu. If *object* is omitted, the form with the focus is used.
menuname	Required. The name of the pop-up menu to display. The specified menu must have at least one submenu.
flags	Optional. A value or constant that specifies the location and behavior of the pop-up menu being displayed.
x	Optional. Specifies the x-coordinate where the pop-up menu is displayed. If omitted, the x-coordinate of the mouse is used.
y	Optional. Specifies the y-coordinate where the pop-up menu is displayed. If omitted, the y-coordinate of the mouse is used.
boldcommand	Optional. Specifies the name of a menu item in the pop-up menu that will be displayed in bold text. If omitted, no items in the pop-up menu will be bold.

To display, for example, the File menu as a pop-up menu on a form (assuming the menu control's name is *mnuFile*), you could use a statement like this:

```
PopupMenu mnuFile
```

Generally, I don't like to take anything for granted, so I explicitly specify objects whenever possible. I would use the following statement instead:

```
Me.PopupMenu mnuFile
```

It's not usually necessary to use any of the optional parameters—the defaults work just fine. However, if you want to adjust the location or behavior of the pop-up menu, use one or more of the constants for the *flags* parameter.

Constant (Location)	Value	Description
vbPopupMenuLeftAlign	0	The left side of the pop-up menu is located at *x*. (Default)
vbPopupMenuCenterAlign	4	The pop-up menu is centered at *x*.
vbPopupMenuRightAlign	8	The right side of the pop-up menu is located at *x*.

Constant (Behavior)	Value	Description
vbPopupMenuLeftButton	0	An item on the pop-up menu reacts to a mouse click only when clicked with the left mouse button. (Default)
vbPopupMenuRightButton	2	An item on the pop-up menu reacts to a mouse click when clicked with either the right or the left mouse button.

Since you must display pop-up menus by explicitly calling the *PopupMenu* method, you have to add code to a mouse event. The proper event from which to display a pop-up menu is the *MouseUp* event, not the *MouseDown* event.

Incorrect:

```
Private Sub lstContacts_MouseDown(Button As Integer, _
    Shift As Integer, X As Single, Y As Single)
    '* Purpose  :  Display a pop-up menu for the contact list.
    On Error GoTo PROC_ERR

    '* If the user clicked with the right button,
    '* show the menu at the default location.
    If Button = vbRightButton Then
        Me.PopupMenu mnuContacts
    End If

PROC_EXIT:
    Exit Sub

PROC_ERR:
    Call ShowError(Me.Name, "lstContacts_MouseDown", Err.Number, _
                Err.Description)
    GoTo PROC_EXIT

End Sub
```

Correct:

```
Private Sub lstContacts_MouseUp(Button As Integer, _
    Shift As Integer, X As Single, Y As Single)
    '* Purpose  :  Display a pop-up menu for the contact list.
    On Error GoTo PROC_ERR

    '* If the user clicked with the right button,
    '* show the menu at the default location.
    If Button = vbRightButton Then
        Me.PopupMenu mnuContacts
    End If

PROC_EXIT:
    Exit Sub

PROC_ERR:
    Call ShowError(Me.Name, "lstContacts_MouseUp", Err.Number, _
                Err.Description)
    GoTo PROC_EXIT

End Sub
```

13.2.2 **Use the mouse pointer to give the user feedback.** Most of the time, the mouse behaves like a one-way street. The user manipulates it to provide information to a program, and the program takes the information generated by the mouse and performs some sort of action. However, the mouse is also capable of sending information to the user by way of its icon.

You change the icon of the mouse pointer by changing the *MousePointer* property of an object. For example, to change the mouse pointer of the *Screen* object to an hourglass, use this statement:

```
'* Set the screen mouse pointer to an hourglass.
Screen.MousePointer = vbHourglass
```

The following table lists the constants for the *MousePointer* property. These constants are system constants and are not part of an enumeration; you won't get a drop-down list of these constants when writing code. Instead, you'll have to use online Help, refer to this table, use the *MousePointer* class provided on the CD, or create your own custom enumeration.

NOTE On the CD you'll find a *MousePointer* class that you can add to your own projects. This class wraps the *MousePointer* property of the *Screen* object into an easy-to-use object, complete with an enumeration for the value constants.

Constant	Value	Description
vbDefault	0	Shape determined by the object (default)
vbArrow	1	Arrow
vbCrosshair	2	Cross (crosshair pointer)
vbIbeam	3	I beam (often used for positioning within text)
vbIconPointer	4	Icon (small square within a square)
vbSizePointer	5	Size (four-pointed arrow pointing north, south, east, and west)
vbSizeNESW	6	Size NE SW (double arrow pointing northeast and southwest)
vbSizeNS	7	Size N S (double arrow pointing north and south)
vbSizeNWSE	8	Size NW SE (double arrow pointing northwest and southeast)
vbSizeWE	9	Size W E (double arrow pointing west and east)
vbUpArrow	10	Up arrow
vbHourglass	11	Hourglass (wait)
vbNoDrop	12	No drop
vbArrowHourglass	13	Arrow and hourglass
vbArrowQuestion	14	Arrow and question mark
vbSizeAll	15	Size all
vbCustom	99	Custom icon specified by the *MouseIcon* property

Although all these icons have a useful purpose, the two used most often are *vbDefault* and *vbHourglass*. When your program is busy processing and can't accept input from the user, display the hourglass by setting the *Screen* object's *MousePointer* property to *vbHourglass*. Users get extremely frustrated and perplexed when the program looks as though it will accept input but it doesn't. This often results in a three-fingered salute (Ctrl+Alt+Delete), which just leads to real complications. Most of the time, you can avoid this simply by displaying an indicator—the hourglass—to show that the program is busy. When the process is finished and control is returned to the user, set the *Screen* object's *MousePointer* property back to *vbDefault*.

The behavior of the *Screen* object's mouse pointer has changed since previous versions of Visual Basic. In earlier versions, setting the *Screen* object's *MousePointer* property to *vbHourglass* changed the pointer to an hourglass, regardless of where on the screen it was. Now, the changes you make to the *Screen* object's *MousePointer* property affect the pointer *only when it's over a window of your application*. This makes sense because although your program might be busy, the user could still switch to a different program and continue working; you don't want to affect the pointer in other programs or within Windows itself.

When a procedure that has changed the mouse pointer finishes what it's doing, it must always set the mouse pointer back to the default. When the mouse pointer's icon is not appropriate for a given situation, it confuses and frustrates users. For instance, leaving the pointer as an hourglass when the system isn't busy leads the user to thinking she can't interact with the program even though she can. Imagine waiting for a program to return control to you when all the while the program has been waiting for you to do something.

Incorrect:

```
Private Sub cmdFillYears_Click()
    '* Purpose  :  Fill a list box with the years from 1900 to 2050.
    On Error GoTo PROC_ERR
    Dim intYear As Integer

    Const c_YearMin = 1900
    Const c_YearMax = 2050

    '* Set the pointer to an hourglass so that the user knows
    '* we're busy.
    Screen.MousePointer = vbHourglass
```

(continued)

```
'* Populate the list box with the range of years.
For intYear = c_YearMin To c_YearMax
    lstYears.AddItem intYear
Next intYear

PROC_EXIT:
    Exit Sub

PROC_ERR:
    Call ShowError(Me.Name, "cmdFillYears_Click", Err.Number, _
                Err.Description)
    GoTo PROC_EXIT

End Sub
```

Correct:

```
Private Sub cmdFillYears_Click()
    '* Purpose  :  Fill a list box with the years from 1900 to 2050.
    On Error GoTo PROC_ERR
    Dim intYear As Integer

    Const c_YearMin = 1900
    Const c_YearMax = 2050

    '* Set the pointer to an hourglass so that the user knows
    '* we're busy.
    Screen.MousePointer = vbHourglass

    '* Populate the list box with the range of years.
    For intYear = c_YearMin To c_YearMax
        lstYears.AddItem intYear
    Next intYear

    '* Restore the mouse pointer.
    Screen.MousePointer = vbDefault

PROC_EXIT:
    Exit Sub

PROC_ERR:
    Call ShowError(Me.Name, "cmdFillYears_Click", Err.Number, _
                Err.Description)
    GoTo PROC_EXIT

End Sub
```

Also correct:

```
Private Sub cmdFillYears_Click()
    '* Purpose : Fill a list box with the years from 1900 to 2050.
    On Error GoTo PROC_ERR
    Dim intYear           As Integer
    Dim intMousePointer   As Integer

    Const c_YearMin = 1900
    Const c_YearMax = 2050

    '* Get the current mouse pointer.
    intMousePointer = Screen.MousePointer

    '* Set the pointer to an hourglass so that the user knows
    '* we're busy.
    Screen.MousePointer = vbHourglass

    '* Populate the list box with the range of years.
    For intYear = c_YearMin To c_YearMax
        lstYears.AddItem intYear
    Next intYear

    '* Restore the mouse pointer.
    Screen.MousePointer = intMousePointer

PROC_EXIT:
    Exit Sub

PROC_ERR:
    Call ShowError(Me.Name, "cmdFillYears_Click", Err.Number, _
                    Err.Description)
    GoTo PROC_EXIT

End Sub
```

13.2.3 When displaying pop-up menus that perform actions on selected list items, always select the item that is clicked before displaying the pop-up menu. Although the right mouse button is used to display pop-up menus, the list box control doesn't recognize the right click as a way to select an item. When you display a pop-up menu with commands that operate on the selected item in a list box control, you must write code to ensure that the item under the mouse when the right click occurred is the item that is selected when the menu appears. This is best done with the *MouseDown* event.

Selecting an item in a list box with the right mouse button is trickier than you might think. Essentially, you have to calculate the row that was clicked by considering the y-coordinate of the mouse and the height of a capital letter. This becomes even more complex when you consider that a list box's container can have one of many different scale modes and that some containers (such as the frame control) don't have scale modes at all! I've created a procedure that you can add to a project and call from the *MouseDown* event of any list box. This procedure determines the row that is clicked and selects the item if there is one at that location. It takes advantage of the fact that the y-coordinate passed to the *MouseDown* event is always in twips, regardless of the scale mode of the container, and it uses the list box's parent to compute the average height of a letter. If you change the font used in a list box or on the parent form to something other than the standard font, this procedure might not work correctly.

```
Public Sub SelectListBoxItemFromY(ctlListBox As ListBox, _
    intButton As Integer, sngYTwips As Single)
'* Purpose  :  Determine which item (if any) in a list box
'*               lies under the y-coordinate, and select it.
'* Accepts  :  ctlListBox - the list box control.
'*               intButton - the mouse button clicked.
'*               sngYTwips - the vertical coordinate. This is
'*               expected in twips, which is the way all MouseDown
'*               events receive it.
On Error GoTo PROC_ERR
Dim intSelectedIndex As Integer

'* If the user clicked the mouse with a button other than
'* the right button, get out.
If intButton <> vbRightButton Then GoTo PROC_EXIT


'* This is a technique for determining which row the user clicked.
'* We use the letter A to determine how high each row is.
'* NOTE: Since the list box can appear in any number of containers
'*       having any scale mode, we use the ScaleMode and ScaleY of
'*       the list box's parent control (usually a form) to make
'*       sure all of the numbers involved are of the same scale.
'*       Remember, y is expected in twips.
intSelectedIndex = (sngYTwips \ _
                ctlListBox.Parent.ScaleY(ctlListBox.Parent. _
                TextHeight("A"), ctlListBox.Parent.ScaleMode, _
                vbTwips)) + ctlListBox.TopIndex
```

```
'* If the selected index is greater than the index of the last
'* item, the empty area below the list was clicked.
'* Otherwise, a valid item was clicked, so select it.
If intSelectedIndex < ctlListBox.ListCount Then
   ctlListBox.ListIndex = intSelectedIndex
End If

PROC_EXIT:
   Exit Sub

PROC_ERR:
   Call ShowError(Me.Name, "SelectListBoxItemFromY", Err.Number, _
               Err.Description)
   GoTo PROC_EXIT

End Sub
```

To use this procedure, simply call it from the *MouseDown* event of a list box control, passing it a reference to the list box, the button, and the y-coordinate, as shown here:

```
Private Sub lstNames_MouseDown(Button As Integer, Shift As Integer, _
      X As Single, Y As Single)
   '* Purpose  :  Display a pop-up menu related to the item
   '*               clicked if the user clicked with the right mouse
   '*               button.
   On Error GoTo PROC_EXIT

   '* Select the item where the user clicked if the user clicked with
   '* the right mouse button.
   Call SelectListBoxItemFromY(lstNames, Button, Y)

   Me.PopupMenu mnuNames

PROC_EXIT:
   Exit Sub

PROC_ERR:
   Call ShowError(Me.Name, "lstNames_MouseDown", Err.Number, _
               Err.Description)
   GoTo PROC_EXIT

End Sub
```

13.3   Create thoughtful and functional message boxes.

The most common way to notify a user about something is to use the *MsgBox* function. The *MsgBox* function is extremely flexible——with it you can ask a question or make a statement. You can also control the type of icon shown (if any), as well as the buttons available to the user. Because creating message boxes is such a common and easy task, the process is often taken for granted and it's easy to create bad message boxes. In this section, I'll discuss the techniques you can use to create better messages.

When writing messages, use a formal tone. Don't use large words, and avoid using contractions. The text should be immediately understandable and not overly fancy. Remember: a message box is not a place to show off your literary prowess; it's a place to convey a simple and clear message to a user. When a message box must ask a question, create an accurate and succinct question so that the user can make an educated decision.

Although sometimes you simply can't avoid displaying a long message, you should limit messages to only two or three lines. You want a user to feel comfortable and in control at all times. Lengthy messages spanning multiple lines not only are harder for a reader to digest but also can intimidate the user, which you absolutely don't want to do.

It's a fact that users make mistakes, and sometimes *they really screw up*. However, it's your job to make them feel as though they haven't done anything wrong, even when they do. If a message comes across as personal, a user will take it personally.

Practical Applications

13.3.1 Create the proper type of message box for a given situation. There are four types of messages: information, warning, critical, and question (or query). Information message boxes should be displayed with the information icon (as shown in Figure 13-9), warning messages with the exclamation icon (Figure 13-10), and critical messages with the red icon with the *X* in it (Figure 13-11). For messages that ask the user a question, display the question mark icon shown in Figure 13-12. To display an icon in a message box, you supply the appropriate constant in the *MsgBox* function's *buttons* parameter. (Note: The *buttons* parameter is actually used to specify the buttons and the icon that are shown.)

Figure 13-9.   *Information message boxes are simple, noncritical notifications. They should display the information icon.*

Figure 13-10.   *Warning message boxes are used to notify the user of something that's fairly important. When the user sees the exclamation icon, the user knows to take note.*

Figure 13-11.   *Critical message boxes are used to notify the user of something that absolutely must be attended to. Don't overuse the critical message icon on less-than-important messages—you'll be crying wolf, and the user won't pay attention when it's necessary.*

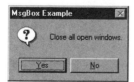

Figure 13-12.   *The question icon should be reserved for messages that ask the user a question.*

The following table lists the constants that specify icons in a message box, their values, and their descriptions.

MsgBox Icon Constant	Value	Description
vbInformation	64	Displays the information icon
vbExclamation	48	Displays the exclamation icon
vbCritical	16	Displays the critical message icon
vbQuestion	32	Displays the question icon

Although you can specify the text to appear in the title bar of a message box in the third parameter of the *MsgBox* function, you're often better off omitting the *title* parameter. When you omit the *title* parameter, Visual Basic uses the text supplied for the application title in the Project Properties dialog box. (See Figure 13-13.) When you allow this to happen, your message boxes will have a more consistent feel because they will always show the name of the program that's displaying them.

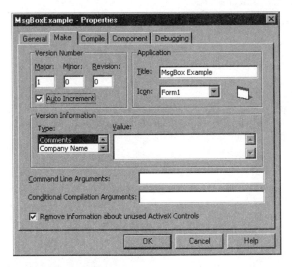

Figure 13-13. *Omit the* title *parameter of a* MsgBox *function so that the title will be set to the application's title as entered in the Project Properties dialog box.*

Incorrect:

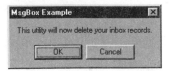

Figure 13-14. *This message box does not have an icon, and therefore it does not provide a visual clue as to its importance.*

Correct:

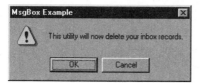

Figure 13-15. *This notification needs to be taken seriously by the user, and the exclamation icon should do the trick. Note that you could also create a Yes/No message box for the same purpose.*

13.3.2   Provide buttons that make sense. Designating the proper icon as described in Practical Application 13.3.1 is just the first step in building a good message box. The message box is capable of displaying many different buttons, and it's up to you to choose which button or buttons will appear in any given message box. The following table lists the constants available for specifying buttons, along with their values and descriptions.

MsgBox Button Constant	Value	Description
vbOKOnly	0	Displays an OK button only
vbOKCancel	1	Displays the OK and Cancel buttons
vbAbortRetryIgnore	2	Displays the Abort, Retry, and Ignore buttons
vbYesNoCancel	3	Displays the Yes, No, and Cancel buttons
vbYesNo	4	Displays the Yes and No buttons
vbRetryCancel	5	Displays the Retry and Cancel buttons

To specify more than one constant for the *buttons* parameter, use *Or*. For instance, to display an OK button along with an exclamation icon, use a statement like this:

```
'* Combine constants for a single parameter by using Or.
MsgBox "Finished updating table.", vbOKOnly Or vbInformation
```

The constants of the message box are system constants and can be used anywhere in your code, and you must take care that you don't interchange them. For example, the *MsgBox* function has a return constant of *vbOK*, indicating that the user clicked the OK button. The constant *vbOK* has a value of 1. If you mistakenly build a *MsgBox* statement by using a statement like the one following, you'll end up with a message box containing an OK button and a Cancel button, not just an OK button:

```
'* This statement has an error. The constant vbOK should only
'* be used to check the return value of the MsgBox function.
MsgBox "Finished updating table.", vbOK Or vbInformation
```

To designate a specific button as the default button (that is, the button that appears with a dark rectangle around it and that is "clicked" when the user presses Enter), add one of the constants in the following table to the *buttons* parameter.

MsgBox Default Button Constant	Value	Description
vbDefaultButton1	0	The first button is the default.
vbDefaultButton2	256	The second button is the default.
vbDefaultButton3	512	The third button is the default.
vbDefaultButton4	768	The fourth button is the default.

Make the default button of every message box a deliberate choice. For example, if you're displaying a message box with a Yes button and a No button and you're asking the user if he wants to format his hard drive, set No as the default button. The order of the buttons on a message box is always the same as the order listed in the *buttons* parameter. For example, to default to the No button in a Yes/No message box, you could use a statement like this:

```
'* The button order is the same as listed in the constant.
'* So button 1 is Yes, and button 2 is No.
If MsgBox("Format c:?", vbYesNo Or vbQuestion Or vbDefaultButton2) _
    Then ...
```

When using the *MsgBox* function to solicit a decision from the user, the function returns one of the values listed in the following table. To ensure that your code is as easy to understand as possible, always refer to the return value by its constant, not by its literal value.

MsgBox Return Constant	Value
vbOk	1
vbCancel	2
vbAbort	3
vbRetry	4
vbIgnore	5
vbYes	6
vbNo	7

The icon, buttons, and default button must all be chosen to work in unison. If, for example, you're not asking a yes/no question, don't use a question mark icon. If you're displaying a critical message prior to performing some task that the user won't be able to undo, provide a Cancel button. Every message box is different, and I can't give you a hard-and-fast rule for every situation. Consider the ideas presented here, and use common sense. Consider what you would want and expect from each message box.

Incorrect:

Figure 13-16. *This message box has a few problems. First, if you're going to update a user's files, provide a Cancel button so that the user can stop and back up the files. If you're not giving an option, there's no need for the message box. Second, you don't press a button, you click it. And, finally, there's no need to tell the user to click anything; that much is obvious.*

Correct:

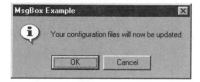

Figure 13-17. *This message box is simple and to the point. Furthermore, the user is given an opportunity to prevent an irreversible process from starting.*

13.3.3 Proofread all messages. This idea is so fundamental that it seems silly to have to mention it. Yet time and time again messages with poor spelling and bad grammar are displayed. If you're not particularly adept at writing, find someone in your organization who is and have that person proofread your messages. Also, if you're localizing a program into a language that's not your native language, find someone who speaks the language fluently to check your messages.

Think of message box text as if it were an important document on company letterhead, signed by your CEO, and sent to all your customers. If your messages are terse, they will reflect negatively on your company. If you've got a particular developer who's a bit short on people skills, write that developer's message box statements or at least proofread them before they're released.

Incorrect:

Figure 13-18.   *Even forgetting the spelling errors, this is rather unpleasant. Can't put what where? Why the exclamation icon?*

Correct:

Figure 13-19.   *Notice the friendlier tone and the information icon. This message box is helpful, as opposed to obnoxious.*

13.3.4   Avoid using technical jargon in a message box. Have you ever tried to explain a programming-related issue to a person who has never programmed before? If so, you're probably familiar with the glazed look that appears on the person's face as a little propeller attached to a yellow and red beanie is pictured atop your head. When you live and breathe a technology, it's easy to forget that not everyone else does. Also, just because a person uses software doesn't mean he or she is a technical person.

Unless your program is written for a very specific vertical market, avoid using technical jargon in your messages. Remember that messages should be clear and concise. When you use technical jargon, you risk confusing the reader. If you find yourself creating a message with technical jargon, consider rewriting the message in a nontechnical way.

Users are continuously interacting with your program. Make it easy for them to navigate your program and execute the functions they need to get their jobs done. When your program must stop the user's work flow to display a notification or get an answer to a question, make sure that it does it in the clearest and most concise manner possible. The smoother the interaction, the more productive (and grateful) the user will be.

Team Projects

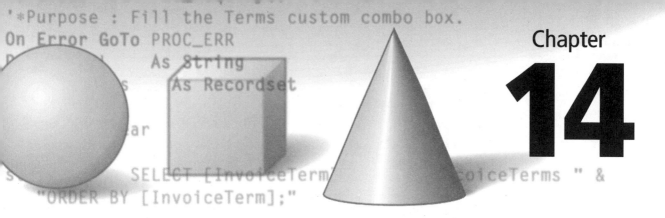

Version Control

Change is inevitable. Creating computer software is more like growing a garden than manufacturing a widget. Although a distributed program file is a static entity, the program itself usually changes—even adapts—over the course of its life. For example, developers usually change a program to correct problems or improve usability. When developers stop enhancing a product, it's often abandoned by users who switch to tools that are more in line with current business paradigms. It's a simple fact that you must improve your product or lose your customers. Although this constant change is good for users (and good for your bottom line), it creates a number of challenges for developers and project managers.

Projects in Microsoft Visual Basic are complex entities, often composed of dozens of source files. In addition, most projects make use of ActiveX controls and are distributed through the use of dedicated installation programs. As you make changes and distribute new versions of a program, it becomes exceedingly difficult to keep the entire process moving forward. For example, have you ever inadvertently compiled an older version of a form in a new program and ended up breaking what was once working? Also, you need to make sure that you add version information to your applications so that installation programs and adventurous users don't end up overwriting a program with a version that isn't current. And you need to have a solid backup plan to ensure that you never lose important program changes.

Goals of Version Control

The goals of version control include

- Compiling the most current and stable components
- Versioning all compiled programs
- Maintaining a history list of changes in versions
- Backing up project and other source files to prevent loss of work and time

---

Directives

14.1 Increment the version number each time you compile a program.

When you compile a program or ActiveX component, a version number is included in the compiled file. This version number is used by installation programs to ensure that files aren't overwritten with older versions. You can view the version number of a file by using Windows Explorer—see Figure 14-1—which makes troubleshooting faulty installations easier.

The version number of a compiled program is not arbitrary. The number is determined by the settings on the Make tab of the Project Properties dialog box, as shown in Figure 14-2. When the Auto Increment check box is selected, Visual Basic automatically increments the version number stored in the project whenever you compile a new distributable file. *You should select this check box in every one of your projects.*

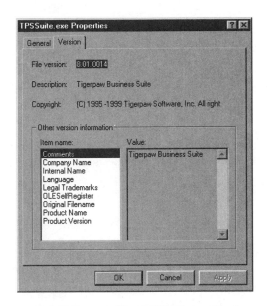

Figure 14-1. *Right-clicking a file in Windows Explorer allows you to view the file's properties, which include the file's version number.*

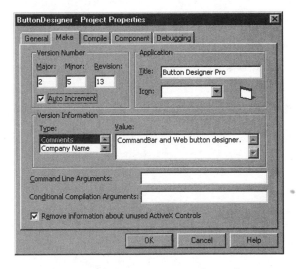

Figure 14-2. *The version numbers you specify in the Project Properties dialog box are part of the distributable file.*

Even if you're only compiling a component for a quick internal test, increment the version number. It's tempting to "not waste" a version number, but this is silly—you can maintain hundreds of minor revision numbers, and it's simply far too risky to have two versions of a compiled program with the same version number.

 N OTE If your installation program supports versioning, maintain incremental versions and a separate version information document for each new version of the installation program that you create.

14.2 Display a program's version number in the About dialog box.

Version numbers greatly aid the customer support process. When a user calls about a problem and you believe the problem is fixed, you need to know what version of the program the user is running to compare it against your internal revision document. It's best to make things easy for the user. Asking a user to open Windows Explorer, find a file, right-click the file, and select Properties (to view the file's properties)—all so that you can determine the file's version—isn't wise.

All professional programs should include an About dialog box. This dialog box usually contains licensing information such as the registered user of the software and a serial number. In addition, most About dialog boxes include the version number of the program. (See Figure 14-3.)

Version numbers are shown in the following format:

Major.Minor.Revision

When displaying version information, keep in mind that the minor revision number is usually shown as four digits right-justified. To display the 28th revision of version 8.1, for example, you'd display

8.1.0028

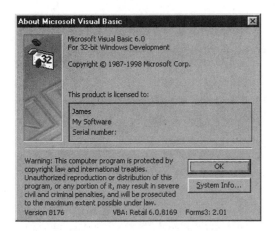

Figure 14-3.   *Include the version of your program in its About dialog box.*

The major, minor, and revision numbers of the program are available as
properties of the App object. Since these properties are always accurate,
use them instead of hard-coding version numbers for display. The following statement can be used to display the version number of a program in a
label control:

```
'* Display the full version information for this program.
lblVersion.Caption = Trim(Str$(App.Major)) & "." & _
                     Trim(Str$(App.Minor)) & "." & _
                     Format(App.Revision, "0000")
```

14.3   Maintain backward compatibility in ActiveX components.

Distributing ActiveX components created in Visual Basic requires that
you give careful consideration to code changes prior to distribution and at
the time you compile a file. You no longer have the "luxury" of worrying
only about breaking sections of your code. You must also make sure not
to break other programs that use the component.

Simply providing unique version numbers in each compile of an update does not in itself ensure that applications using the component won't have any problems. The relationship between the new version of a component and an older one, and the extent to which they are interchangeable, is called *version compatibility*. When you distribute an update to a component, make sure that the new component is backward compatible with previous versions of the component so that existing applications won't be broken.

You might distribute an updated component for many reasons. Perhaps you've fixed bugs or added new features. Sometimes the changes to a component are minor and only occur *within* existing functions. Programs that use the updated component are blind to the changes and are able to use the component without any problems. When a new version of a component is created so that it doesn't break applications that use a previous version, it's said to have *backward compatibility*.

Suppose that you've created the following procedure in a distributed DLL. (This function takes two numbers, multiplies them, and returns the result—of course you would never use such a cumbersome technique to multiply two numbers, but it serves well to illustrate a point.)

```
Public Function Multiply(intNumber1 As Integer, intNumber2 _
    As Integer) As Long
'* Purpose  :  Multiply two numbers.
'* Accepts  :  intNumber1 and intNumber2 - the numbers
'*              to multiply.
'* Returns  :  The result of multiplying the numbers.
On Error GoTo PROC_ERR
Dim intCount   As Integer
Dim lngResult As Long

lngResult = 0

'* Add the second number to itself. Do this as many times as
'* specified by the first parameter.
For intCount = 1 To intNumber1
    lngResult = lngResult + intNumber2
Next intCount

Multiply = lngResult
```

```
PROC_EXIT:
   Exit Function

PROC_ERR:
   Call ShowError(Me.Name, "Multiply", Err.Number, Err.Description)
   GoTo PROC_EXIT

End Function
```

Although this function works, it is by no means efficient. Now, assume you realize that you can perform this task by using the multiplication operator (*), so you change the procedure:

```
Public Function Multiply(intNumber1 As Integer, intNumber2 _
      As Integer) As Long
   '* Purpose  :  Multiply two numbers.
   '* Accepts  :  intNumber1 and intNumber2 - the numbers
   '*               to multiply.
   '* Returns  :  The result of multiplying the numbers.
   On Error GoTo PROC_ERR

   Multiply = intNumber1 * intNumber2

PROC_EXIT:
   Exit Function

PROC_ERR:
   Call ShowError(Me.Name, "Multiply", Err.Number, Err.Description)
   GoTo PROC_EXIT

End Function
```

Because you changed only the internals of the function—not the way the function is called or what it returns—the programs using the existing version of the DLL can use the new version without modifications. The new component is backward compatible with the previous version of the component.

Some changes to ActiveX components aren't so benign. Say you developed an ActiveX DLL that provides the following method:

```
Public Sub AddRecord(strFirstName As String, strLastName As String)
   ⋮
End Sub
```

Now, because of users' requests, you decide that you want the function to also accept a phone number. You change the definition to

```
Public Sub AddRecord(strFirstName As String, strLastName As String, _
    strPhoneNumber As String)
    ⋮
End Sub
```

When you compile the new DLL and distribute it to users, existing applications can no longer use the component! This happens because the heading of the method (procedure) has changed, making the new DLL incompatible with the older version. For existing applications to be able to use the function in the new DLL, the existing applications would need to be modified, recompiled, and redistributed.

 N **OTE** The text in this section refers to Class IDs (CLSIDs), globally unique identifiers (GUIDs), and other terms related to ActiveX components and the system Registry. It's beyond the scope of this book to teach you these concepts. Instead, this book shows you how to use your existing knowledge of these topics to ensure component compatibility across revisions.

For a component to be fully backward compatible, all the conditions listed below need to be met. The new version must

■ **Have the exact same CLSID and type library identifiers as the previous version.** The CLSID is the GUID that uniquely identifies a component in the system Registry. If a component is compiled with a CLSID that's different from a previous version, existing applications won't be able to use the new component.

■ **Support all the members (that is, properties, methods, and events) of the previous version.** You can add new properties, methods, and events without affecting compatibility. However, deleting an existing property, method, or event will break applications that use the component.

■ **Ensure that all properties, methods, and events have the same Dispatch IDs as the previous version.** Dispatch IDs are the unique identifiers of a component's members. Dispatch IDs (referred to as *Procedure IDs* in Visual Basic) are usually assigned by Visual Basic, but you can assign them manually by using the Procedure Attributes dialog box.

■ **Ensure that all properties, methods, and events have the same parameters and parameter types as the previous version.** Not only do all the existing properties, methods, and events need to be supported, you can't modify their interfaces. Adding an additional parameter to an event, for example, causes the component to lose backward compatibility.

■ **Exhibit the same functionality for all the properties, methods, and events of the previous version.** You can change the "guts" of a procedure as much as you like without technically breaking backward compatibility. However, if you modify the functionality of a procedure, you will cause problems with programs that use the component. With this in mind, feel free to change the inner workings of a procedure, as long as you don't deviate from the original functionality.

Visual Basic lets you create a component with one of three levels of compatibility:

■ No Compatibility

■ Project Compatibility

■ Binary Compatibility

You set the level of compatibility for a project on the Component tab of the Project Properties dialog box, as shown in Figure 14-4.

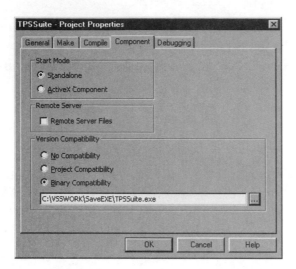

Figure 14-4. *The Version Compatibility setting is used at compile time to make new versions remain compatible with previous versions.*

Relinquishing Compatibility

To relinquish backward compatibility, select No Compatibility. Each time a project is compiled with the No Compatibility option selected, Visual Basic assigns a new CLSID to the component as well as new procedure identifiers. This is usually the least desirable option of the three levels of compatibility.

No Compatibility is useful for creating a new version of a component that won't replace an older version. This allows both versions of the component to exist peacefully on the same machine. When you use the No Compatibility option to produce a new version of a component, you should change the Project Name property of the project and compile the project with a filename different than that of the previous version. That way you'll create a completely unique component that won't overwrite the previous version or clash with it in any way. All existing programs continue to use the older component. For a program to use the new component, its source code will have to be modified and then recompiled.

Maintaining Project Compatibility

When you compile a project that uses the Project Compatibility setting, Visual Basic keeps the type library identifier of the previous component, and all class IDs from the previous version are maintained as well. Procedure IDs are retained only if binary compatibility can be maintained. This setting allows you to open projects that use previous versions of the component, but it doesn't ensure that they will run without modifications. If the type library CLSID were changed, the project couldn't load the component at all because it would be referencing an identifier that was no longer valid.

 N OTE The Visual Basic documentation states that for the purpose of releasing compatible versions of a component, Project Compatibility is the same as No Compatibility.

Perhaps you've experienced Visual Basic being unable to load an ActiveX control because it was no longer available on the development computer. Visual Basic doesn't know what to do in this situation, so it replaces all instances of the component with picture box controls.

When Project Compatibility is selected, the text box at the bottom of the Project Properties dialog box is enabled. In this text box, you enter the name of the component with which to maintain compatibility—this file should be a previous version of the compiled component.

 N OTE Always keep a copy of each compiled version of a component somewhere safe. If you lose a compiled component file, you lose the ability to create new components that are backward compatible with the file.

Remember that selecting the Project Compatibility option does not ensure that a project using the component will run without modifications, only that projects will still have a valid reference to the component's library.

Maintaining Total Compatibility

The Binary Compatibility option is the only option that truly enforces compatibility between components. When you compile a project with Binary Compatibility selected, the new component has the same CLSID and procedure identifiers as its previous version. Applications that use the previous version of the component can use the new component without having to be modified or recompiled.

Simply selecting Binary Compatibility does not force Visual Basic to prevent you from making changes to a project that would render it incompatible with a previous version. However, if you do make changes that would prohibit backward compatibility (such as changing a Procedure ID by using the Procedure Attributes dialog box), Visual Basic will warn you of that fact at compile time. (See Figure 14-5.) If you choose to ignore this warning, you sacrifice backward compatibility.

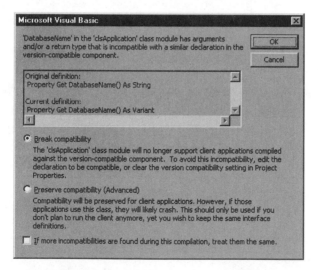

Figure 14-5. *Visual Basic tells you when you are creating an incompatible component. You can then alter your approach or go ahead and break compatibility.*

When creating an ActiveX component, you must be keenly aware of compatibility issues. In most situations, Binary Compatibility is the best option and No Compatibility is the worst. If you truly want no backward compatibility, create a new component by changing the project name and the name of the compiled program.

14.4   Document changes in a Readme file.

Product development often occurs at a rapid rate, yet it can span months or years. Because it's impractical to expect a person or a team to remember all the various changes that are made and in what versions those changes were made, it's important to maintain a journal of program changes. Usually, this journal is written as a Readme file.

Most users are familiar with Readme files. A Readme file is a document that usually accompanies a program during a new installation or an update. Users view the Readme file to learn about program changes that might or might not have made it into the product documentation. Use the Readme file as a vehicle to notify users of important changes and additions.

You can choose to maintain two versions of a Readme file: one for users and one for internal use. Generally, Readme file information for users is of a more general nature than that in your internal documents. Users don't need to know the specific technical implementation of a feature, just that the feature is available and how to access it. However, internal documents are used as references by developers, and therefore they need to contain specific information. You can maintain two documents, or you might choose to maintain one document and remove the items intended for internal use prior to distributing the file with the product.

You can put just about anything you want in a Readme file. Many companies choose to include a welcome letter, contact information, and marketing information. My advice is to keep the Readme file as focused as possible. If you want to distribute a lot of nontechnical information, consider putting it into other document files and including a reference to those files in the Readme document. Regardless of what other types of information you do include in the Readme file, you should always provide revision information.

As you make changes or enhancements to your product, document them in the Readme file in a clear and concise manner. It's important to associate all items in the Readme file with a specific revision of the program. When distributing a Readme file, you can choose to lump all revisions under one version number rather than showing all the various revisions numbers between releases, but do keep track of the changes in *each specific revision* for internal use. Sooner or later, you're going to need to know the exact version in which a change occurred.

14.5 Back up your files.

Too often I hear about a company or individual that has lost data and has no current backup. (This happens more frequently than you'd think.) Before computers became mainstream, ignorance was the most common reason for this sad state of affairs. However, even then, ignorance was a marginal excuse. Most software documentation includes information on the necessity of backing up files. Now, the need to back up files is well understood, and CD-ROM burners, tape units, and large hard drives are so common and inexpensive that it's inexcusable not to back up your files.

Of course, your particular situation should dictate the type of backup plan you employ. If few changes are made to a project, a weekly backup might be sufficient. For most development shops, nightly backups are the norm. Don't forget to rotate your media. At times, backup media can go bad, and backups can become corrupted. It's best if you keep at least five successive backups. In addition, you should archive backups of important milestones such as product releases.

 NOTE Consider this: You have a problem, and you need to go to a backup. No problem—you always back up your files. Soon you find out that the file you need isn't there because the file or its folder wasn't specified in the backup plan. It's happened to me a few times and to others I know as well. You should periodically restore a backup just to make sure that everything you want backed up is being backed up. It's easy to forget to add a folder to your backup plan, and this mistake can be disastrous. The time to find out you're not backing up a file is *not* when you need it.

14.6 Use Microsoft Visual SourceSafe to maintain versions of source code.

Keeping backup files of all revisions of all project files is next to impossible. For complex projects, you should seriously consider using a program such as Visual SourceSafe to manage your projects. Visual SourceSafe keeps track of all of the revisions of all files in a project, allowing you to easily revert to a specific revision when necessary. Chapter 15, "Source Code Control," explains the implementation of Visual SourceSafe in detail.

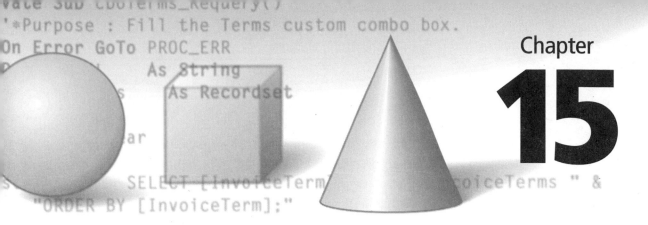

Source Code Control

Managing source code in a team environment is a difficult job; doing so when many developers are involved and no source code tool is employed is almost impossible. Microsoft Visual SourceSafe is a tool that ships with the Enterprise edition of Microsoft Visual Basic, but there's some speculation that the tool was meant to remain an internal application and not be released to the general public. (By the way, Microsoft didn't create Visual SourceSafe; the company purchased it.) Although Help text exists for Visual SourceSafe, the program's general workings and the process of setting up Visual SourceSafe in a production environment are not that well documented. In addition, Visual SourceSafe doesn't have the polish of most Microsoft applications—it contains many functional and physical characteristics that fall far beneath the standards of Microsoft Windows applications. For instance, one of Visual SourceSafe's three components (Visual SourceSafe Administrator) doesn't even have a File menu! Also, many of the program's menu items weren't placed on the menus that make the most sense.

The complexity of implementing Visual SourceSafe in a development environment, coupled with its nonstandard appearance and less-than-adequate documentation, prevent many people from successfully implementing and using Visual SourceSafe. Many are discouraged from even trying. I've known a number of highly technical people who were unable to get Visual SourceSafe up and running—one was an MCSE!

Nonetheless, Visual SourceSafe *works*, and if you take the time to implement it in your team environment, you'll be glad you did. Rather than offering directives that will help you create better code, my goal in this chapter is teaching you how to use a tool that will drastically reduce the amount of resources needed to manage a large product and a team of developers, a tool that will easily handle situations almost impossible to deal with without some sort of integrated solution.

Identifying the Challenges of Team Development

Professional software development is often performed by more than one programmer. As more and more developers become involved in a project, managing the work performed by all the developers becomes exponentially more difficult. A team-developed project can quickly become a multiheaded beast, ready to strike at any time. Some of the challenges inherent with team development are

- Making sure that multiple developers aren't modifying the same code and objects at the same time

- Preventing developers from overwriting the work of others

- Tracking versions of the software

- Centralizing project files

When two developers modify the same code at the same time, someone's going to lose. Generally, it's the first programmer to finish the modifications who loses the work—the second developer overwrites the first programmer's changes. It can be quite a task to make sure that developers don't "stomp" on each other as a project progresses. Also, it's imperative that multiple programmers don't waste time working on the same problem.

Version tracking can also be a challenge in a team environment. With so many changes to so many source files taking place, it's difficult to get a snapshot of the project in any particular state. As developers make changes to different files, or even to the same files, tracking the changes over time becomes increasingly complicated.

Visual Basic projects often consist of dozens of different files, and trying to find the optimum way to manage these files can be frustrating. Allowing only one developer to work on the project at a time is obviously not a solution. Should you let each developer modify a full version of the source project on his or her local computer and e-mail you a batch of changes? Not really; project files need to be better organized than that and easily accessible. The challenges multiply with every developer added to the team. Reducing the complexity of the situation (as well as reducing the possibility of costly errors) is critical, and Visual SourceSafe will definitely help you in this regard.

Understanding Visual SourceSafe

What *is* Visual SourceSafe? This is a question that's difficult to answer. Visual SourceSafe is a tool comprising the following three components:

- An administrator program. Used to manage tasks such as setting up source code control and creating user accounts.

- A user's program. Visual SourceSafe Explorer allows each developer to manage project files.

- An add-in to Visual Basic. Provides an integrated solution for managing Visual Basic project files under source code control.

Visual SourceSafe allows you to

- Manage all sorts of source files, including text, graphics, resources, and sounds

- Control who has access to source code files

- Know who is working on what source code files

- Make sure only one person at a time can modify a source file

- Revert to previous versions of source files or merge current changes with earlier revisions

- Maintain a current version as well as revisions in a centralized location

As I've said, more than one competent system administrator has given up on using Visual SourceSafe to manage team development, and this is not because of a lack of skill on the administrator's part or because Visual SourceSafe doesn't do what it's supposed to do. Rather, Visual SourceSafe is unnecessarily difficult to set up with the little documentation provided in Help. Before you can begin setting up source code control, you need to understand the basic principles involved.

First, when a project is under source code control, no developer makes changes directly to the master copy of the project. Instead, each developer works with his or her own copy of the source code files—a developer checks out files when ready to change them, much as you check out a library book. When a developer is finished making modifications, he or she checks in the file or files. Throughout the entire process, a complete copy of the project is kept in the developer's working folder. (I'll explain working folders later in this chapter.) Although you have access (read permissions) to all files in the project, you can alter only those files that you have checked out. While you have a file checked out, no other user is allowed to check it out (with the exception of the master project file).

 OTE   To prevent you from making changes to files you have not checked out, Visual SourceSafe designates and marks files as read-only. When you actually check out a file, Visual SourceSafe removes the read-only flag.

Setting Up Visual SourceSafe

To implement source code control, first create a Visual SourceSafe database. Once you've created a Visual SourceSafe database, you can add a Visual Basic project to it. This is most easily done with Visual SourceSafe Administrator, shown in Figure 15-1. To start Visual SourceSafe Administrator, choose Programs from the Start menu, and then choose Microsoft Visual SourceSafe and Visual SourceSafe 6.0 Admin from the submenus.

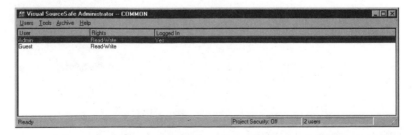

Figure 15-1.   *Use Visual SourceSafe Administrator to configure source code control.*

Creating a Visual SourceSafe Database

Visual SourceSafe is installed with a default source code database titled Common. When placing projects under source code control, it's best to start by creating your own source code database. When you do this, you'll begin to notice that Visual SourceSafe isn't always the most intuitive program. Most Windows applications let you create documents (including databases) by using items on a File menu. However, in Visual SourceSafe, you create databases by using the Tools menu. (Note that there isn't a File menu available in Visual SourceSafe Administrator.)

To create a Visual SourceSafe database, follow these steps:

1. Choose Create Database from the Tools menu.

2. Enter the name of the folder in which you want to create the source code database. (See Figure 15-2.) This folder should be a new, empty folder placed on the network where all developers can access it. Make sure that all developers who'll use the project have full access to this folder and its subfolders.

3. Click OK to commit your folder selection.

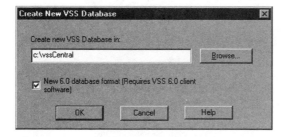

Figure 15-2.   *Create each new Visual SourceSafe database in its own folder.*

 OTE   You don't actually specify a name for the new Visual SourceSafe database; you specify the folder in which it is created.

Opening a Visual SourceSafe Database

In applications such as Microsoft Word or Microsoft Access, when you create a new document or database, the new object is automatically opened and ready to use. This is not how it works with Visual SourceSafe. After you create a Visual SourceSafe database, you must explicitly open the database. To open the database, choose Open SourceSafe Database from the Users menu. (Remember: sometimes you'll have to explore the menus to find the function you need.)

After choosing Open SourceSafe Database, you're shown the Open SourceSafe Database dialog box, as shown in Figure 15-3. At first, your new database won't appear in the list. Although Visual SourceSafe created the database for you, it doesn't remember it. You'll have to click the Browse button to locate and select the Visual SourceSafe database file you've created. (See Figure 15-4.)

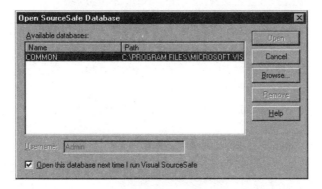

Figure 15-3. *Visual SourceSafe doesn't remember the database it just created, you must locate the database manually.*

Figure 15-4. *Visual SourceSafe saves its databases with the extension .ini, but not all .ini files are Visual SourceSafe databases.*

OTE Although the extension .ini is commonly used for text files of a specific format throughout Windows, Visual SourceSafe actually uses the same extension for its databases! The interface and behavior of Visual SourceSafe deviates from accepted standards in many ways, and therefore it is not an exemplary model of standardization. However, if you can get past these shortcomings, you'll find a very useful tool that can help you deal with many administrative challenges.

Adding Users to a Visual SourceSafe Database

Each new Visual SourceSafe database is created with an Admin and a Guest user. You'll need to create a custom user account for each developer who will access the project while it's under source code control. When a project under Visual SourceSafe protection is opened in Visual Basic, the person opening the project has to log in as a valid user. If you create passwords for the users, each user will have to enter a password as well. By making each user log in to the Visual SourceSafe database, you'll have a level of security, you'll be able to determine which files each and every user presently has checked out, and you'll be able to review version history for each user.

To add a new user to a Visual SourceSafe database, follow these steps:

1. Choose Add User from the Users menu to display the Add User dialog box shown in Figure 15-5.

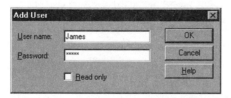

Figure 15-5.   *Each user who will have access to the protected project must have a valid user account.*

2. Enter the name of a user and the user's password. Leave the password field blank if you don't want to enforce passwords.

3. To grant the user read-only access to files under source code control, select the Read Only check box. Don't select this check box if you want the user to be able to modify files.

4. Click OK to save the new user's information. The new user then appears in the main Visual SourceSafe Administrator window. (See Figure 15-6.)

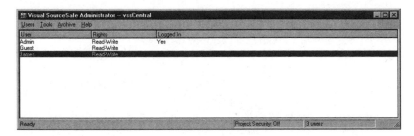

Figure 15-6.   *All users of a Visual SourceSafe database are shown in Visual SourceSafe Administrator, along with their rights and whether or not they are logged in to the database.*

Although you can add users at any time, always start with at least one custom user. Also, even if you don't assign passwords to all the user accounts, consider adding a password to the Admin account to prevent other users from running Visual SourceSafe Administrator and modifying your configuration. To add a password to the Admin user, select the user in the list and choose Change Password from the Users menu.

Placing a Visual Basic Project Under SourceSafe Control

To place a Visual Basic project under source code control, you must add the project and all of its files to the SourceSafe database. This can be a tedious and error-prone process if done manually. However, there is an easy way to add an entire Visual Basic project to source code control, and that's through Visual Basic itself.

To add a Visual Basic project to Visual SourceSafe, follow these steps:

1. Start Visual Basic, and open the project you want to add to Visual SourceSafe.

2. Visual SourceSafe includes a Visual Basic add-in component. You access the features of the add-in component on the SourceSafe submenu that is automatically added to the Tools menu in Visual Basic. Choose Add Project To SourceSafe from the SourceSafe submenu, as shown in Figure 15-7.

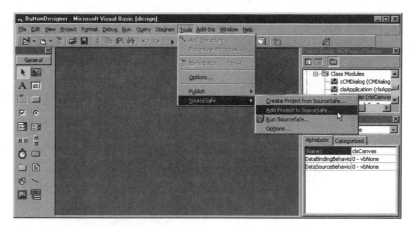

Figure 15-7.   *Add an entire Visual Basic project to source code control by using the SourceSafe add-in menu.*

3. After choosing to add the Visual Basic project to source code control, you're asked to log in to the Visual SourceSafe database, as shown in Figure 15-8. Enter your user name and password (if applicable), and make sure that the proper Visual SourceSafe database is specified in the Database text box. If the database displayed isn't the correct one, click Browse to locate and select the proper database.

4. Click OK to log in to Visual SourceSafe and add the project to source code control.

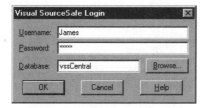

Figure 15-8.   *To perform any functions with Visual SourceSafe, you must log in as a valid user.*

5. After you log in to Visual SourceSafe, you're shown the Add To SourceSafe Project dialog box, as shown in Figure 15-9, which displays the current project tree of the active Visual SourceSafe database. You can have more than one project in a Visual SourceSafe

database. If projects already exist in the active Visual SourceSafe database, they'll appear in this dialog box. Use this dialog box to specify the name of the project as well as its location in the database organizational tree. Usually, accepting the defaults is adequate.

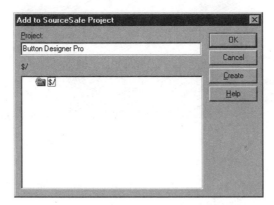

Figure 15-9.   *Use this dialog box to name a project and to specify its location in the Visual SourceSafe database organizational tree.*

6. Next, you are asked to specify which files to add to source code control. (See Figure 15-10.) Generally, you'll want to add all Visual Basic project files to source code control. All files are selected by default, so you can simply click OK to continue.

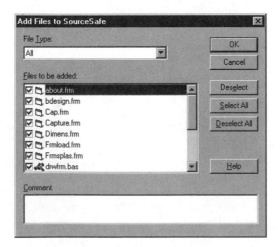

Figure 15-10.   *Although you can selectively add files to source code control, it's best to add all of your Visual Basic source files.*

After you select the files to place under source code control, Visual Source-Safe will display a dialog box as it adds the files to the current Visual SourceSafe database. If the project is very small, the dialog box might appear and disappear so fast that you won't notice it. When Visual Source-Safe is finished, the Visual Basic Project Explorer window refreshes, and you'll see new icons for each file in the project, as shown in Figure 15-11.

Figure 15-11. *Files under source code control appear in the Project Explorer with icons indicating their Visual SourceSafe status, such as available, checked out by the current user, or checked out by another user.*

The files under source code control appear with an icon of a document and a lock. When a file is checked out, a red check mark is placed on the icon's document.

Visual Basic Projects and Visual SourceSafe

For the most part, development of a Visual Basic project under source code control is similar to your work on an ordinary project. The primary difference is that you must check out files to modify them. I've said that when you check out a source code file it's much like checking out a book at the library and taking it home. You can make changes to the book because you have it—although you shouldn't do this to a library book!—but no other person can make changes to it until you check it in and that person checks it out. However, unlike a small library that houses only one copy of each book, Visual SourceSafe provides as many read-only copies of every source code file as necessary for every developer to be able to view the file. This is necessary because you can't edit and debug a form, for example, without having the entire project in which the form resides.

 NOTE When you check out a file in the Visual Basic integrated development environment (IDE) that has a corresponding binary file (such as the .frx file that corresponds to a form's .frm file), the binary file is automatically checked out as well.

Designating a Working Folder

Before developers begin to work with a project under source code control, some setup must be performed on each development machine. Creating a *working folder* for each developer is the first step. A working folder is a folder containing a copy of the entire project. *Each developer must have a unique working folder that is not shared by any other developer.* No developer opens a "master" project. Instead, each developer opens the copy of the project that resides in that developer's working folder.

When you use the Add Project To SourceSafe menu item in Visual Basic to add the current project to Visual SourceSafe, the project is treated as the working project and the folder in which it resides is automatically designated as the current user's working folder. Once the project is under source code control, there's no master project that can be opened in Visual Basic. Instead, the source files are stored in a complex structure in the folder in which the active Visual SourceSafe database resides. As users check files in and out, the master Visual SourceSafe project is updated. *It's absolutely critical that you regularly back up the entire contents of the Visual SourceSafe database folder, including all subfolders.*

Since the master Visual SourceSafe project is not stored in the same format as Visual Basic project files—and therefore you cannot open the master project directly—you need to have a working copy of the Visual Basic project to do any development using Visual Basic. The developer who adds the project to source code control by following the steps outlined previously already has a working copy. However, you must create a working folder and a working copy of the project for all other developers.

To create a custom working folder, use Visual SourceSafe Explorer, shown in Figure 15-12. To start Visual SourceSafe Explorer, choose Programs from the Start menu, and then choose Microsoft Visual SourceSafe and Microsoft Visual SourceSafe 6.0 from the submenus. The current working folder is shown in the right pane below the toolbar. Notice that the user logged in to Visual SourceSafe in Figure 15-12 has no working folder.

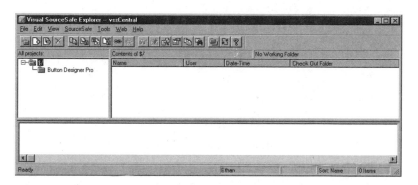

Figure 15-12. *Each developer manages his or her project by using Visual SourceSafe Explorer.*

To create or change the current working folder of a developer, follow these steps:

1. Log in to Visual SourceSafe as the user whose working folder you want to create. This is best done from the machine that the developer will use, to prevent problems with relative paths and drive mappings.

2. Choose Set Working Folder from the File menu to display the Set Working Folder dialog box shown in Figure 15-13.

3. Enter the path and folder name of the developer's working folder. To create a new folder, enter the name and path in the text box *first* and then click Create Folder.

4. Click OK to use the designated working folder.

 OTE Each and every developer must have a unique working folder; do not attempt to create a shared working folder. Since each developer will have a distinct working folder, you don't have to create working folders on a shared drive. However, the master Visual SourceSafe database must reside on a shared drive.

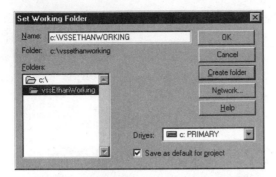

Figure 15-13. *Create or change working folders by using the Set Working Folder dialog box.*

Creating a Working Copy of the Project

Once you've designated a working folder, you have to create a working copy of the Visual Basic project with which the developer can work. To do this, select the project name in the left pane of Visual SourceSafe Explorer. When you select the project, the pane on the right fills with the list of all files under source code control for the selected project. (See Figure 15-14.)

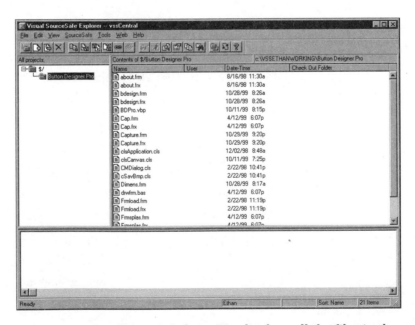

Figure 15-14. *Selecting a Visual SourceSafe project displays all the files in the project.*

With the project selected, choose Get Latest Version from the SourceSafe menu. Visual SourceSafe asks you to confirm the working folder, as shown in Figure 15-15. If the working folder is correct, click OK to accept the defaults and create a working project.

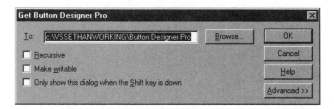

Figure 15-15. *Whenever you retrieve the latest version of a project, validate that the files are being pulled to the correct working folder.*

Checking Out Files by Using Visual SourceSafe Explorer

Most of the time, you'll check files in and out through the Visual Basic IDE. However, there will be times when you'll want to use Visual SourceSafe Explorer. For instance, although you can tell that a file is checked out by another user by looking at the icon displayed in Visual Basic's Project Explorer, you can't tell who has a file checked out. Visual SourceSafe Explorer offers this as well as other information and functionality not available within the Visual Basic IDE. Since you'll be using Visual SourceSafe Explorer at times, you should be familiar with checking files in and out through Visual SourceSafe Explorer's interface.

To check out a file by using Visual SourceSafe Explorer, follow these steps:

1. Select the file or files. To select multiple files, use the Ctrl and Shift keys in conjunction with clicking an item or items.

2. Right-click the selected file or files to display a shortcut menu.

3. Choose Check Out, as shown in Figure 15-16. (Note that Check Out is also available from the SourceSafe menu.)

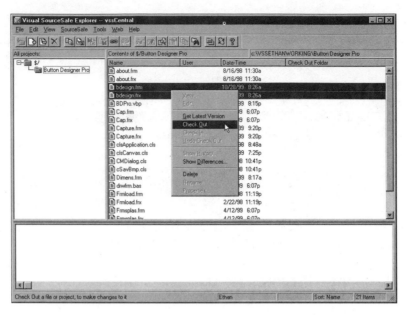

Figure 15-16. *Use Visual SourceSafe Explorer to check out files only when necessary. Using the Visual Basic IDE is a better way to check out files.*

 N OTE   When you check out a file—such as the .frm file of a form object—from within the Visual Basic IDE, Visual SourceSafe knows to check out the corresponding .frx file automatically. However, when you check out such a file by using Visual SourceSafe Explorer, you must check out the associated binary file manually or you will have problems.

The only file that can be checked out by more than one developer at a time is the main project file (.vbp). Whether a given developer should check out the project file depends on what the developer is doing. For instance, to add a new form to a project, you must have rights to modify the .vbp file because information on all forms in a project is maintained within the .vbp file; if you don't have the project's .vbp file checked out, you cannot add new forms to the project. Also, if you use the Increment Version option when compiling distributable components, Visual Basic needs to be able to write the new version information to the .vbp file, so once again you'll have to have the project file checked out to do this.

When a file is checked out to a user, its icon changes—a red check mark and border are added—making it very easy to determine which files are checked out. (See Figure 15-17.) In addition, the name of the user who has a file checked out is displayed in the list next to the file, as well as the working folder containing the checked out version of the file.

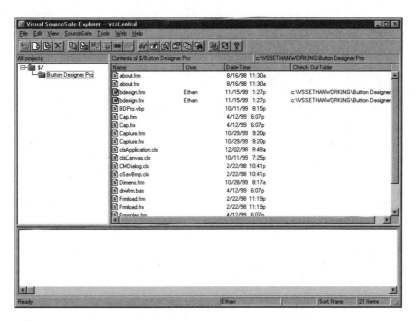

Figure 15-17. *Visual SourceSafe Explorer makes it easy to determine who has a file checked out and where the working copy is located.*

Once you've set up a working folder and retrieved the latest versions of the source files, you're ready to begin using the project with Visual Basic. To do so, open the working copy of the project in the working folder.

Checking Files In and Out from the Visual Basic IDE

Although you can check files in and out by using Visual SourceSafe Explorer, most of the time you'll do this directly from within Visual Basic. When you have a file checked out, the file's icon in the Project Explorer contains a red check mark, as shown in Figure 15-18. Unfortunately, the only visual clue indicating that another user has a file checked out is the border of the document icon—its color will have changed from black to dark gray. This is hard to notice when you're running in a high resolution mode. To check out an object file (or files), right-click the object and choose Check Out, as shown in Figure 15-19.

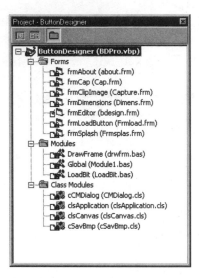

Figure 15-18. *Each file you have checked out appears with a red check mark in its icon.*

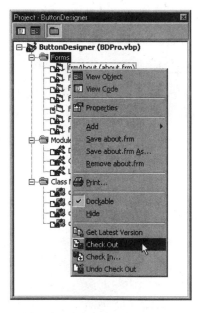

Figure 15-19. *Right-clicking an object in the Project Explorer window accesses the Visual SourceSafe functionality applicable to the object.*

Once you have an object (comprising one or more files) checked out, you can make changes to it as you do any object in a project not under source code control. If you attempt to make changes to an object that you do not have checked out, you'll receive an error similar to that shown in Figure 15-20.

Figure 15-20. *When you don't have a file checked out, you have only read rights for the file. Attempting to edit such a file generates an error similar to this one.*

To check in a file that you've modified, right-click the file's icon in the Project Explorer window and choose Check In from the shortcut menu. (Refer back to Figure 15-19.) When you elect to check in a file, the Check In Files To SourceSafe dialog box shown in Figure 15-21 is displayed.

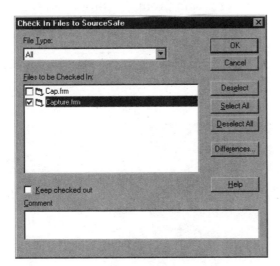

Figure 15-21. *You can check in more than one file at a time by using this dialog box.*

Check In Files To SourceSafe is a very useful dialog box, which lets you check in multiple files at once. No corresponding dialog box allowing you to check out multiple files at one time exists in the Visual Basic IDE. To check out multiple files simultaneously, you have to use Visual Source-Safe Explorer.

The Check In Files To SourceSafe dialog box displays all files that you currently have checked out. When you check in a file, your changes replace the original file in the Visual SourceSafe project. *This is the only way that a developer can make changes to the master project.* If you plan to continue working with the files, select Keep Checked Out. Select all the files that you want to check in, and click OK.

At times, you might make changes to a file that you have checked out and later find that you don't want to commit those changes. To undo a file checkout, right-click the object in the Project Explorer window and choose Undo Check Out from the shortcut menu. (Refer to Figure 15-19.)

Adding New Files to a Project Under Source Code Control

When you add a new object to a project under source code control, Visual SourceSafe won't do anything with the new file until you attempt to save it. At that point, Visual SourceSafe prompts you to add the file to Visual SourceSafe, as shown in Figure 15-22.

 OTE If you do not have the main project file checked out, Visual SourceSafe won't allow you to add a file to the project.

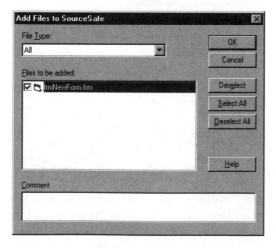

Figure 15-22. *After saving a new file, Visual SourceSafe displays its Add Files To SourceSafe dialog box, allowing you to place the file under source code control.*

Each user who adds new files to a project should save the new files in his or her working folder. When you add the file to Visual SourceSafe and save it in your working folder, Visual SourceSafe adds the file to the master project in its own format. Users obtain copies of new files by pulling the latest version of the project file, as I'll discuss in the next section.

 OTE Visual SourceSafe has a number of quirks, and here's one that's particularly annoying: When you add a new file to Visual SourceSafe, you are not given the option of keeping the file checked out to you. To continue making modifications to the file, you'll have to check the file out manually (as discussed earlier in this chapter).

Getting the Latest Version of Files

When a developer checks in files, other users don't automatically receive the new files. To get copies of newly created files, or copies of files changed by other users, you must explicitly obtain the latest version of the project files. You can do this using Visual SourceSafe, or you can do this from within the Visual Basic IDE. You can also have Visual SourceSafe get the latest version of files automatically when you open a project—or have it prompt you when you open a project—by using the Source Code Control Options dialog box shown in Figure 15-23. To access this dialog box in Visual Basic, choose SourceSafe from the Tools menu and then choose Options. Note that you can also use this dialog box to tailor how Visual SourceSafe treats adding new files and removing existing files from your Visual Basic project.

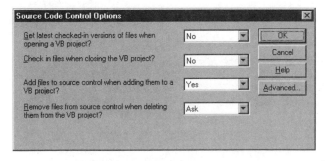

Figure 15-23. *Use the Source Code Control Options dialog box to streamline the interaction between you and Visual SourceSafe.*

When you retrieve the current version of files under source code control, the latest version of each file is retrieved and placed into your working folder, overwriting any older versions there. *Visual SourceSafe will not overwrite any files that you have checked out.* At any time, you can right-click an object in the Project Explorer window and click Get Latest Version to retrieve the current version of a file. This is useful when you know that another developer has checked in changes to a specific file.

In addition to getting the latest versions of files through the Visual Basic IDE, you can also get them through Visual SourceSafe Explorer by selecting the file or files and then choosing Get Latest Version from the Tools menu. When you do this, Visual SourceSafe shows you the dialog box in Figure 15-24. The dialog box asks you to confirm the folder in which you want to place the latest version of the selected file or files—the working folder by default—and allows you to set a few options.

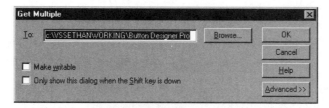

Figure 15-24. *When using Visual SourceSafe Explorer, you have a little more control when getting the latest version of files than you do from within the Visual Basic IDE.*

One setting of particular importance is the Make Writable check box. Earlier in this chapter, I discussed how Visual SourceSafe sets the read-only flag of files that you do not have checked out. It does this to prevent you from making changes to these files. If you want the ability to modify files you do not have checked out, select the Make Writable check box. Visual SourceSafe will then create copies of the files in your working folder, but it will not set the read-only flag. However, this essentially removes the file or files from Visual SourceSafe control, and you might encounter problems if you alter the files.

If you choose to get the latest version of a file that you currently have checked out and that you have modified, Visual SourceSafe displays the dialog box shown in Figure 15-25. You must be very careful when dealing with this dialog box. If you choose to replace the file, you'll overwrite your changes with the latest checked-in version of the file. Your best bet 99 percent of the time is to select the Apply To All Items check box and then click Leave.

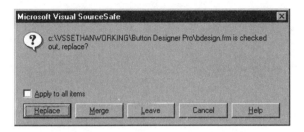

Figure 15-25. *When you see this dialog box, stop and consider your actions carefully before proceeding.*

Comparing Revisions

Visual SourceSafe maintains a full history of revisions to every file under source code control. To view the history of a file, select the file in Visual SourceSafe Explorer and choose Show History from the Tools menu to display the History Options dialog box shown in Figure 15-26. You can use this dialog box to tailor the history list, but most of the time you'll probably use the defaults.

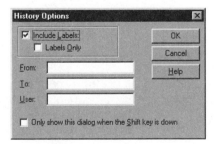

Figure 15-26. *Use the History Options dialog box to tailor the history list. For instance, you might choose to view history for only a specific user, for a date range, or for both.*

Clicking OK in the History Options dialog box commits your selections and displays the History dialog box. (See Figure 15-27.) This dialog box shows you all revisions of the file. A revision is essentially a version of the file as it was checked in by a user. Each time a new version of the file is checked in, it becomes a new revision.

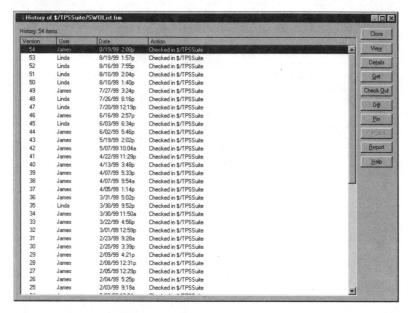

Figure 15-27.   *This History dialog box shows you all revisions of a file and even lets you compare any two revisions of a file.*

One of the most powerful features of the History dialog box is the ability to compare two revisions. To view the differences between any two revisions, select two revisions by clicking the first item and then clicking the second item while holding down the Ctrl key. Once you have two files selected, click Diff to view the differences between the two files.

After clicking Diff, the Difference Options dialog box is displayed, as shown in Figure 15-28. This dialog box shows you the two files that are being compared, along with some additional options.

If you want to compare a certain revision to the file in your working folder (perhaps to see what changes you have made), use the Browse button to locate and select the file from your working folder for either the Compare or the To text box. If you select only one file in the History dialog box and click Diff, the file is automatically compared to the ver-

sion in your working folder. Once you are satisfied with the settings—
the defaults work well most of the time—click OK to view the differences.

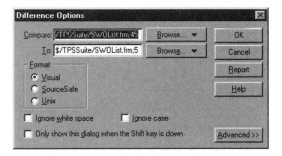

Figure 15-28. *Use the Difference Options dialog box to tailor the way files are compared.*

The Differences Between window shown in Figure 15-29 has two panes.
Each pane has the contents of a single file. All differences between the
two files are shown color-coded. Deleted lines appear in blue, changed
lines are red, and inserted lines are green. The Differences Between window is display-only; you can't make changes to either of the files. However, you can copy text from either file to the clipboard and then paste the
text into your project.

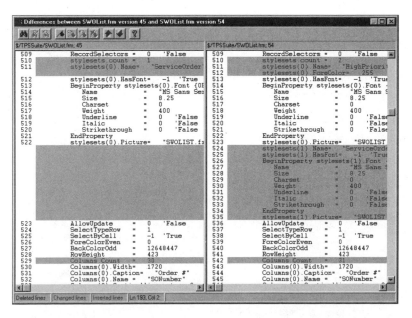

Figure 15-29. *Differences between two files are clearly highlighted with an appropriate color.*

NOTE   The fact that you can copy text is not immediately apparent because right-clicking on selected text does not give you a shortcut menu. However, you can highlight text to select it and then use the keyboard command Ctrl+C to copy the selected text.

Visual SourceSafe is a powerful tool that can greatly enhance the efficiency and reliability of team development. Attempting to manually accomplish some of the operations that are performed automatically by Visual SourceSafe takes quite a bit of effort. Some of the actions performed by Visual SourceSafe, such as allowing only one person to modify a file at a time and the ability to compare versions of a file, are almost impossible to perform any other way. If you develop projects as part of a team—even if that team is only two developers—you should seriously consider using Visual SourceSafe to manage your development efforts.

F

F1 key, 74
F5 key, 110
False value, 89, 231, 241
fan-in and fan-out, 31–32, *32*
File menu commands, 283
files
    backing up, 339, 342
    binary, 15, 356, 360
    .ini file extension, *350,* 351
    logging errors to text, 130–34
    Readme, 341–42
    Visual Basic (*see* projects)
    Visual SourceSafe database
        (*see* databases, Visual
        SourceSafe)
Fixed Dialog style, 255, *255*
Fixed Single style, 256–57, *257*
Fixed ToolWindow style,
    258–59, *259, 260*
flow control constructs, 229–47
    avoiding *GoSub* statements,
        243–44
    documenting, 243
    documenting nested, with
        end-of-line comments,
        239–40
    formatting expressions,
        241–43
    goals of, 230
    GoTo statements, 244–47
    If...End If, 230–34
    overview of, 229–30
    Select Case...End Select,
        234–39
    using *On Error Goto* for,
        116–22
focused variables, 80–81, 82
folders
    designating working,
        356–57, *357, 358*
    for object templates, 14–15,
        14, 15, 19–20, *19*
    paths and object templates,
        21
    for project templates, 16, *17*
    sharing working, 357
    Visual SourceSafe database,
        349, *349*
For Each...Next constructs,
    223–28, 277
formatting characters for each
    developer, 190–91

formatting code, 145–77
    benefits of, 145–49
    expressions, 241–43
    goals of, 149
    indenting comments, 193
    indenting continuation
        lines, 156–59
    indenting declarations to
        show subordination,
        168–69
    indenting *For...Next*
        constructs, 210, 215
    indenting to show
        organizational structure,
        160–68, *160*
    menus, 281–85, *282*
    using line continuation
        character, 151–56
    using single statements per
        line, 102, 150–51
    using white space to group
        statements, 169–77
forms, 254–65
    assigning access keys to
        command buttons, 303–4,
        304, 305
    avoiding morphing, 264–65
    border styles, 254–59, *255,
        256, 257, 258, 259, 260*
    controls on (*see* controls)
    creating command buttons,
        302–3
    disabling templates, 18, *18*
    keyboard navigation, 298–99
        (*see also* keyboard
        navigation and
        interaction)
    pop-up menus (*see* pop-up
        menus)
    setting maximum length of
        data-bound controls,
        305–7, *306, 307*
    setting tab order of, 299–301,
        301, 302
    startup positions, 260–64,
        261, 262, 263
    templates, 14–15, *14*
    unloading, 264
For...Next constructs
    commenting, 201–2
    GoTo statement vs., 221–23
    looping through arrays,
        226–27
    using, 205–16

frame controls, 275–76, 279–80,
    301
Friend keyword, 39–41
functionality, backward
    compatibility and, 337
Function keyword, 26
Function procedures. *See also*
    procedures
    calling, 45–46
    defined, 25, 26
    documenting return values,
        198
    retrieving return values, 45,
        46–47
    Variant return values, 101

G

global constants, 20–21, 30, 66.
    See also system
    constants
globally unique identifiers
    (GUIDs), 336
global scope, 39
global variables
    commenting, 202–3
    parameters vs., 20–21, 30, 41
    problems of, 103–4
GoSub statement, 243–44
GoTo statements
    case of line labels, 65, 118,
        246–47
    indentation of line labels,
        167–68
    line numbers and labels, 117
    looping constructs vs.,
        221–23
    single exit points and, 36
    using, 244–47
grammar mistakes, 324
Guest user, 351
GUIDs (globally unique
    identifiers), 336

H

hard-coded values
    numbers (*see* magic
        numbers)
    in object templates, 20–22
    strings, 59
height of single-line controls,
    265–67, *266, 267*
Help menu commands, 285

The manuscript for this book was prepared and submitted to Microsoft Press in electronic form. Text files were prepared using Microsoft Word 2000. Pages were composed by Microsoft Press using Adobe PageMaker 6.52 for Windows, with text in Melior and display type in Frutiger Condensed. Composed pages were delivered to the printer as electronic prepress files.

Cover Designer
Girvin Strategic Branding and Design

Cover Illustrator
Glenn Mitsui

Interior Graphic Artist
Michael Kloepfer

Principal Compositor
Barb Runyan

Principal Proofreader/Copy Editor
Roger LeBlanc

Indexer
Shane-Armstrong Information Systems

About the Author

James Foxall is Vice President of Development and Support for Tigerpaw Software, Inc. (*www.tigerpawsoftware.com*), an Omaha, Nebraska, Microsoft Certified Solution Provider specializing in commercial database applications. James manages a commercial suite of programs designed to automate contact management, marketing, service and repair; proposal generation; and inventory control and purchasing. James's experience in creating certified Office Compatible software has made him an authority on application interface and behavior standards for the Microsoft Windows and Microsoft Office environments.

James has written well over 100,000 lines of commercial production Microsoft Visual Basic code in both single-programmer and multiple-programmer environments. He is also the author of numerous books, including *Discover Visual Basic 5*, *Access 97 Secrets*, *Access for Windows 95 Secrets*, and the *Access Bible (Gold Edition)*, and he has written articles for *Access/Office/VBA Advisor Magazine*. James, a Microsoft Certified Professional, is an international speaker on Microsoft Access and Visual Basic. When not programming or writing about programming, he enjoys spending time with his family, playing guitar, doing battle over the chess board, listening to Pink Floyd, playing computer games, and (believe it or not) programming!

System Requirements

To run the sample programs on the CD, you must have the following:

- Windows 95, Windows 98, Windows NT 4, or Windows 2000
- Visual Basic 6

To view the electronic book on the CD, you must have the following:

- Windows 95, Windows 98, Windows NT 4 Service Pack 3, or Windows 2000
- Internet Explorer 4.01 or later and the HTML Help components

The Autorun.exe program in the Ebook folder will install the HTML Help components if you do not already have them and will install Internet Explorer 5 if you do not already have Internet Explorer 4.01 or later. For more detailed information about system requirements for the electronic book, see the Readme.txt file in the Ebook folder.

MICROSOFT LICENSE AGREEMENT

Book Companion CD

IMPORTANT—READ CAREFULLY: This Microsoft End-User License Agreement ("EULA") is a legal agreement between you (either an individual or an entity) and Microsoft Corporation for the Microsoft product identified above, which includes computer software and may include associated media, printed materials, and "online" or electronic documentation ("SOFTWARE PRODUCT"). Any component included within the SOFTWARE PRODUCT that is accompanied by a separate End-User License Agreement shall be governed by such agreement and not the terms set forth below. By installing, copying, or otherwise using the SOFTWARE PRODUCT, you agree to be bound by the terms of this EULA. If you do not agree to the terms of this EULA, you are not authorized to install, copy, or otherwise use the SOFTWARE PRODUCT; you may, however, return the SOFTWARE PRODUCT, along with all printed materials and other items that form a part of the Microsoft product that includes the SOFTWARE PRODUCT, to the place you obtained them for a full refund.

SOFTWARE PRODUCT LICENSE

The SOFTWARE PRODUCT is protected by United States copyright laws and international copyright treaties, as well as other intellectual property laws and treaties. The SOFTWARE PRODUCT is licensed, not sold.

1. **GRANT OF LICENSE.** This EULA grants you the following rights:

    a. **Software Product.** You may install and use one copy of the SOFTWARE PRODUCT on a single computer. The primary user of the computer on which the SOFTWARE PRODUCT is installed may make a second copy for his or her exclusive use on a portable computer.

    b. **Storage/Network Use.** You may also store or install a copy of the SOFTWARE PRODUCT on a storage device, such as a network server, used only to install or run the SOFTWARE PRODUCT on your other computers over an internal network; however, you must acquire and dedicate a license for each separate computer on which the SOFTWARE PRODUCT is installed or run from the storage device. A license for the SOFTWARE PRODUCT may not be shared or used concurrently on different computers.

    c. **License Pak.** If you have acquired this EULA in a Microsoft License Pak, you may make the number of additional copies of the computer software portion of the SOFTWARE PRODUCT authorized on the printed copy of this EULA, and you may use each copy in the manner specified above. You are also entitled to make a corresponding number of secondary copies for portable computer use as specified above.

    d. **Sample Code.** Solely with respect to portions, if any, of the SOFTWARE PRODUCT that are identified within the SOFTWARE PRODUCT as sample code (the "SAMPLE CODE"):

    i. **Use and Modification.** Microsoft grants you the right to use and modify the source code version of the SAMPLE CODE, *provided* you comply with subsection (d)(iii) below. You may not distribute the SAMPLE CODE, or any modified version of the SAMPLE CODE, in source code form.

    ii. **Redistributable Files.** Provided you comply with subsection (d)(iii) below, Microsoft grants you a nonexclusive, royalty-free right to reproduce and distribute the object code version of the SAMPLE CODE and of any modified SAMPLE CODE, other than SAMPLE CODE, or any modified version thereof, designated as not redistributable in the Readme file that forms a part of the SOFTWARE PRODUCT (the "Non-Redistributable Sample Code"). All SAMPLE CODE other than the Non-Redistributable Sample Code is collectively referred to as the "REDISTRIBUTABLES."

    iii. **Redistribution Requirements.** If you redistribute the REDISTRIBUTABLES, you agree to: (i) distribute the REDISTRIBUTABLES in object code form only in conjunction with and as a part of your software application product; (ii) not use Microsoft's name, logo, or trademarks to market your software application product; (iii) include a valid copyright notice on your software application product; (iv) indemnify, hold harmless, and defend Microsoft from and against any claims or lawsuits, including attorney's fees, that arise or result from the use or distribution of your software application product; and (v) not permit further distribution of the REDISTRIBUTABLES by your end user. Contact Microsoft for the applicable royalties due and other licensing terms for all other uses and/or distribution of the REDISTRIBUTABLES.

2. **DESCRIPTION OF OTHER RIGHTS AND LIMITATIONS.**

    - **Limitations on Reverse Engineering, Decompilation, and Disassembly.** You may not reverse engineer, decompile, or disassemble the SOFTWARE PRODUCT, except and only to the extent that such activity is expressly permitted by applicable law notwithstanding this limitation.

    - **Separation of Components.** The SOFTWARE PRODUCT is licensed as a single product. Its component parts may not be separated for use on more than one computer.

    - **Rental.** You may not rent, lease, or lend the SOFTWARE PRODUCT.

    - **Support Services.** Microsoft may, but is not obligated to, provide you with support services related to the SOFTWARE PRODUCT ("Support Services"). Use of Support Services is governed by the Microsoft policies and programs described in the user manual, in "online" documentation, and/or in other Microsoft-provided materials. Any supplemental software code provided to you as part of the Support Services shall be considered part of the SOFTWARE PRODUCT and subject to the terms and conditions of this EULA. With respect to technical information you provide to Microsoft as part of the Support Services, Microsoft may use such information for its business purposes, including for product support and development. Microsoft will not utilize such technical information in a form that personally identifies you.

- **Software Transfer.** You may permanently transfer all of your rights under this EULA, provided you retain no copies, you transfer all of the SOFTWARE PRODUCT (including all component parts, the media and printed materials, any upgrades, this EULA, and, if applicable, the Certificate of Authenticity), **and** the recipient agrees to the terms of this EULA.

- **Termination.** Without prejudice to any other rights, Microsoft may terminate this EULA if you fail to comply with the terms and conditions of this EULA. In such event, you must destroy all copies of the SOFTWARE PRODUCT and all of its component parts.

3. **COPYRIGHT.** All title and copyrights in and to the SOFTWARE PRODUCT (including but not limited to any images, photographs, animations, video, audio, music, text, SAMPLE CODE, REDISTRIBUTABLES, and "applets" incorporated into the SOFTWARE PRODUCT) and any copies of the SOFTWARE PRODUCT are owned by Microsoft or its suppliers. The SOFTWARE PRODUCT is protected by copyright laws and international treaty provisions. Therefore, you must treat the SOFTWARE PRODUCT like any other copyrighted material **except** that you may install the SOFTWARE PRODUCT on a single computer provided you keep the original solely for backup or archival purposes. You may not copy the printed materials accompanying the SOFTWARE PRODUCT.

4. **U.S. GOVERNMENT RESTRICTED RIGHTS.** The SOFTWARE PRODUCT and documentation are provided with RESTRICTED RIGHTS. Use, duplication, or disclosure by the Government is subject to restrictions as set forth in subparagraph (c)(1)(ii) of the Rights in Technical Data and Computer Software clause at DFARS 252.227-7013 or subparagraphs (c)(1) and (2) of the Commercial Computer Software—Restricted Rights at 48 CFR 52.227-19, as applicable. Manufacturer is Microsoft Corporation/One Microsoft Way/Redmond, WA 98052-6399.

5. **EXPORT RESTRICTIONS.** You agree that you will not export or re-export the SOFTWARE PRODUCT, any part thereof, or any process or service that is the direct product of the SOFTWARE PRODUCT (the foregoing collectively referred to as the "Restricted Components"), to any country, person, entity, or end user subject to U.S. export restrictions. You specifically agree not to export or re-export any of the Restricted Components (i) to any country to which the U.S. has embargoed or restricted the export of goods or services, which currently include, but are not necessarily limited to, Cuba, Iran, Iraq, Libya, North Korea, Sudan, and Syria, or to any national of any such country, wherever located, who intends to transmit or transport the Restricted Components back to such country; (ii) to any end user who you know or have reason to know will utilize the Restricted Components in the design, development, or production of nuclear, chemical, or biological weapons; or (iii) to any end user who has been prohibited from participating in U.S. export transactions by any federal agency of the U.S. government. You warrant and represent that neither the BXA nor any other U.S. federal agency has suspended, revoked, or denied your export privileges.

DISCLAIMER OF WARRANTY

NO WARRANTIES OR CONDITIONS. MICROSOFT EXPRESSLY DISCLAIMS ANY WARRANTY OR CONDITION FOR THE SOFTWARE PRODUCT. THE SOFTWARE PRODUCT AND ANY RELATED DOCUMENTATION ARE PROVIDED "AS IS" WITHOUT WARRANTY OR CONDITION OF ANY KIND, EITHER EXPRESS OR IMPLIED, INCLUDING, WITHOUT LIMITATION, THE IMPLIED WARRANTIES OF MERCHANTABILITY, FITNESS FOR A PARTICULAR PURPOSE, OR NONINFRINGEMENT. THE ENTIRE RISK ARISING OUT OF USE OR PERFORMANCE OF THE SOFTWARE PRODUCT REMAINS WITH YOU.

LIMITATION OF LIABILITY. TO THE MAXIMUM EXTENT PERMITTED BY APPLICABLE LAW, IN NO EVENT SHALL MICROSOFT OR ITS SUPPLIERS BE LIABLE FOR ANY SPECIAL, INCIDENTAL, INDIRECT, OR CONSEQUENTIAL DAMAGES WHATSOEVER (INCLUDING, WITHOUT LIMITATION, DAMAGES FOR LOSS OF BUSINESS PROFITS, BUSINESS INTERRUPTION, LOSS OF BUSINESS INFORMATION, OR ANY OTHER PECUNIARY LOSS) ARISING OUT OF THE USE OF OR INABILITY TO USE THE SOFTWARE PRODUCT OR THE PROVISION OF OR FAILURE TO PROVIDE SUPPORT SERVICES, EVEN IF MICROSOFT HAS BEEN ADVISED OF THE POSSIBILITY OF SUCH DAMAGES. IN ANY CASE, MICROSOFT'S ENTIRE LIABILITY UNDER ANY PROVISION OF THIS EULA SHALL BE LIMITED TO THE GREATER OF THE AMOUNT ACTUALLY PAID BY YOU FOR THE SOFTWARE PRODUCT OR US$5.00; PROVIDED, HOWEVER, IF YOU HAVE ENTERED INTO A MICROSOFT SUPPORT SERVICES AGREEMENT, MICROSOFT'S ENTIRE LIABILITY REGARDING SUPPORT SERVICES SHALL BE GOVERNED BY THE TERMS OF THAT AGREEMENT. BECAUSE SOME STATES AND JURISDICTIONS DO NOT ALLOW THE EXCLUSION OR LIMITATION OF LIABILITY, THE ABOVE LIMITATION MAY NOT APPLY TO YOU.

MISCELLANEOUS

This EULA is governed by the laws of the State of Washington USA, except and only to the extent that applicable law mandates governing law of a different jurisdiction.

Should you have any questions concerning this EULA, or if you desire to contact Microsoft for any reason, please contact the Microsoft subsidiary serving your country, or write: Microsoft Sales Information Center/One Microsoft Way/Redmond, WA 98052-6399.